Classic Writings on Instructional Technology

INSTRUCTIONAL TECHNOLOGY SERIES

Classic Writings on Instructional Technology. Donald P. Ely and Tjeerd Plomp, Editors.

Instructional Technology: Past, Present, and Future. 2d ed. Gary J. Anglin, Editor.

Classic Writings on Instructional Technology

Donald P. Ely

ERIC Clearinghouse on Information & Technology
Syracuse University
Syracuse, New York

Tjeerd Plomp

University of Twente
Enschede, Netherlands

1996
Libraries Unlimited, Inc.
Englewood, Colorado

LIBRARIES UNLIMITED, INC.
P.O. Box 6633
Englewood, CO 80155-6633
1-800-237-6124

Constance Hardesty, *Project Editor*
Sheryl Tongue, *Composition*

Excerpts from AUDIO-VISUAL METHODS IN TEACHING by Edgar Dale, copyright 1946 by Holt, Rinehart and Winston, Inc.

Library of Congress Cataloging-in-Publication Data

Classic writings on instructional technology / Donald P. Ely, Tjeerd Plomp [editors].
    xix, 257 p. 17x25 cm. -- (Instructional technology series)
    Includes bibliographical references and index.
    ISBN 1-56308-230-6
    1. Educational technology. 2. Instructional systems--Design.
3. Teaching--Aids and devices. 4. Audio-visual education. I. Ely, Donald P. II. Plomp, Tjeerd. III. Series.
LB1028.3.C617   1996
370.3'078--dc20   96-3668
                                      CIP

Contents

Part 2
Design and Development Functions

Design and Development   91

Evaluation   109

Part 3
Delivery Options

Media   167

Methods and Techniques   181

Part 4
The Profession

Professions in the Audio-Visual Field   229

Introduction

Most books are stimulated by events or needs experienced by individuals. This one is no different. Both editors participated in the design of an educational technology curriculum at the University of Twente in Netherlands in the early 1980s. In an attempt to describe the content of a new curriculum, a review of the literature was necessary. Questions about the "core" literature, "seminal" works, and the "roots" of the field led to a search that continues today. This book is a progress report.

At about the same time, one of the editors was teaching a course on Perspectives of Educational Technology, a graduate seminar that attempted to communicate the geography of the field—the conceptual contributions of the people, events, legislation, ideas, and movements that have helped to shape the profession. Logical resources for such an endeavor are the publications of the field—the written history of the profession. Then the next step is to ask: What publications are the classics of the field—those books and articles that have withstood the test of time and are still read and quoted? Mark Twain described a classic as "something everyone wants to have read and nobody wants to read." What would happen if *you* were to create a list of classics? It is not easy, as we found out.

Even when a reasonably satisfactory list is created, how does one locate the articles themselves, many of which have disappeared over the years? Sometimes a colleague has squirreled away a copy in a personal archive, or a library still has the paper copy or a microfiche. Wouldn't it be helpful if all these classic works could be brought together in one volume? At least it would save searching for articles that are now obscure. It might also help to document the history of the field through its literature. This book is an attempt to make such important articles readily available. It also attempts to provide a partial conceptual history of the *primary* works that often are sidestepped for more recent interpretations of the older gems. When historians do history, they go to the original sources, not secondary interpretations and digests. The editors have attempted to collect the original articles that are difficult to find. Insistence on original works always raises questions about more contemporary writings by professors and practitioners in the field. There are such books (e.g., Anglin 1995), and they certainly complement this publication. But they do not offer the original—the primary work upon which many of today's ideas are based. Therefore, without apology, we present the classics, naked and unashamed.

The Selection Process

What initially seems like a fairly routine task becomes a nightmare because each educational technology professional has his or her own ideas about which articles are classics. One editor prepared a list based on his own experience and the frequency of citations in major works, such as the histories of Reiser (1987) and Saettler (1990) and the encyclopedia articles of Eraut (1989) and Clark and Salomon (1986). When the second editor joined the team, there was agreement on more than half of the original titles and suggestions for alternate and additional titles. The list was still too long, and there was some disagreement about some of the titles. Clearly, a broader perspective was needed.

A list of tentative titles was sent to individuals who were members of the Professors of Instructional Development and Technology (PIDT) group in the United States and to several leaders in European countries who teach courses in which the publication might be used.

Thirty-five titles were included on the original list, and the respondents were asked to use the following criteria in making their judgments:

1. The article or chapter is one of the first to introduce important concepts.

2. It is original and does not borrow extensively from other sources.

3. It is often quoted as a primary reference by current authors.

4. It is recognized by academics who are experienced in the field.

5. It has lasting value; it is not just a historic document that was popular at the time it was published.

The respondents expressed their opinions using the following recommendations:

1. Definitely include; one of the best articles in this area.

2. Seriously consider; this is an important article.

3. If you have space, this would be a good article.

4. Do not consider; there are other articles that are better.

5. I am not familiar with this title.

Respondents were also asked to nominate other titles that should be considered for inclusion in the collection.

More than 30 individuals reacted to the original list of 35 titles. There was a high level of agreement on about half the titles and suggestions for 36 more works, a half dozen of which were mentioned more than once. Several new perceptions and ideas that would influence selection emerged from the comments of the respondents. They include:

■ There are books that ought to be considered classics. The editors felt that a representative article or a chapter from a book could be included in the collection. For example, Gagné's *Conditions of Learning* (1965) has a surrogate article that communicates the conceptual essence of the book.

■ North American educational technologists are much less familiar with articles published in Europe; for example, Davies (1978). The editors felt that their combined experience in North America and Europe was sufficiently valid to make judgments about selecting European articles, even though the articles are relatively unknown in North America.

■ Despite descriptions and instructions about the classics and the criteria for expressing opinions, many respondents requested articles that are more up-to-date. Many felt there are more recent publications that better represent contemporary thinking. For example, several respondents recommended using the new 1994 Association for Education Communications and Technology (AECT) definition (Seels and Richey 1994) rather than the 1977 AECT definition. Of course contemporary thinking is better represented by the 1994 publication than the 1977 work, but it is difficult to call a recent publication a classic! The editors had to veto the suggestions for more contemporary listings because they would violate the basic premise that the articles are "first to introduce the concept" and "often quoted as a primary reference," as indicated in the list of criteria.

■ The number of new titles introduced by the respondents caused some reflection by the editors. Clearly, all of them could not be added, but some initial titles could be dropped in favor of suggestions that seemed to make more sense. Several changes were made as a result of this input.

A further check on the utility of the proposed articles was their use in a graduate seminar held just before the final selection was made. Students read and reacted to a wide spectrum of articles, many of which were on the original list. They expressed their opinions regarding the value to them as they were about to enter the profession. Their opinions added useful input and a reality check, because the students represent the ultimate users for whom the book is intended. Manal El-Tigi and Jason Ravitz, graduate students at Syracuse University, made valuable contributions to the selection process.

The table of contents sent to the publisher contained 30 articles of various lengths. The publisher's review of the text when adjusted to a uniform typographical format indicated twice the number of pages that had been estimated. At this point there was a further reduction by the editors emphasizing several criteria: (1) difficulty of access, (2) older items, (3) core literature, and (4) published in the United States (since the primary users would be in North America). This wrenching task left 17 of the 30 articles.

The conclusion based on the experience of the selection process is that each educational technologist has his or her own list of classic articles from the professional literature. This idiosyncratic opinion is based on such factors as the university in which graduate study was done, courses taught by the individual, and the satisfaction received from a specific publication at one time or another during one's professional career. The final decision as to what to include is a mix of the editors' personal favorites, the votes of professional colleagues, and the input of students who will be the readers of this volume.

Organization of the Book

Initially it seemed appropriate to use AECT's most recent definition of instructional technology (Seels and Richey 1994) as the organizing structure since so much effort went into the development of that book. However, the articles selected did not seem to fit into this ready-made pattern. After all, the domains in that definition emerged from thinking that was represented in many of the articles selected for inclusion. However, the original sources were more an artifact of history—an evolution of thinking that emerged over time. There was no organizational scheme that shaped the field; rather, there were pieces that were loosely linked to each other and eventually were considered to be useful to the field. Therefore, an alternative conceptual framework had to be created for the classic works. The framework appears to be more historical and begins with some of the earliest works that first introduced new concepts. It is expanded by later writings that built on the earlier foundations.

The table of contents categorizes the classic articles into a framework that can be used as is, but it can be adapted for special uses. For example, each of the articles can fit into one of the domains described in the current AECT definition (Seels and Richey 1994), even though all aspects of each domain are not represented in this collection. We considered creating new categories (after the selection of articles from various facets of the field's development) as another way of organizing the field. The fit of the articles to the structure is not always perfect, and there are some overlaps between categories. It may be better to acknowledge the inadequacy of any organization scheme and simply move on to the writings themselves since they are the heart and the reason for this publication.

Using Classic Works

This book can be used as a resource of articles that are frequently used in educational technology courses. It can be used by professionals in the field as a reference volume for items often cited in the literature. It can be used as a history of the field's development through some of the relevant literature. It can be used as support for descriptions of the domains that make up the field. It can serve as a source of documents that introduce ideas that have become the conceptual roots of educational technology.

Users will want to expand the contents. The basic volume is a beginning; personal additions will enrich the content and permit local use that fits specific needs.

Conceptual Organization

There is no single conceptual organization of educational technology that is acceptable to all professionals. Since the field emerged during the post-World War II period, the profession has struggled with its own purpose and identity. The preoccupation with definition from 1963 (Ely) to 1994 (Seels and Richey) is an example of the continuing effort to clarify the ambiguities. It seems that each person views the field with a personal perspective based on the individual's experience with those aspects of the field that fall within the scope of one's daily work. When it comes to organizing the classic works, one scheme would appear to be almost as logical as the next. The editors have chosen to use the following approach:

1. Definition and Conceptual Background
   The Field and Its Definition
   Theory and Rationale

2. Design and Development Functions
   Design and Development
   Evaluation

3. Delivery Options
   Media
   Methods and Techniques

4. The Profession
   Professions in the Audio-Visual Field

Definition and Conceptual Background

The field and its definition. Educational technology has different meanings for different people. To some, it is a process for analyzing instructional problems and devising, implementing, evaluating, and managing cost-effective solutions to those problems in all aspects of human learning. For others, it is the process of designing curricula and instruction following system models. Still others view the field through the hardware and software that deliver education and training. It is the first meaning, a problem-solving process, that encompasses the other two meanings and is used as the organizing principle for the first section of the book.

The articles in this section describe the field: what it is and what its practitioners do. The AECT chapter (beginning on page 3) is taken from a longer work, *The Definition of Educational Technology* (1977). In this chapter, the authors present the field in its many dimensions and attempt to create a unified definition. It is an outgrowth of the 1963 and 1972 attempts to do the same thing. It is a report of the Definition and Terminology Committee of the AECT and represents the collective view of individuals who were involved in the evolution of the field over the years. It is included here because it was the first comprehensive definition that built on previous works, and it has endured longer than any other definition. It has been replaced by Seels and Richey (1994) *Instructional Technology: The Definition and Domains of the Field.*

Ivor K. Davies' article, "Educational Technology: Archetypes, Paradigms and Models" (page 15), is often quoted in reference to the problem-solving orientation of the field. It presents multiple viewpoints regarding the scope and direction of the field. Davies concludes that there is one "archetype" (and several paradigms) that best represents the field. He endorses problem solving as the most appropriate emphasis.

Robert Heinich's query, "Is There a Field of Educational Communications and Technology?" (page 31) is answered by an analysis of functions that various professionals perform. He tries to describe the role of specialists by using curriculum development, course planning, and instructional implementation as basic operational levels. He concludes that there *is* a field of educational communications and technology and that there are three major domains: (1) curricular and instructional design, (2) instructional product design, and (3) media services. Heinich champions the "larger vision" of a "broad framework" as the best way to characterize the field.

Each of these articles provides a different insight into the field of educational technology. Taken together they help the professional, as well as others, to understand the purpose and substance of the field. The essence of each article has been incorporated into the current definition: "Instructional technology is the theory and practice of design, development, utilization, management and evaluation of processes and resources for learning" (Seels and Richey 1994, p. 1). This current definition builds on the 1977 AECT definition in its use of functional areas (domains). It reflects the audiovisual and engineering archetypes of Davies more than his problem-solving approach while maintaining Heinich's "broad framework."

The 1994 definition focuses more on the domains of the field than on the meaning of the terminology. Each domain (design, development, utilization, evaluation and management) describes what professionals *do* rather than what the field *is*. The only reference to problem solving is in the domain of evaluation where "problem analysis" is viewed more operationally as "needs assessment" and "front-end analysis." Whether this volume will become a classic in the future is yet to be decided.

Theory and rationale. What thinking supports the decisions that professionals make? Why do most specialists approach design using a systematic approach? What has led to the current swing away from behaviorism toward cognitive and constructivist thinking? The articles in this section represent a spectrum of theories and supporting rationales that explain some of the "whys." The major elements come from systems concepts, communication theory, learning psychology, and instructional psychology. Both learning and instructional technology are discussed from their behaviorist and constructivist approaches.

For most design decisions there are reasons for embracing one approach rather than another. Educational technology is known for its system viewpoint. That fact can be traced to the opening presentation of the 1956 Lake Okoboji Audiovisual Leadership Conference by Charles F. Hoban Jr. (page 57). Hoban was one of the first, if not the first, to recognize that educational technology was composed of many elements and that, unless these elements were considered together, there was very little pedagogical purpose in considering them one at a time. This concept was furthered by Churchman's keynote address at a conference on systems approaches to education held at Syracuse University in 1964 (page 39) and James D. Finn's series of articles on instructional technology in *Audiovisual Communication Review* in the early 1960s. (A representative article, "A Walk on the Altered Side," begins on page 47). There are others, of course, but these three authors seem to describe several significant origins of systems thinking in educational or instructional technology.

Communication theory was a major influence in the early development of the field. The pioneer work of Shannon and Weaver (1949), especially the supplementary chapter written later by Warren Weaver spelled out the dimensions of communication theory that had implications for application in the instructional setting. Unfortunately, it is not included here. Others (Berlo 1960; Schramm 1954) used Shannon and Weaver as the basis for their works on applications of communications theory to practical events. Much of the communications theory today has found its way into instructional design practice and is often merged with concepts of learning and instructional theory, especially in the presentation of information to learners and the use of feedback. In the 1950s and 1960s, communications theory and practice dominated the field, especially for professionals who were deeply involved in the classroom use of media. Communications theory provided a rationale for their day-to-day work.

Learning theory was the emphasis of a special issue of the research journal *Audiovisual Communications Review* (Meierhenry 1961). The first definition of the field endorsed by the professional association (Ely 1963) used learning theory as one contributing element to the field. (The other contributing element was communications theory.) As programmed learning became more prominent, learning psychologists such as Skinner (1958) and Lumsdaine (1964) joined the movement. Even today their pioneering works speak to those who are developing computer-assisted learning.

Transitional thinking based on a behavioral orientation but moving toward a constructivist approach is represented by the work of Romiszowski (1981). His *Designing Instructional Systems: Decision Making in Course Planning and Curriculum Design* (1981) was clearly rooted in the behaviorism of the 1960s and 1970s, but there is evidence in Romiszowski's work that he seeks to move beyond mere behavior to the larger sphere of cognitive psychology.

Later, Charles Reigeluth introduced new ideas in the area of instructional theory as it applied to design. His edited volume *Instructional Design Theories and Models: An Overview of the Current Status* (1983) presented a spectrum of theories related to instructional design for the first time. The blending of learning theory and instructional theory have offered sound bases for both research and development. They are currently manifest in much of the computer-assisted instruction and learning literature. The work of Merrill (1983), Merrill, Li, and Jones (1990), and Jonassen (1991) have opened up a new era of constructivism, which reduces the influence of behaviorism. Jonassen's 1991 article was one of the first to identify constructivism as a major paradigm shift.

In 1964, Lumsdaine anticipated the merging of learning and instructional theories in his article "Educational Technology, Programed Learning, and Instructional Science" (page 65). This landmark article discussed the contributions and eventual merger of physical science knowledge and principles with the concepts and principles of the behavioral sciences. It is included in the book largely because it represents both a historical and a transitional point of view. The figure depicting the merger of the various physical science and behavioral science contributions is, in itself, a classic.

It is difficult to include every article that has contributed to the theory and rationale of educational technology. The representatives that are included here provide original works that have made contributions to the intellectual evolution of the field. They represent four major roots of the field: systems, communication, learning theory, and instructional theory. Some may argue that other fields contributed. For example, management, education (pedagogy), and engineering are often considered to be fundamental contributors. Some of these areas are discussed in subsequent sections of this introduction with appropriate articles selected to represent these fields.

Design and Development Functions

Design and development. This section focuses on the intellectual activities that undergird the process of design and development. One of the most influential persons in this area has been Robert Gagné. His first edition of *Conditions of Learning*, published in 1965, clearly set the standard for application of psychological principles to the design of instruction. The article, "Learning Hierarchies" (page 93), is representative of his work at that time. Later he joined Leslie Briggs in authoring *Principles of Instructional Design*—a book that was destined to shape the thinking and practice of professional instructional designers.

Other facets of design and development were considered for inclusion in this section but did not survive the final cut. The inventory of instructional design and development models by Andrews and Goodson (1980) has been reprinted several times in other collections of influential writings and therefore is not reprinted here. It compares many of the instructional design models that were being used at the time. Earlier, Tosti and Ball (1969) rode the wave of behaviorism in describing one of the first media selection procedures based on principles of learning psychology. Their approach is still useful today. Keller (1987) was the first to seriously introduce concepts of motivation in the design and development process. His ARCS model has been used frequently in both research and application.

Evaluation. Evaluation entered instructional design and development through the back door. Never up front as part of early design models, it was later included as an afterthought. Initially, evaluation was considered nice to do, but not essential. The introduction of behavioral science, in the thinking of many educational technologists, required evaluation to determine whether or not the objectives had been reached. Later, needs assessment and front-end analysis emerged at the beginning of the process and evaluation became an integral part of the systematic approach. It was only then that practitioners looked around for foundational support and found it in the work of Ralph Tyler. The 1942 "General Statement on Evaluation" became relevant for instructional designers about 30 years after it was published in the *Journal of Educational Research*. Tyler's later work "New Dimensions in Curriculum Development" (page 161), offers an overview of his approach to curriculum development in words that speak to educational technologists. From the United Kingdom came Derek Rowntree's *Educational Technology in Curriculum Development* (1974), which has had considerable influence on the field in Europe. Robert Stake's "countenance" article (1967) (page 143), further pointed directions for evaluation that had direct implications for the field of educational technology even though it was not intended for that specific audience.

The more theoretical approach of Tyler and Stake found operational outlets in Roger Kaufman's seminal works on needs assessment (1972; 1977 [included in this volume beginning on page 111]; 1979) and in Donald Kirkpatrick's work on "Techniques for Evaluating Training Programs" (1979; included in this volume beginning on page 119). The contributions of Michael Scriven (1967) and Daniel Stufflebeam (1983) are significant in the minds of many practitioners in the education community at large as well as in the work of instructional designers. Space limitation prevented inclusion in this volume.

Delivery Options

Media. In the early post-World War II period, the focus of the field was on media—audiovisual media. The success of training with media during the war led to a newfound enthusiasm among those who were involved in the development and delivery of training in the various branches of the military. This success was attributed to media *per se*, and advocates among the veterans promoted audiovisual media as revolutionary tools for learning in the classroom. There was not much research supporting the use of media at that time, but the results from military training seemed to speak louder than any research.

It was in this environment that Edgar Dale's Cone of Experience was well received and used as a supporting rationale for the use of media. The Cone was introduced in Dale's first edition of *Audio-Visual Methods in Teaching* (1946) even though the concrete to abstract continuum concept was used in earlier works (Hoban, Hoban, and Zisman 1937). (An excerpt from Dale's book appears in this volume beginning on page 169.) The Cone of Experience captured the imagination of audiovisual advocates and provided a reasonable rationale for promoting the use of media in teaching and learning. Dale's interest in communication and teaching conferred a legitimacy that helped to gain acceptance of the Cone. The concept was central to each of the three editions of Dale's classic text (1946, 1954, 1969) with minor modifications in the second and third editions.

Research about the use of media in education began with the film utilization studies of Wood and Freeman (1929) at Chicago and Knowlton and Tilton (1929) at Columbia. After a relatively quiet period in the 1930s, postwar research efforts were picked up by Carpenter and Greenhill (1956) at Pennsylvania State University, May (1958) at Yale, and Meierhenry (1952) at Nebraska. These classic studies were supported by the military, foundations, and film producers themselves. For the most part, they were attempting to "prove" the value of motion pictures in education.

Clark's 1983 comprehensive review of media research is an overview and summary of research in the field. It is also a critique, especially of the earlier research, and offers recommendations for future research. It is one of the most frequently quoted articles about media research today and has led to a lively exchange of opinions among professionals in the field. The dominant question seems to be: Can students learn from media? Clark maintains that this is the wrong question and offers alternative hypotheses about ways in which learning from media might occur.

Methods and techniques. Clark (1983) maintains that the way media are used determines the effectiveness of learning, not the media themselves. This proposition is supported more by scholars and researchers outside the field of educational technology than by those inside the field. In this section of the book, three influential authors emphasize methods and techniques that have influenced the improvement of learning. They emphasize change in the role of the teacher. Keller (1968) and Skinner (1958) suggest that the teaching function can be altered and improved by following an instructional design procedure that is focused on the individual learner. Keller (1968) describes procedures for a personalized system of instruction (PSI) that begins with the individual learner (see page 183). Skinner (1958) suggests that the use of "teaching machines," programmed for use by individual learners, offers an alternative to lecturing by a teacher. These articles illustrate a shift from group instruction to individual instruction. Another proponent of individualized learning was Carroll (1963), who first outlined the procedures for mastery learning that were later picked up by Bloom (1968) and Block (1979). Skinner's 1954 article, "The Science of Learning and the Art of Teaching" (in this volume beginning on page 199), describes one aspect of instructional design from a psychologist's viewpoint. He maintains that more frequent and appropriate reinforcement in the teaching/learning process would improve learning. He suggests that a mechanical device (a "teaching machine") could be one way to provide individual student reinforcement without burdening the teacher with the task. The suggestion is further developed in his 1958 article, "Teaching Machines" (in this volume beginning on page 211).

The Profession

Information about the educational technology profession can be found throughout the literature of the field. Most of it is concerned with trends, the content of professional education, salary structures, surveys of academic programs, and prospects for the future. Less frequent are the critical writings about the field—its ethics, values, and direction. This last section of the book presents a view that is constructively critical of the field. James D. Finn influenced the profession more than any other single person during its formative post-World War II years. As co-founder of the *Audio-Visual Communication Review* (later known as the *Educational Communications and Technology Journal* and *Educational Technology Research and Development*), Finn addressed the profession in the very first issue. "Professionalizing the Audio-Visual Field" (1953) has become a beacon for the field. (The article appears in this volume beginning on page 231). It has served as a foundation for the definition of the field (1977) and for the establishment of professional education programs. It continues to serve as a measure of growth for the AECT, the successor of the Department of Audio Visual Instruction (DAVI). Finn's "six characteristics of a profession" establish criteria for the field of educational technology and are still used as measures of professional status.

From England, the voice of David Hawkridge, first director of the Institute of Educational Technology in the British Open University, is heard in "Next Year, Jerusalem! The Rise of Educational Technology" (1976), which does not appear in this volume. Hawkridge provides a historical perspective of the field from the work of its earliest precursors through its twentieth century contributors. He considers the early work in programmed instruction from both sides of the Atlantic and the emerging influence of professional journals, government, and professional organizations. The projections he makes from his 1976 perspective are amazingly contemporary. His understanding of the field in the United States is thorough and accurate, and his first-hand knowledge of educational technology in his own country is impeccable—a unique combination! From the United States, Morgan (1978) describes the evolution of the field from the early days of programmed instruction to the "maturity" of the field in the 1970s. He recounts the contributions of behavioral psychology to the theory and practice of educational technology.

A Final Comment

It is apparent that these are dated articles. Most of them come from the three decades following the end of World War II. Each article is representative of the author's contributions to the field of educational technology. There are ten times the number of articles contained in this volume that constitute the core literature of the field. Some are within the range of dates used here; many more are published later. The contents of this book are classics as noted by many practitioners in the field. There probably would not be 100 percent agreement among all the individuals who participated in the nomination process. We hope that the reader will review the bibliography for a list of many works that have helped to establish the field as a profession.

The Field and Its Definitions

The Definition of Educational Technology: A Summary

**Association for Educational
Communications and Technology**

A concept as complex as educational technology requires an equally complex definition. The following definition—all 16 parts—are meant to be taken as a whole; none alone constitutes an adequate definition of educational technology.

1. *Educational technology* is a complex, integrated process involving people, procedures, ideas, devices, and organization, for analyzing problems and devising, implementing, evaluating, and managing solutions to those problems, involved in all aspects of human learning. In educational technology, the solutions to problems take the form of all the *Learning Resources* that are designed and/or selected and/or utilized to bring about learning; these resources are identified as Messages, People, Materials, Devices, Techniques, and Settings. The processes for analyzing problems, and devising, implementing and evaluating solutions are identified by the *Educational Development Functions* of Research-Theory, Design, Production, Evaluation-Selection, Logistics, Utilization, and Utilization-Dissemination. The processes of directing or coordinating one or more of these functions are identified by the *Educational Management Functions* of Organization Management and Personnel Management. The relationships among these elements are shown by the Domain of Educational Technology Model [see fig. 1]. The definitions of the elements in the Domain of Educational Technology are given in tables 1, 2, and 3 [see pages 6–12].

Educational technology is a theory about how problems in human learning are identified and solved.

Educational technology is a field involved in applying a complex, integrated process to analyze and solve problems in human learning.

Educational technology is a profession made up of an organized effort to implement the theory, intellectual technique, and practical application of educational technology.

From: Association for Educational Communications and Technology. 1977. The definition of educational technology: A summary. In *The definition of educational technology*, 1–16. Washington, D.C.: AECT. Reprinted with permission.

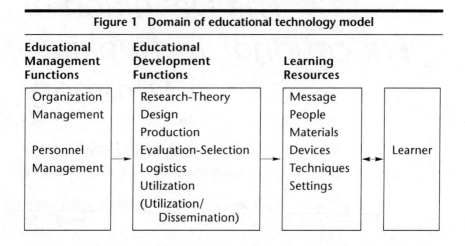

Figure 1   Domain of educational technology model

2. Educational technology is often confused with "technology in education."

Technology in education is the application of technology to any of those processes involved in operating the institutions which house the educational enterprise. It includes the application of technology to food, health, finance, scheduling, grade reporting, and other processes which support education within institutions. Technology in education is *not* the same as educational technology.

3. Educational technology is often confused with "instructional technology."

Instructional technology is a sub-set of educational technology, based on the concept that instruction is a sub-set of education. Instructional technology is a complex, integrated process involving people, procedures, ideas, devices, and organization, for analyzing problems, and devising, implementing, evaluating and managing solutions to those problems, in situations in which *learning is purposive and controlled*. In instructional technology, the solutions to problems take the form of *Instructional System Components* which are prestructured in design or selection, *and* in utilization, and are combined into complete instructional systems; these components are identified as Messages, People, Materials, Devices, Techniques, and Settings. The processes for analyzing problems and devising, implementing, and evaluating solutions are identified by the *Instructional Development Functions* of Research-Theory, Design, Production, Evaluation-Selection, Utilization, and Utilization-Dissemination. The process of directing or coordinating one or more of these functions are identified by the *Instructional Management Functions* of Organization Management and Personnel Management. The relationships among these elements are shown by the Domain of Instructional Technology Model [see fig. 2]. The definitions

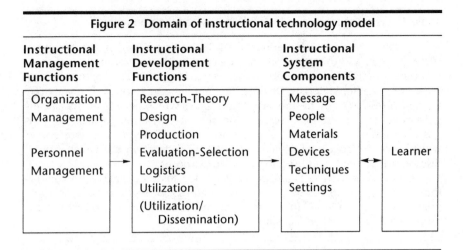

Figure 2   Domain of instructional technology model

Instructional Management Functions	Instructional Development Functions	Instructional System Components	
Organization Management Personnel Management	Research-Theory Design Production Evaluation-Selection Logistics Utilization (Utilization/ Dissemination)	Message People Materials Devices Techniques Settings	Learner

of the elements in the Domain of Instructional Technology are given in tables 1, 2, and 3.

Thus, all of instructional technology fits within the parameters of educational technology, while all of educational technology does not fit within the parameters of instructional technology. If instructional technology is in operation, then of necessity, so is educational technology; the reverse is not necessarily true. In educational technology, the Development and Management Functions are *more inclusive* because they apply to more Learning Resources than just Instructional System Components—they include all resources that can be used to facilitate learning.

4. The definition of educational technology constitutes a Theory because it meets the criteria of: existence of a phenomenon, explanation, summarizing, orientation, systematizing, gap identification, generating strategies for research, prediction, and a principle or set of principles.

5. Educational technology has a unique Intellectual Technique—an approach to solving problems. Each development and management function has an individual technique associated with it. However, the intellectual technique of educational technology is more than the sum of these parts. It involves the systematic integration of the individual technologies of these functions, and their interrelationships, into a complex, integrated process to analyze whole problems and create new solutions. It produces a synergistic effect, yielding outcomes not totally predictable based on the individual elements operating in isolation. This indigenous intellectual technique is unique to educational technology; no other existing field uses it.

6. Educational technology has practical applications. The existence of resources for learning, and the performance of the development and management functions, constitute the most basic and explicit evidence of this practical

Table 1   Learning resources/instructional system components

Learning Resources (for Educational Technology)—all of the resources (data, people, and things) which may be used by the learner in isolation or in combination, usually in an informal manner, to facilitate learning; they include Messages, People, Materials, Devices, Techniques, and Settings. There are two types: (a) resources by design—those resources which have been specifically developed as "instructional system components" in order to facilitate purposive, formal learning, and (b) resources by utilization—those resources which have not specifically been designed for instruction but which can be discovered, applied, and used for learning purposes.

Instructional System Components (ISC) (for Instructional Technology)— those learning resources which are prestructured in design or selection *and* utilization, and combined into complete instructional systems, to bring about purposive and controlled learning.

Resource or Component	Definition	Examples
Message	Information to be transmitted by the other components; takes the form of ideas, facts, meanings, data.	Any subject matter/content, e.g., the history of the Greeks; Ohm's Law; World Series results; the parliamentary system of government; conjugation of the verb "to be."
People	Persons who are acting to store and/or transmit Messages.	Teacher; student; actor; speaker.
Material	Items (traditionally called media or software) which usually store Messages for transmission by devices; sometimes self-displaying.	Overhead transparency; slide; filmstrip; 16mm motion picture; 8mm motion picture; videotape; record; audiotape; programmed instruction materials; computer-assisted instruction program; book; journal.
Device	Items (traditionally called hardware) which transmit Messages stored on Materials.	Overhead projector; slide projector; filmstrip projector; 16mm film projector; 8mm film projector; videotape recorder; television set; record player; radio; tape recorder; dial access information retrieval system console; teaching machine; talking typewriter; computer output devices.

Table 1 Learning resources/instructional system components *(continued)*

Resource or Component	Definition	Examples
Technique	Routine procedures or precast molds for using Materials, Devices, Settings, and People to transmit Messages.	Computer-assisted instruction; programmed instruction; simulation; gaming; discovery; inquiry; field trip; team teaching; individualized instruction; self-instruction; group instruction; lecture; discussion.
Setting	The environment in which the Messages are received.	*Physical:* school building; instructional materials center; library; studio; classroom; auditorium. *Environmental:* lighting; heating; acoustics.

application. In addition, the application of educational technology affects the organizational structure of education because: (1) it moves the impact of educational technology to the curriculum strategy (and perhaps determination) level; (2) it permits four types of educational patterns—people resources alone, other resources used by (and controlled by) people, people in shared responsibility with other resources (combined into educational systems using mediated instruction), other resources (mediated instruction) alone; (3) it makes possible the existence of alternative institutional forms for facilitating learning, and can serve all these types of alternative institutions. These applications have significant impact on the specific processes of education: they change the techniques of doing, and the people who do, content determination (including standardization, choice, quantity, and quality), design, production, and evaluation of instruction, and interaction with, and assessment of, learners. The result leads to a drastic change in the role of school systems and the individual teacher.

7. Educational technology has guidelines for training and certification. There is a competency-based framework for training people who perform tasks in educational technology. The framework is based on groupings of tasks from various functions within the domains of educational and instructional technology. The groupings reflect specialties within the field as well as levels of performance within the specialty area. The specialties are: (1) instructional program development, (2) media product development, and (3) media management. The three levels of task complexity are aide, technician, and specialist. AECT currently has guidelines for training programs for, and certification of, technicians and specialists in each of the three specialty areas, and is developing procedures for the implementation of those guidelines.

8. Educational technology has provisions for the development and implementation of leadership. Leadership within the profession is carried out

Text continues on page 13

Table 2 Educational/instructional development functions

Functions which have as their purpose analyzing problems, and devising, implementing, and evaluating the Learning Resources/Instructional System Components solutions to these problems.

Function	Definition	Examples
Research-Theory		
Purpose:	To generate and test knowledge (theory and research methodology) related to the functions, Learning Resources and Instructional System Components and learners.	To conceptualize theoretical models. To conduct research projects. To analyze research data.
Outcome:	Knowledge which can act as an input to the other functions.	To generate new ideas. To test validity of model. To test hypotheses.
Activity:	Seeking information, reading it, analyzing it, synthesizing it, testing it, analyzing test results.	Reads proposal. Compares model with known data. Formulates specific hypotheses.
Design		
Purpose:	To translate general theoretical knowledge into specifications for Learning Resources or Instructional System Components.	To design programmed instruction materials. To develop instructional modules for individualized instruction. To design equipment systems.
Outcome:	Specifications for production of Learning Resources and Instructional System Components, regardless of format or resource.	To write general objectives. To determine medium. To describe technical systems.
Activity:	Analyzing, synthesizing, and writing objectives, learner characteristics, task analyses, learning conditions, instructional events, specifications for Learning Resources and Instructional Systems Components.	Analyzes objectives. Synthesizes objectives/ sequence/content/media. Arranges materials in sequence.

Table 2 Educational/Instructional development functions *(continued)*

Function	Definition	Examples
Production		
Purpose:	To translate specifications for Learning Resources or Instructional Systems Components into specific actual items.	To produce audiotapes. To direct motion picture. To write computer programs for computer-assisted instruction.
Outcome:	Specific products in the form of test versions, prototypes, or mass-produced versions.	To make slides into test filmstrips. To decide on music/sound effects. To match audio and visuals.
Activity:	Operating production equipment, drawing, laying out, writing, building products.	Mixes narration tape and sound. Sequences slides using viewer. Operates motion picture camera.
Evaluation-Selection		
Purpose:	To assess acceptability of actual produced Learning Resources or Instructional System Components in terms of criteria set by other functions, and to develop models for this assessment.	To pilot test prototype instructional materials. To preview and select instructional materials. To develop evaluation models and techniques.
Outcomes:	(a) Evaluation for Design: effectiveness of Learning Resources or Instructional System Components in meeting their objectives. (b) Evaluation for Production: acceptability of items in meeting production standards. (c) Evaluation for Evaluation: evaluation models. (d) Evaluation for Selection: acceptability of items for acquisition for a specific purpose.	To identify problems with materials. To identify objectives not met. To insure acceptable sound quality.

Table continued on next page

Table 2 **Educational/instructional development functions** *(continued)*

Function	Definition	Examples
Outcomes: *(continued)*	(e) Evaluation for Utilization: acceptability of items for meeting learning objectives in actual use.	
Activity:	Analyzing quality in terms of standards.	Observes students using materials. Analyzes possible uses of materials. Compares data and objectives.
Logistics		
Purpose:	To make Learning Resources and Instructional System Components available for other functions.	To have equipment ready as needed. To provide delivery service. To catalog materials.
Outcome:	Ordered, stored, retrieved, classified, catalogued, assembled, scheduled, distributed, operated, maintained, and repaired Learning Resources and Instructional System Components.	To cross-index materials. To locate materials for delivery. To keep repair history. To repair filmstrip projector.
Activity:	Ordering, storing, retrieving, classifying, cataloging, assembling, scheduling, distributing, operating, maintaining, repairing Learning Resources and Instructional System Components.	Threads movie projector. Assigns media code from list. Plans new scheduling system.
Utilization		
Purpose:	To bring learners into contact with Learning Resources and Instructional System Components.	To help student use learning activity. To monitor individualized and self-instruction. To help student select learning activities and to meet objectives.

Table 2   Educational/Instructional development functions *(continued)*

Function	Definition	Examples
Outcome:	Facilitation and assessment of student learning.	To analyze student learning style. To present information. To encourage interest in learning activity.
Activity:	Assigning, preparing learner for, presenting, assisting, and following up Learning Resources and Instructional System Components; testing learners.	Discusses with student. Compares learning activities with learning style. Compares pre- and post-tests.
Utilization-Dissemination		
Purpose:	(A special subfunction of Utilization.) To bring learners into contact with information about educational technology.	To consult on materials design and use. To teach photography course. To explain individualized instruction project. To increase use of learning resources center services by teachers.
Outcome:	Dissemination of information about educational technology.	To provide models for designing instruction. To improve use of mediated instruction by teachers. To answer questions about individualized instruction project. To demonstrate projector. To explain learning resources center services to teachers.
Activity:	Taking in and giving out information about educational technology.	Defines learning resources center services available. Writes professional articles. Views microteaching lesson. Role plays teacher using mediated instruction.

Table 3 Educational/instructional management functions

Functions which have as their purpose the directing or controlling of one or more of the Educational/Instructional Development Functions or of other Educational/Instructional Management Functions to ensure their effective operation.

Function	Definition	Examples
Organization/ Management		
Purpose:	To determine, modify, or execute the objectives, philosophy, policy, structure, budget, internal and external relationships, and administrative procedures of an organization performing one or several of the Development functions or the Management functions.	To administer/direct project which includes two or more functions. To monitor and change operation of center. To provide secretarial services in an audio-visual center.
Outcome:	Policy, budget, plans, coordinated activities, administrative operations.	To prepare budget. To identify organization needs. To ascertain jobs to be done.
Activity:	Defining, writing, and carrying out procedures leading to the outcomes.	Reviews purchase orders. Designs new organizational model. Analyzes problems in project.
Personnel- Management		
Purpose:	To interact with and/or to supervise the people who perform activities in the functions.	To supervise personnel in graphics unit. To improve communications between technicians and artists. To staff projects.
Outcome:	Interpersonal interaction, discussion, supervision, employment, and personal development.	To evaluate work performed. To encourage discussion. To supervise the repair person.
Activity:	Discussing with and speaking to other people.	Negotiates with personnel department. Questions applicants. Talks with new employees.

through various leadership conferences and internship programs. In addition, educational technology fulfills a leadership function in the field of education through participation in joint groups, grants, and publications.

9. Educational technology has an association and professional communications. There is at least one professional association directly concerned with educational technology—the Association for Educational Communications and Technology. In addition to facilitating communication among members through its annual convention and three periodic publications, it serves to develop and implement the standards and ethics, leadership, and training and certification characteristics of the profession.

10. Educational technology acknowledges itself as a profession through its professional association and the activities it performs.

11. Educational technology operates within the larger context of society. It advocates being a concerned profession—concerned about the uses to which its techniques and applications are being put. Further, as a profession, it has taken stands in favor of intellectual freedom, in favor of affirmative action, against stereotyping in materials, and in favor of enlisting technology in support of humane and life-fulfilling ends.

12. Educational technology operates within the total field of education. In its relationship to other professions also involved in the field it advocates a coequal and cooperative relationship among these professions.

13. Since the definition presented here meets all the criteria for the existence of a theory (preceding items 1–4), educational technology is a theory about how problems in human learning are identified and solved. Since the definition meets all the criteria for the existence of a field (preceding items 1–6), educational technology is a field involved in applying a complex, integrated process to analyze and solve problems in human learning. Since the definition meets all the criteria for the existence of a profession (preceding items 1–12), educational technology is a profession made up of an organized effort to implement the theory, intellectual technique, and practical application of educational technology. The definitions of educational technology as a theory, a field, and a profession are congruent—with each being derived directly from the one which precedes it.

14. Persons are members of the field of educational technology if they perform activities that fall within the Domain of Educational Technology, based on the theoretical framework of, and employing the intellectual technique of, educational technology.

15. Persons are members of the profession of educational technology if they already meet the criteria for operating within the field; spend a majority of their time performing one or more of the Domain of Educational Technology functions; subscribe to the standards and ethics of the profession; and have the training and certification required by the profession; are involved in developing their own leadership abilities; are members of the association and participate in its communications through reading its journals and attending its meetings; acknowledge themselves as members of the profession; are concerned professionals—examining the ends to which their skills are put and accepting those values set forth by the profession; and relate to other professionals on a coequal and cooperative basis. These people may be called "educational technologists."

16. "The concept of instructional or educational technology is totally integrative. It provides a common ground for all professionals, no matter in what aspect of the field they are working. It permits the rational development and integration of new devices, materials, and methods as they come along. The concept is so completely viable that it will not only provide new status for our group, but will, for the first time, threaten the status of others" (Finn, 1965, p. 193).

"The educational future will belong to those who can grasp the significance of [educational and] instructional technology" (Finn, 1964a, p. 26).

Educational Technology: Archetypes, Paradigms and Models

Ivor K. Davies

His Majesty's Ministers, finding that Gulliver's stature exceeded theirs in the proportion of twelve to one, concluded from the similarity of their bodies that he must contain at least 1728 (or 12³) of theirs, and must needs be rationed accordingly.

Jonathan Swift

Like education itself, educational technology has undergone considerable change over the last twenty years. Although the old fears about technology still exist, particularly when technology is narrowly conceived, the basic concepts are gradually being absorbed into the mainstream of educational thought and practice. Imagination and technology, aided by a renewed sense of craftsmanship in teaching, have together enlarged the possibilities of knowledge, action and moral obligation. At the same time, however, whilst imagination and technology have expanded the possibilities or range of choices available to educators, they have also made it more difficult to foresee the full consequences of the choices made and the actions taken.

Technology, contrary to popular belief, is not necessarily confined to the *means* by which educators realise their ends. Technology also raises anew questions about the nature of the ends themselves. It forces us to reflect on the morality of what we are about, by its very insistence on defensible choices. By opening up the range of possibilities, technology in and of education has caused us to reflect upon, and sometimes to reconsider, the manner in which selections are made, as well as the purposes for which they are being considered. In other words, the very richness of the alternatives now available to us, together with potential for increased effectiveness, forces us to reflect on the ethical nature of what we have in mind. Unfortunately,

---

From: Davies, I. K. 1978. Educational technology: Archetypes, paradigms and models. In *Contributions to educational technology*, vol. 2, edited by J. A. Hartley and I. K. Davies, 9–29. London: Kogan Page. Reprinted with permission. Copyright Ivor K. Davies.

the deep satisfaction, sense of creativity, and feelings of accomplishment that can be experienced in the *doing* of educational technology are too often preferred to the related, but very different, pleasures of *contemplating* educational technology. Yet contemplation and responsibility go hand in hand, one without the other is meaningless.

Problems of Choice

The problem of the standard or criteria against which choices are made from the range of technological alternatives available is, therefore, becoming a matter of enhanced importance to both the theory and practice of education. What is "best" is not only a technological question, but also an ethical one. A defensible choice, at the very least, involves addressing both of these issues, and, in so doing, raises yet again basic questions regarding the nature of education. Different sets of criteria reflect different values, and the idea of value is implicit in the very term "education". Richard Peters (1959) speaks of education as initiation into worthwhile activities, and goes on to suggest that:

> Education relates to some sort of processes in which a desirable (e.g., valued) state of mind develops. It would be as much a logical contradiction to say that a person has been educated and yet the change was in no way desirable as it would be to say that he had been reformed and yet had made no change for the better … something of value should be passed on … the truth is that being worthwhile is part of what is meant by calling it education.

Thus, tightly bound up with the idea of education is the underlying notion that education is implicitly worthwhile, and that what students learn should be valuable. Since educational technology should contribute to the worthwhileness of the experience, the issues of relevance and justification must constantly be addressed by the technologist. Judgements as well as decisions must be constantly made and questioned.

A *judgement* is a choice between "right" and "wrong"; a choice between "good" and "bad" or "true" and "false". The goal is to determine who is "guilty" and who is "innocent." This is achieved by weighing the evidence, having previously determined what information will be admissible, and then making a pronouncement or judgement. Implicit in the process is the role of an outside arbiter who forms an authoritative opinion one way or another, providing that there is a case to answer and that it is within jurisdiction. A *decision*, on the other hand, is a choice between a range of alternatives, none of which is probably more right than the others. At the very best, a decision is likely to involve selecting between alternatives that are "almost right" and "probably wrong," and, at the very worst, between a range of alternatives between which there is little to choose. Implicit in the process is the role of an inside person, who has the necessary authority to resolve the issue by making a choice appropriate to the circumstances.

In a very real sense, decisions are made prior to an event, before any action has been taken, whereas judgements are more likely to be made after the event when a course of action has been implemented. This distinction is important, in the context of educational technology, for all too often it is overlooked. An educational technologist chooses between the alternatives available by making appropriate decisions on the basis of a set of principles and procedures valued by the profession and founded in a theory or paradigm. The experiences and results that stem from these decisions, however, should subsequently be judged in terms of their worth in an educational endeavour. The question "What is desirable, and why is it desirable?" is the fundamental and most far-reaching problem facing education. Yet, it is not a question that lends itself to a final answer. All that is possible is to consider it rationally, and for the technologist to attempt to identify the relative merits of the solutions that are proposed for meeting current educational demands. Care should be taken, however, to leave the door open, so that fresh solutions and new evidence can be considered as they become available. As long as the question is constantly being raised, and educational judgements made, educational technologists will be better able to make decisions more likely to contribute to initiation into worthwhile and morally defensible experiences.

The Nature of Educational Technology

The effectiveness of any form or organised activity largely depends upon an organisation's ability to achieve its goals, fulfil the needs of its members, maintain itself internally, and to adapt to its environment. If an organisation fails to realise these goals, it is "unhealthy", or steadily ineffective. If an organisation realises them, it is "healthy", and able to learn through experience, free to change, and free to respond to new circumstances. Educational technology is concerned with these problems in an educational context, and it is characterised by its disciplined approach to a creative organisation of resources for learning. In order to make this contribution to the "health" of an educational institution, curriculum, programme, course or lesson, an educational technologist uses a body of established principles, know-how and procedures. Indeed, the original meaning of the word "technology" was concerned with know-how or method, and it was only with the Great Exhibition of 1851 that the word became overly associated with machines.

Although in one very real sense there has always been a technology *of* education (teachers, for instance, use their voices to excite as well as to explain; chalkboards and books have become such commonplace items in classrooms that few think of them as a form of media; lesson planning is a form of systematic development, etc), its "modern" antecedents are clearly discernible in the so-called educational revolution of the late 1950s. Sir Eric Ashby (1967) actually distinguishes four revolutions in education. The first occurred when society began to differentiate out varying roles, and the task of educating the young was partly shifted from parents to teachers and from homes to schools. The second occurred with the adoption of the written word as an alternative to oral instruction, whilst the third revolution came with the invention of printing which resulted in a wider availability of books. The fourth revolution, Ashby argues, was foreshadowed by developments in electronics, particularly developments in the area of radio, telephone, television, projectors, recorders (both sound and picture), and computers.

The term "revolution", particularly in the context of education, is distasteful, but the four developments that Ashby identifies have certainly had, and are still having, a remarkable effect on educational practice. Each has brought along a set of problems, still largely with us today. Each has led less to an enlargement of the intellectual realm, and more to a reinforcement of existing traditional institutions and practices—but on a different scale. The problem of the respective responsibilities of the home and school still troubles us today, and the role of the teacher and of the learner in the theatre of education is a matter of continuing concern. The uneasy competition between the written and oral traditions in education is with us still, whilst the present escalating prices of printed books are bringing renewed problems to classroom teachers and students alike. The developments of the fourth or electronic revolution (already in general use in educational research, in growing use in administration, and in some use in the information and library sciences) are now beginning to affect the teaching-learning processes. They are making possible independent study, an enriched variety of courses and methods of instruction, easier access to education, a lessening of routine teaching responsibilities and duties, as well as a more analytical and creative approach to subject matter. Unfortunately, the cost is a very heavy one, not only in terms of money, but even more importantly in terms of the centralising effects that each revolution has introduced into the organisation of education. Whilst some people are concerned with the problems that can come from de-humanising education, too few appear to be concerned with the greater problems which stem from the centralisation of education.

Ashby's four revolutions, if we must continue to use the term, also highlight another problem with educational technology, as it has been utilised. In each case, there has been a tendency, in most instances stemming from inertia, to use the fruits of technology merely to replicate, on a larger and grander scale, traditional institutions and practices (the Open University is a major exception to this rule, as are some of the curriculum development projects of the Schools' Council for Curriculum and Examinations). Instead of viewing educational technology as an opportunity for renewing educational practice, it has, too often, been conceived as a means of doing what has always been done—only more efficiently. Too few educators and parents, until perhaps the "Great Debate" which took place in Britain in 1977, have overly concerned themselves with asking whether, what can undoubtedly be done more efficiently, ought to be done at all. Something else is needed, and educational technology ought to be a part of it, but this entails questioning the underlying assumptions we make about technology *in* education. Indeed, technology is probably considerably less self-limiting than our own perception or view of it.

The Three New Educational Technologies

Some years ago, Francis Crick, winner of the Nobel Prize for his work on DNA, was asked why it was that only a few scientists made important discoveries. Professor Crick thought for a while, and then said that there were many reasons. Sometimes, it was due to an absence of the necessary resources, or even a lack of opportunity. A piece of experimental evidence could be wrong. Rarely, however, was the failure due to an absence of the necessary facts; usually they were there all the time. The most important reason, he went on to say, was usually that people were handicapped by assumptions that they were not aware they were making. So it is with the assumptions we make about the nature of the educational technology. Indeed, three different technologies can be discerned in the literature, depending upon the assumption made. They can be conveniently referred to as Educational Technology One, Two and Three (Davies, 1972).

Educational Technology One

Educational Technology One is essentially a "hardware" approach, stressing the importance of aids for teaching. Its origin lies in the application of the physical sciences and engineering to the problems of education. This concept tends to dominate most of the classical writings on educational technology. It assumes that a technology of machines is intimately related to a technology of teaching, and that progressive views in education, therefore, are closely associated with possession of the latest projector, language laboratory or computer.

Technology is seen as a means of mechanising or automating the process of teaching with devices that transmit, amplify, distribute, record and reproduce stimuli materials, and thus increase the teacher's impact as well as widen the potential audience. In other words, teachers can use Technology One to deal more efficiently with larger and larger groups of students, increase the power of their teaching, and reach beyond the boundaries of the school or classroom— all without necessarily increasing the cost of students taught, and sometimes even reducing it.

Educational Technology Two

Educational Technology Two is essentially a "software" approach, stressing the importance of aids to learning. Its origin lies in the application of behavioural science to the problems of education. This concept tends to dominate most of the current writings on educational technology, particularly in the areas of curriculum, course and instructional development. It assumes that a technology of message design (founded firmly on goal setting, task analysis, motivational principles and evaluation) lies at the heart of efficient learning.

Technology is seen as a means of providing the necessary know-how for designing new, or renewing current, worthwhile learning experiences. Machines and mechanisation are viewed merely as instruments of presentation or transmission. The procedures of curriculum and course development (the predominant British terms) as well as instructional development (the current American term) characteristic of this approach largely revolve around: identifying appropriate aims, goals and objectives; selecting relevant content and subject matter; choosing contrasting learning methodologies, activities and experiences so as to make for a worthwhile and rewarding course of study; and then evaluating not only the success of the resulting learning experience but also the effectiveness of the very development techniques employed.

Teachers can also use Technology Two as a means of enhancing their own teaching. If they are inexperienced, Technology Two provides guidelines or procedures; if they are experienced teachers, Technology Two can be used as a springboard for further craftsmanship. Indeed, much of the curriculum and course renewal that has characterised European and North American education over the last ten years (at primary, secondary and tertiary levels), as well as a great deal of military and industrial training, is a product of the interest that has been taken in Educational Technology Two. The activity is also a testimony to the efficacy of the development procedures available, as well as a warning of the limitations that can be expected if enthusiasm and systematic development activities lose sight of the ultimate "name of the game".

Educational Technology Three

Educational Technology Three combines the "hardware" and "software" approaches of the other two technologies. It rejects systematic development (i.e., step-by-step, rigidly mechanical or mechanistic procedures) as the *only* way of proceeding, in favour of a systemic (i.e., organic rather than mechanistic) set of procedures focusing rather more deeply on the processes as well as on the products of teaching and learning. It applies system analysis concepts to education, and its bias is somewhat less towards the individual *per se* and rather more towards the group or team within which an individual plays a role. The quality and relevance of the overall experience is one of the major concerns of Technology Three, and accordingly it assumes that the environment within which teaching and learning take place is as important as the actual processes themselves. Authority and organisation in the school, in so far as they are related to both curricular and pastoral matters, and as they affect individuals, groups, institution and community, are subjects of concern. No teacher or student is free to act in total isolation, and neither is an institution like a school or university able to carry on its business without affecting others (see Richardson, 1975). Everything is part of a whole or a living system, and the "health" of that system is a matter of primary concern, not only for its continued well-being but also for its very survival.

Educators can use Technology Three as a means of enhancing the worthwhileness of what they are about. Whilst Technology One is largely concerned with transmission-reception problems, and Technology Two with purposeful shaping of behaviour, Technology Three is warmly human in its total and integrated approach. Its emphasis is on a range of contrasting skills, from which selections can be made depending upon the nature of the problem posed. It is fundamentally a problem-solving approach, heavy in its diagnostic interest and inquiry orientation. Technologies One and Two can be used, as appropriate, but the orientation and reasons for their use are wider and broader than might otherwise be perceived.

Educational Technology Three, with its primary orientation towards a systemic approach, is characteristically faced with one underlying question. Identifying the boundary of the system, within which problems are occurring, is a matter of enormous practical difficulty. What at first sight might appear to be a nice, self-contained difficulty, can soon become a matter of complexity involving a greatly enlarged context. It is as if "everything nailed down is coming loose". Whilst such a discovery might be intellectually exciting, it places an enormous burden of responsibility on the technologist. It is impossible, in the real world, to dismantle everything every time some change is required. Common sense, alone, suggests that there is an underlying advantage, in most cases, to a piecemeal approach, in which one moves by successive approximations towards some desired future. Indeed, this is likely to be one of the reasons why educators so dislike the term "revolution" as applied to their professional area, with all its connotations of a utopian blueprint—desirable, perhaps, but so out of tune with the realities. Reality for Educational Technology Three is to identify problem boundaries, to deal with the immediate situation, but without always calling for too drastic a remedy. The problem is one of effectiveness, not necessarily one of efficiency.

The skills of effectiveness are particularly revealing as far as they reveal the underlying priorities of a Technology Three approach. They include:

- *sensitivity*, so that the needs of the total situation, both people and task, can be sensed
- *diagnostic ability*, so that the nature of the problem or difficulty can be identified and communicated
- *decision making*, so that appropriate actions can be selected from a wide range of possible alternatives
- *flexibility*, so that it is possible to implement whatever the situation demands or requires
- *action skills*, so that routine and mechanistic tasks of implementation can be efficiently carried out

Above all, to borrow from Peter Drucker (1966), Educational Technology Three requires an understanding of where a teacher's and student's time goes. It requires a knowledge of how to gear efforts to results, rather than to activities which generate only busy work; how to build on their own and their students' strengths, rather than on their weaknesses. It involves making the right decisions based on "dissenting opinions", rather than on a "consensus of the facts". All this means focusing upon opportunities, rather than on problems, and on those few key areas that will produce outstanding results, rather than on trying to achieve everything and fail through lack of time (see Davies, 1976).

Archetypes, Paradigms and Models of Educational Technology

As in any area of disciplined inquiry, educational technologists never theorise in a vacuum. The way in which an educational problem is stated, the principles and concepts that are used, all provide a starting point. Empirical data, assumptions, professional perspectives are all used to illuminate the situation, as well as to suggest a range of appropriate strategies and tactics that might be employed. Other factors, as Phillips (1971) points out, can influence such theorising; factors such as simplicity, robustness, elegance and sophistication are often important, as is coherence with established theories in education and educational technology. In other words, educational technologists always have a theory, sometimes crude and at other times highly sophisticated, that shapes the way a situation is seen, and influences the values that surround it. Since there is little currently in the literature that seeks to examine the theories of educational technology, it is important to use this opportunity to take stock—so that the papers making up this volume can be viewed in the light of the different positions they represent and the values that they espouse.

Three terms are often used in the general literature dealing with disciplined acts of inquiry, all of which have quite specific technical meanings. The three terms are "archetype", "paradigm" and "model". Since the term "model" is often used in the literature of educational technology, usually with a lack of precision, it is important to consider what is being said and more often suggested when the term is employed. Indeed, the literature of educational technology, and more especially that of curriculum, course and instructional development, is replete with competing models, all of which suggest different ways of proceeding, and most of which appear to indicate values more appropriate to engineering than to an education.

An Archetype

The viewpoint or perspective used by someone engaged in an act of inquiry is most often referred to as an "archetype" or "root metaphor". It acts as a loose theoretical framework or prototype, a primordial image or pattern that seems constantly to recur throughout the professional literature. More importantly, it is consistent enough in its occurrence to be considered a universal principle or algorithm for thought and action.

The term, which was first used in English around 1605, is part of the vocabulary of historians, anthropologists and psychologists. Jung (1922) uses the term in the context of a "primordial image", a "psychic residue", which constantly tends to repeat itself in human experience. Frazer, in *The Golden Bough*, uses the word to trace elemental patterns of myth and ritual, which recur in the legends and ceremonials of diverse cultures. The term has also been used in literary criticism (by Wilson Knight, Robert Graves and Northrop Frye) to identify narrative designs, character types or images which are said to be identifiable in a wide range of writings. The term is also meaningful in educational technology as a descriptor for the myths, dreams and ritualised modes of professional conduct, which—rather than be seen for what they are—have often been taken for what they are not. They hold the profession together, offer a language of belief, and bind the community in a set of common acts and assumptions. The current myth of concern and the liturgy of action, as evidenced by the basic *engineering* archetype, threatens to become for educational technology a limitation to further creative efforts.

A Paradigm

An archetype can serve a number of different paradigms, but more usually only one paradigm is involved—although the paradigm may be presented differently or in varying degrees of detail or complexity. In essence, a paradigm is a more concrete conceptualisation of an underlying idea or theory, involving definitions, statements and interrelationships between the statements. Some refining has taken place so that a coherent tradition of research and practice is possible. The paradigm, which is usually qualitative in nature, may be expressed in words, in numbers or in some other type of visual display. A diagram, illustrating important relationships by means of a series of boxes and arrows, is often used. In this way, a unique description of the phenomena can be portrayed, underlying methodologies indicated and research questions worthy of further study suggested. The paradigm may also be used to help explain events previously unexplained.

Unlike the archetype, a paradigm rarely represents a dramatic new orientation, nor does it attempt to offer a "world view" or wide embracing perspective of the nature of reality. It is much too limited and applied for that. However, as in educational technology, a particular paradigm can be recognised in two important ways:

- it is sufficiently novel and appealing to attract an enduring group of adherents away from competing ways of proceeding
- it is sufficiently open-ended to allow adherents to pursue all sorts of problems in a manner that allows them to refine and define the details of the basic paradigm, as well as to attract new adherents.

To put it another way, it can usually be assumed that where there is a small group of people working together, with shared values and concerns, the liturgy and rituals of their activities indicate that there is likely to be a shared paradigm. The paradigm acts as a cohesive and binding force for their work.

Once a paradigm or series of paradigms has been proposed, there will still be details and ambiguities to be identified and resolved. This type of activity will commonly result in different variations of the basic paradigm design. The basic principle remains, but the emphasis, priorities and particulars may change. In fact, the number of paradigm variations can be endless, and often a new paradigm is promised when nothing more than another variation is proposed. So it is with educational technology, and even more particularly with curriculum, course and instructional development. The paradigms that are currently available are worryingly limited, although the variations offered seem endlessly lacking in anything creatively different.

A Model

Curriculum, course and instructional development is rich in so-called "models", which in the manner of the preceding discussion are technically paradigms. A model, which usually has a quantitative dimension, is a much more specific and detailed representation of reality. Just as a child's model car bears a quantitative relationship to the real thing, so that the distance between the rear wheels on the model can be used to calculate the distance between them on the real car, so a model in science bears a quantitative relationship to reality. A map is a model, distances on the map represent distances on the ground, a mathematical equation is a model, and so is a photograph. Simulators are also models, as are some games.

The idea of modelling is hardly new. Early astronomers made models of the universe as they conceived it, engineers made models of the bridges and aquaducts they designed, and architects have long made models of the buildings they wished to build. What is new, is the recognition that is currently given to models, and the extent to which they are currently employed as a basis for intellectual activity. Three main reasons suggest themselves for this growth and ready acceptance (Starr, 1971). First, the deliberate manipulation of people and organisations is ethically questionable and in many cases now unlawful. Secondly, the amount of uncertainty with which professional people have to deal has been increasing rapidly, so that errors are more probable at a time when the costs (human and financial) associated with them are increasing at an alarming rate. Finally, as a result of developments in operations research, our ability to build models that are good representations of reality has improved to such a degree that there has been increased interest and confidence in their usefulness.

The underlying purpose of building a paradigm is to falsify it, so that it can be replaced with a more accurate portrayal. On the other hand, the underlying purpose of building a particular model is to exploit or use it in the solution of a particular problem. Models are usually specific to a particular phenomenon, and quite different models may represent the same phenomenon from quite different paradigmatic viewpoints. Exploiting Bohr's principle of complementarity in physics as a paradigm, for instance, it is possible to model "light" both as particles travelling as straight lines, and as a series of wave trains without being inconsistent. The great property of the paradigm is its "suggestive power", whereas the importance of the model lies in the manner in which it is possible to formulate associated hypotheses so that they can be tested.

In educational technology, few of the models—with the possible exception of the models of Aptitude-Treatment Interaction (ATIs)—have been tested, with the worrying result that so much of the empirical investigations have taken place without reference to an underlying theory. Instead, the field has been overly characterised by a vast amount of small pieces of self-contained research, which is often difficult to put together into a coherent framework useful as a guide for future action. An attempt to make such a contribution has been made in the area of pre-instructional strategies (Hartley and Davies, 1976), where the empirical findings concerning behavioural objectives, pre-tests, advance organisers and overviews have been reviewed in an attempt to indicate their several roles in a range of contrasting instructional situations.

Objective and Subjective Paradigms in Educational Technology

As we have already seen, the concept of educational technology implies for many people a systematic approach to learning "in which one tries to develop means to achieve given ends and persists in one's attempts to find solutions to problems" (MacKenzie, Eraut and Jones, 1976). The basic and all pervasive archetype appears to be an engineering one, and the associated paradigms are heavily biased towards the kinds of objectivity traditionally valued in science as normally perceived (see Kuhn, 1970). This has led to a suspicion amongst educators that the notion of objectivity is the *only* paradigm possible in educational technology, especially in the areas of curriculum, course and instructional development. It is as if perception, consensually validated, is the only professionally acceptable way of knowing and understanding reality. Yet an alternative is available, and an alternative that is particularly valuable in the domain of educational technology. This alternative involves the notion that there is available a subjective paradigm, and that both objectivity and subjectivity are themselves assumptions.

The very process of observation, in an educational context, interferes with what is being observed, as it does in any other situation, so that the phenomenon observed is changed by the very act of observing it. Eddington (see Heisenberg, 1958) put the matter dramatically when he wrote:

> We have found that where science has progressed the farthest, the mind has but regained from nature that which the mind put into nature. We have found a strange footprint on the shores of the unknown. We have devised profound theories, one after another, to account for its origin. At last, we have succeeded in reconstructing the creature that made the footprint. And lo! It is our own.

The inescapable conclusion to be drawn would appear to be that there are limits to objectivity, and that knowledge leads back to the people engaged in the act of inquiry. Problems are solved by people, and the data they collect is contaminated by the people making the very act of observation and perception, analysis and evaluation. This thought, however, is so alien to some traditional ways of thinking developed by educational technologists, although not to many teachers in the humanities, that it has only been in the last few years that any attempt has been made to accommodate the idea by developing a new archetype based not on engineering but on creative problem solving. Lateral, rather than vertical, thinking (see de Bono, 1976), like Zen, has become a fashionable and useful archetype with associated paradigms.

A great deal of the present concern in education with morality and ethical matters can be viewed as a direct contribution of the subjective paradigm. Poole (1972), for instance, argues that since the "body is the locus of all ethical experience, all experience is, because spatial, ethical. There can be no act which does not take place in ethical space. There can be no 'flaccid' act, no act devoid of all significance, no unconditioned act." In other words, knowledge and responsibility are both aspects of the subjective paradigm and ethical concerns have little or no role in a world seen from the viewpoint of an objective paradigm. Such a thought is of particular importance to educational technology, since the antecedents of so many of its procedures are clearly discernible in the principles of behaviourism. The very advantages claimed for behaviourism, as viewed from the perspective of the objective paradigm, raise important ethical questions for education when viewed from the alternative perspective of the subjective paradigm. Dogmatism and scepticism, however, are human failings associated with both paradigms, and at the very end technologists are still faced with the problem of making a judgement and a series of associated decisions about technology.

Three Archetypes and Three Paradigms of Educational Technology

In the light of the preceding discussion, it is possible to identify three archetypes that have developed in educational technology. The first archetype is an audio-visual one, and although initially developed in the media field in the 1930s it became particularly important in the years following the second world war. The second archetype is an engineering one, which came into prominence with the emerging interest in programmed learning in the early 1960s and is still with us to a very large extent to this day. The third archetype is a problem-solving one, highly related to the creative process, which is currently emerging as a focal point of the more innovative curriculum, course and instructional development activities currently under way in both the United Kingdom and the United States.

Each one of these archetypes has led to the development of a series of related paradigms. Although more than one paradigm has developed for each of the "root metaphors", the differences are more in detail than in substance. Accordingly, it is possible to indicate the major concerns and development procedures by looking at one paradigm for each of the three archetypes. For the sake of illustration, a metaphor is used for each paradigm in order to indicate the flavour of the underlying approach. As with all figurative language, the metaphors should not be taken literally or even too seriously. Figure 1 illustrates both the three paradigms of educational technology, and their associated metaphors. [Figure 1 was not available for reprint.] In each case, additional boxes, circles and arrows could have been added to the diagrams, as well as more labels. The aim, however, has not been to be as exhaustive as possible, but to convey the major thrust of each of the three contrasting approaches.

The Audio-Visual Archetype

The Audio-Visual Archetype predates the other archetypes of educational technology, which perhaps explains why media departments in so many of our universities have associated with them, as an apparent anomaly, curriculum, course or development activities. The associated metaphor is one of a gum-ball machine, "you put in your money and you are given something to chew on." So it is with the associated paradigm. Educational technology or, more accurately, the associated audio-visual "hardware" can be used to: aid classroom presentations and teaching; serve as a means of improving classroom demonstrations by allowing students to experience what normally would not be available to them; help solve logistical problems (as in the use of radio and television, films and sound tapes) by enabling teachers to deal with learners located in different parts of the country; enrich teaching and learning by becoming an integral part of both processes; and, finally, offer a novel form of instrumenting assessment and testing procedures by making available computers and other machines so as to automate and speed up the whole examination process.

The Engineering Archetype

The Engineering Archetype came into being with the advent of programmed learning, and the application of behaviouristic technology to both teaching and learning as a result of the influence of Professor B F Skinner in the early 1960s. Operant conditioning, and the shaping of behaviour, became part of a radically new technology in education and, at the same time, generated a good deal of emotion for and against educational technology itself. A great deal of the initial effort, therefore, involved comparing the respective performance of classroom teachers and teaching machines in order to demonstrate the advantages of the new methodology. It was a similar technique to that still used in medicine and pharmacology, where a new procedure or drug is tested in a comparative situation, with one group given the new treatment and the other a placebo. The metaphor, in both instances, is that of a slot-car race, in which one car is raced against another in order to see who wins.

The underlying paradigm in educational technology normally takes the form of a series of boxes and arrows, usually with a feedback loop, indicating a step-by-step approach to development work. Almost always there is a clear beginning (definition of objectives), and almost always a terminal step (evaluation). Indeed, the initial and terminal steps have become so threatening to classroom teachers that a great deal of emotion has been generated on the subject of defining objectives and evaluating teaching. The debate, however, really centres around the mechanistic character of the paradigm, and the notion that it is possible to regard each one of the different activities associated with development work as self-contained entities. Unfortunately, the debate has sometimes led a few technologists to design even more complicated and detailed paradigms, with even more feedback loops, rather than examine the underlying assumptions.

The Problem-Solving Archetype

The Problem-Solving Archetype began to be adopted around 1973 to 1974, and, although still not characteristic of the everyday activities of the majority of educational technologists, it is fast becoming an alternative way of seeing. The associated metaphor is that of a chess game, in which players engage in an intellectual activity for which there is no one set of appropriate moves. Intense concentration, ability to foresee the future consequences of current actions, flexibility, and acquired skill and learning experience are all essential prerequisites for success *and* a rewarding experience. So it is with educational technology. In the educational context some sort of dissatisfaction should preface development activities, and the overall goal should then be to reach a state of satisfaction as quickly as possible. In order to accomplish this, an educational technologist brings to the situation a range of skills (observation, analysis, synthesis, etc). The order, and manner, in which they are then used depends upon the character of the problem, and the aim in mind. There is no one best way, and no one way of proceeding. Neither is there one optimal solution. Everything depends upon the situation, and the skills available.

Four Classes of Problem

Generally speaking, four broad classes of problem can be recognised in the work of an educational technologist, each associated with a set of appropriate ways of tackling them. The four classes of problem can be identified as: problems of deviation, problems of improvement or renewal, problems of prediction, and problems of acceptance. Problems of deviation occur when there is a gap or deviation from some known standard, and the gap is of sufficient magnitude to warrant some form of corrective action. Examples of this will be found in the present concern amongst parents and teachers with the ability of children to engage in the fundamental skills of reading, writing and reckoning when they leave school.

Problems of improvement or renewal are basically concerned with situations where there is a perceived need to bring about some improvement. This may involve renewing what is being experienced, as well as improving what is being accomplished. Any programme or course can become, over the years, out of tune with the times, and reflection and development are necessary to bring it back into the mainstream. An example of this kind of activity in educational technology is to be found in the growing concern with needs assessment, and the importance of examining the source of many of the ideas underlying the curriculum. Where objectives come from is a much more important question than how they should be written or identified.

Problems of prediction are gradually becoming more frequent in the experience of educational technologists. They basically involve situations in which there is a need to anticipate emerging or future changes in society and the economy, which are likely to have significant effects upon education. An example of this might be found in industry, where the development of a new process entails training workpeople to operate a plant before it has even been constructed. Predicting the training needs, in such a situation, is a demanding operation, for one is really carrying out a task analysis before the event. However, the weight of the evidence is very strong in favour of such techniques, and work in this area has been carried out by the author and his students over the last three years in both the chemical and coke industries.

Problems of acceptance have always faced us. The problems of dealing with planned change are paramount, and the diffusion and adoption of ideas is a matter of prime importance in education. Although a wide range of strategies and tactics are available to the educational technologist, resistance and inertia often present seemingly insuperable barriers. Overcoming these is no mean task, and the educational technologist is intimately involved in their solution.

Conclusion

Educational technology is coming of age. Three contrasting archetypes are available, and each has had developed a set of related paradigms for future action. It has, at last, been generally realised that there is no one best way of proceeding, and that there can be no one educational technology. Scepticism and dogmatism have had their day, and for the educational technologist, as for Kant in his *Critique of Pure Reason*, "the critical path is alone open." Criticism, or evaluation, is becoming the underlying theory of educational technology, rather than merely a sub-component of the process. Educators devoting themselves to technology, however it is conceived, without a sense of distinctive purpose, can never be more than second-class citizens. Educators, on the other hand, who devote themselves to technology, with a conception of criticism, evaluation or reflection as the basic theory, place educational technology in its proper light as having a central rather than peripheral role in matters of educational concern. It is this point that we are fast reaching, but our success will depend upon our ability to develop useful models for action.

References

Ashby, E (1967) Machines, understanding and learning: reflections on technology in education, *The Graduate Journal.* 7(2): 359–73

Black, M (1962) *Models and Metaphors.* Ithaca, New York : Cornell

Davies, I K (1972) *The Management of Learning.* London : McGraw Hill (published as *Competency Based Learning* in the USA)

Davies, I K (1976) *Objectives in Curriculum Design.* London & New York : McGraw Hill

de Bono, E (1976) *Teaching Thinking.* London : Temple Smith

Drucker, P F (1966) *The Effective Executive.* New York : Harper & Row

Frazer, J G (1871) *The Golden Bough.* London : Macmillan

Hartley, J and Davies, I K (1976) Pre-instructional strategies: the role of pre-tests, behavioural objectives, overviews and advance organizers, *Review of Educational Research* 46(2): 239–65

Heisenberg, W (1958) *The Physicist's Conception of Nature.* London : Longman

Jung, C (1922) On the relations of analytical psychology to poetic art. In *Contributions to Analytical Psychology.* London : Paul Trench and Trubner

Kuhn, T S (1970) *The Structure of Scientific Revolutions.* Chicago : University of Chicago Press

MacKenzie, N, Eraut, M and Jones, H C (1976) *Teaching and Learning: an Introduction to New Methods and Resources in Higher Education.* Paris : UNESCO Press

Peters, R S (1959) *Authority, Responsibility and Education.* London : Routledge & Kegan Paul

Phillips, D C (1971) *Theories, Values and Education.* Melbourne, Australia : Melbourne University Press

Poole, R (1972) *Towards Subjectivity.* New York : Wiley

Richardson, E (1975) *Authority and Organization in the Secondary School.* London : Macmillan

Starr, M K (1971) *Management: a Modern Approach.* New York : Harcourt Brace Jovanovich

Is There a Field of Educational Communications and Technology?

Robert Heinich

The president of the Association does a lot of traveling around the country speaking at many conferences and meetings. During my year as president, I talked to three different mixes of audience—sometimes to an audiovisual association, sometimes to a joint meeting of audiovisual and library people (often carried out in a subtly charged atmosphere), sometimes to an officially merged group.[1]

In the course of the year, I had at least one of my rather smug assumptions shattered. I had expected at those meetings attended by librarians to have to explain the background of the field of educational technology. I assumed that people with a library background might not understand some of the tap roots of educational technology because many of them had been somewhat outside the movement when television, programed instruction, CAI, "packaged" curricular innovations, *etc.*, were introduced and developed.

By and large, I believe my assumption was accurate, but I was encouraged by their evidences of concern with the processes of instruction which these innovations implied. But what really surprised me was the extent to which the audiovisual people, to whom I thought this would be old hat, were not aware of the broader implications of educational technology and the ways in which the developments of the last 15 or 20 years have changed the nature of the field we're in.

At the Fourth General Session of the 1972 Association for Educational Communications and Technology Convention in Minneapolis, Past-President Robert Heinich delivered a presentation entitled, "Is There a Field of Educational Communications and Technology?" This article is based on that presentation. At the time this paper was published, Robert Heinich was professor of education, Indiana University, Bloomington.

From: Heinich, R. M. 1973. Is there a field of educational communications and technology? *Audiovisual instruction* 18(5):44–46. Reprinted with permission of Association for Educational Communications and Technology.

I found that when many of the people at these meetings talk about joining the audiovisual and library groups, they are really talking about combining or not combining warehouses and warehouse personnel. Those in favor of combining see it as a way to get a bigger warehouse! Doing so *does* introduce the notion of instructional media—all of the "things" of instruction in a handy one-stop location. (Assuming, of course, that balance among the "things" is maintained and all services continued—but that's another story.) Often missing from this picture, however, is the concept of instructional technology. There is little thought, for example, given to the process of instructional development—and assisting teachers select materials is *not* instructional development. Housing of resources and their distribution is of chief concern.

This has brought us to a crossroads in the historic development of the media field. Up to now, the world of media hasn't experienced the division that occurred in the world of books a long time ago. Librarians have long lived with the distinction between textbooks and library (resource) books. The former is the province of the curriculum people, while the latter falls under the jurisdiction of the librarian. How easy it is for someone brought up in that tradition to slip comfortably from "library books" to "library media," not even consciously realizing that "text media" is the logical companion term. But do we really want the world of media to split this way? Do we really want text media to wander over into the curriculum department, thereby probably losing the participation in the curriculum development process inherent in instructional technology? Are we really only concerned with the supplementary resources of instruction? For example, when dealing with a program such as BSCS, do the media components of the instructional system and how they function within the program fall within our area of expertise and influence, or are we concerned only with those additional biology materials added to the library (or IMC)? In other words, what is the nature of our participation in the instructional process?

As I said before, up to now the world of media has not been split, but media warehousing, historically simply a consequence of instructional decision making, if allowed to become a thing in itself, can be the occasion for an unwanted change. I say unwanted because I don't believe we really seek the split. I think this is the larger issue raised by the presentation, "The Common Quest," at the Special General Session at the Minneapolis Convention. The issue is not whether it is a good thing to bring all media together but, rather, what does bringing them together mean to us in terms of a broader vision.

Historically, the service concept inherent in warehousing fits an instructional configuration not amenable to the full potential of educational technology. The steps of traditional instructional planning and implementation tend to follow a linear, sequential arrangement. While some interaction certainly takes place, the different groups of people represented by the boxes in Figure 1 tend to make discrete decisions, passing along those decisions down the line to the next group. Feedback from the learner normally is monitored only by the same group (teachers) making the specific instructional decisions. Evaluation in this scheme of things is a private process.

Instructional technology, on the other hand, requires that goal setting, curriculum planning, and instructional implementation teams work together in

Figure 1

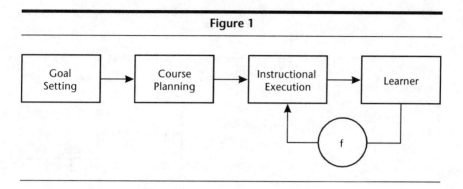

Figure 2

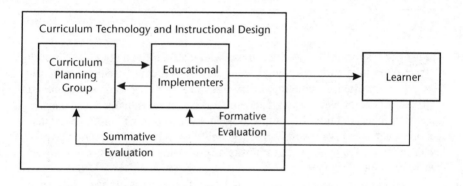

planning the instructional process. Decisions that once could be delayed until the moment of interface with the student now must be built into the system design. Parallel rather than linear planning and decision making are characteristic of what I have referred to in Figure 2 as, "Curriculum Technology and Instructional Design"—an awkward phrase, perhaps, but one which does imply that technological processes can be applied to curricular as well as instructional analysis. In this configuration, the planning group and implementers work together within a framework of shared responsibility. Evaluation also becomes a shared responsibility and as a result is transformed into a "public" process.

The principle of accountability is counter to that of exclusivity of evaluation, producing a good deal of the current unease that teachers have about manifestations of accountability, such as cost-effectiveness. From our vantage point, we must remember that television, programed instruction, and other system approaches to instruction have contributed significantly to the notion that evaluation of instructional performance must be a "public" (open) process,

Figure 3

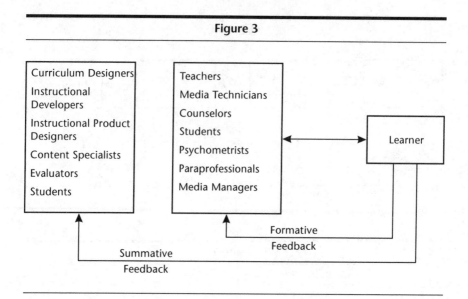

and not the responsibility solely of those who instruct. Evaluation of televised instruction is inherently open to all who view it—students, teachers, supervisors, and, very often, the public. The try-out and revision process of programed instruction is at the very heart of accountability—if the student doesn't learn, the program is at fault. In fact, a fundamental axiom of our field is that technology makes instruction visible. Technology "records" instruction, bringing to open view a process that traditionally remains invisible behind closed classroom doors.

Two kinds of evaluation have long been integral parts of the media field: one to provide data to those responsible for designing media so that revisions may be made on the basis of tryouts with samples of the target audience; the other to provide data to those responsible for curricular and instructional planning so that products can be evaluated on the basis of effectiveness with the intended population. These two kinds of evaluation have recently been labeled formative and summative respectively. Figure 2 shows how each serves the appropriate group.

Figure 3 expands the diagram to illustrate the kinds of professional specialties involved in each of the two main groups in Figure 2. These lists are by no means inclusive, simply illustrative. Notice that content specialists, not teachers, are listed in the planning group. Teachers haven't been "invented" yet. They do appear in the implementation group. Similarly, evaluators appear at the left, psychometrists at the right; instructional product designers at the left, media technicians at the right. These examples are chosen deliberately to show differences in function between the two activities. In practice, many may be the same people who must be skilled at adjusting role to function being performed.

This approach to instructional development makes it possible to rearrange instructional relationships regardless of our institutional configurations. The learner can become the center of the process. We don't necessarily need intermediaries between curriculum planning, instructional resources, and the learner; these resources can be made available to learners directly. Technology is a way of increasing the options available to students, bringing to them the best we have.

Two broad trends in technology underscore the above and have within them the power to affect profoundly our educational institutions. One is our capability, through cable and satellite, to deliver instruction wherever the learner is. The second, through cartridges, cassettes, and print, allows the student to take instruction with him wherever he goes. Both challenge the territoriality of our current institutions. Together they can create new institutional configurations.

Two examples are the Open University and the off-campus degree programs. The Open University in England is predicated on the assumption that almost all instructional needs of students can be taken care of through space and time—by telecommunications and Her Majesty's postal service. The way in which instruction is designed at the open university is probably the best current exemplar of instructional technology.

Let's return to Figure 3 and a closer look at the field we're in. The broad categories of professional concern to our field can be listed as:

- curricular design
- instructional design
- instructional product design
- evaluation of instructional products
- media service management
- media production

  . . .

- broad-band delivery systems

Our roles in the first two are participatory; these are the two areas of broad system planning by interdisciplinary teams. In the others, however, we can and should be responsible for direction. By instructional product design I mean the development of reliable, replicable instruments of instruction based on learner analysis, task analysis, and environmental design and evaluation. How well skilled we are in this area may be the key to participation in instructional and curricular design. If our expertise stops at the media service management level (the warehouse concept), the likelihood of our being involved in curricular and instructional design decreases sharply.

I have appended broad-band delivery systems primarily to warn us not to allow separation of delivery systems from the instructional design concept. We must retain professional concern for how content is organized as well as how it is delivered.

I would like to make a point by further reducing the field to three classes of function:

Domain of Instructional Technology

1. Curricular and Instructional Design
2. Instructional Product Design
3. Media Services

A deep concern of mine, after traveling around last year, is that we tend to base certification on item three, media services, ignoring the other areas. Too frequently, *programs* are based solely on item three. Sometimes I found a tendency to regard the district level program simply as a projection of the building program. The district level is where leadership in the broad perspective of instructional technology can best take place, and to define the district program as a servant to the building program is to throw away our chief path to professional growth in the schools. We must *base* our programs and our top levels of certification on curricular and instructional design.

I realize it is difficult for anyone raised in a service tradition to assume a more central curricular and instructional role, but it must be done. This is not to say that every person in the field must respond to this new challenge and responsibility; but it *is* saying that every *program* should. My plea to those who choose not to respond is don't get in the way of the program—stand aside, keep your still needed function, and let one of the new breed carry the program forward.

Yes, there *is* a field of educational communications and technology with a large cluster of professional specialties that logically belong within our historic purview. Whether we will be able to maintain the cluster as a cohesive unit or whether it will fragment is still to be seen. The answer, of course, depends on our response. The easy route is to define us in reference to media services. If we do, given current pressures, we can expect to see paraprofessionals moving into what we thought to be professional positions. The safe route is the larger vision of the broad framework of educational communications and technology.

Notes

1. Please bear with my use of outmoded vocabulary. I'm deliberately using those terms to separate origins of professional orientation and offer apologies to media generalists, specialists, instructional technologists, et al.

Theory and Rationale

On the Design of Educational Systems

C. West Churchman

This article is concerned with the application of the philosophy of system sciences to the study of education. A system, in the *Oxford Dictionary's* terms, is a "whole compounded of parts." The concept has always been popular in intellectual circles. Indeed, many claim that the goal of science is to create a "system of knowledge," a whole of which the bits of known fact make recognizable parts. Today, we see frequent reference to traffic systems, urban systems, weapon systems, information systems. All professions are called upon to join up in the system parade, lest federal grants and other luxurious sources of funds dry up because the leaders of the professions have failed to recognize the new age.

Of course, as any astute entrepreneur knows, a first step in the direction of modernization is simply to call a spade a heart: instead of talking about school districts, call them school systems. Instead of saying that the school boards are studying budgets and plans for the coming year, say that they are engaged in system design and development.

Is there much more to the recent emphasis on systems besides renaming traditional approaches to the study of education? We all fall victim now and then to our enthusiasms, and these lead us to emphasize one aspect of our lives to the detriment of the rest. Throughout the ages men have exhorted other men to consider the whole and not to neglect any essential part. Are we in the midst of an old fad under a rejuvenated name?

The answer is a complicated one. There is a hard core of honest work being done to bring about a clearer and more useful concept of systems, in order to assist the harassed managers of systems in their almost heroic efforts to maintain some form of stability. As one might expect, this work goes under a number of different names and makes use of many different resources. Names like operations research, management science, system engineering, system development, and system science are all common. Workers in these fields use mathematics, behavioral science, economics, statistics, computers, and even the science of philosophy from time to time. But despite these more sophisticated and precise methodologies, the challenge still remains: What is different about systems research these days? In answering the challenge, this article will describe some thinking that has gone on about the whole and relate this thinking in a general way to the field of education.

From: Churchman, C. W. 1965. On the design of educational systems. *Audiovisual instruction* 10(5):361–365. Reprinted with permission of Association for Educational Communications and Technology.

The Whole System: Two Philosophies

Even as far back as the Greek philosophers, men construed two ways of thinking about the whole that makes up a system. One philosophy insists that the thinker begin with the simple parts, understand them thoroughly, perfect them if he can, and then begin building the parts together into an edifice that eventually becomes the entire structure. Modesty and diligence characterize this philosophy: one must work very hard on what one clearly understands and can feasibly change, before he goes off into more complicated and less tried pathways. One only earns the right to talk about wholes when one has been sufficiently trained in the parts. The opposite philosophy holds that we must begin with a concept of the whole; otherwise we shall never know how to identify the parts, much less how to improve them. Daring and creativity are the hallmarks here, as well as hours of contemplation and debate. Again, one must earn a right, but in this case the right to act. Before changes are introduced in the parts, what the overall goals should be must be thought through, as boldly as possible.

These two philosophies still have their strong representatives in the theories of education. On the one hand, there are those who see the task of improvement as consisting of a series of steps toward excellence: better teacher education, better buildings, better teacher-student relations, and so on. Every suggestion for change must be examined in its own light and adopted if it is indeed a step toward excellence. On the other hand, there are those who keep asking why we have schools and universities at all, especially in their modern form. They insist that it does no good to improve the teacher, or paint the classroom, or add more counselors, if the conception of the whole educational system is wrong to start with. These are the great reminders, shouting outside the walls to the deaf ears of the insane inmates bent on polishing their meaningless tools.

Essentially, this debate is about the costs entailed in any plan of developing educational systems. A plan that emphasizes the parts must pay the cost of failing to consider the whole, and a plan that emphasizes the whole must pay the cost of failing to get down to the real depth with respect to the parts.

It would be very nice indeed if we could measure these two costs and thus find the right compromise. Unfortunately, we are very far indeed from providing such cost-benefit analyses for system studies. In lieu of such a method, we may look instead at a fairly simple "principle" of system design that may suggest enough to guide us.

Housekeeping: The Obvious Principle

There is one obvious principle, well known to all designers, including housewives: "When you see a mess, clean it up!" If your boy owns a puppy, there is no sense in sitting down and wondering what the purpose of boys and dogs really is before you set to work getting things clean again. In all systems, big and small, irrationalities get in and disrupt the process in awkward ways. Presumably, some well-chosen steps will result in clearing away these undesirable features so that the system can operate as intended.

Let us call the activity of straightening up a crooked situation "housekeeping," hoping that the analogy the name implies will prove to be of some help. Note that housekeeping is intended to straighten out an existing system; it leaves the overall goals invariant as it works on the parts that have gotten out of order. It does not raise the horrendous question, what is this system all about? Or, rather, it does not do this unless the task of housekeeping becomes so frustrating, or boring, or costly, that the question more or less asks itself.

In large systems, housekeeping is not usually a simple task. That is, some analysis is required before one knows what steps should be taken. Consider, for example, the technique of operations research known as "waiting line theory." During registration week at a large university like the University of California at Berkeley, one often sees incredibly long lines of students waiting to register in various courses or to be advised by members of the faculty. A casual observer of this process might well claim that some housekeeping is needed here. But a little more scrutiny would show that it is not all that simple. If we hire more people to register the students, then what shall we do with them after the school starts? We can't use occasional employees for this task, because the adviser has to know the details of the system. The analysis of the problem consists of four components: the cost of the "service units," the cost of waiting, the probable arrival of students for service, and the probable time required to service each one. With some reliable evidence on each of these four aspects, we can decide whether the existing system really is functioning rationally or not.

Notice that this housekeeping task does not raise the question whether registration of students, in the manner now performed at the University, is really desirable. It takes the present policy as a "given" and works to see whether the policy is being implemented effectively.

Obviously the housekeeping principle needs to be more precisely phrased if it is to help us in setting our plans for system study. Indeed, the housekeeping principle seems to operate at several levels, and at each higher level there are greater difficulties in interpreting its meaning.

First are procedures clearly detrimental to the system that no one in the system really wants, but that no one ever has had time to think about. The outside observer often sees how to correct these defects and finds no serious difficulty in gaining acceptance of his recommendations.

Second are procedures that result in long delays and inadequate servicing of faculty or students which appear to be the result of the bad bookkeeping, or office management, or assignment of personnel. Perhaps system procedures techniques, or industrial engineering, or even the mathematical methods of linear programing will provide better plans which may gain acceptance and not disturb the overall system.

Third are procedures that seem to be inadequately carried out in the light of advancing technology. Perhaps the newer technology should be applied.

It is at this last level where the strategy of system research becomes very difficult to determine properly.

Instruction: Is It a Housekeeping Problem?

The difficulty is illustrated by the question: how do you do system research on instruction? The term "instruction" is interpreted to mean the activity centering in the classroom, usually consisting of an interface of teacher and a group of students, together with the peripheral support activities the classroom requires. We all know of the development of new technologies involving new media for instruction, for example, so-called programed instruction.

Programed instruction in many ways looks like an example of "level three" of a housekeeping problem. In many of our courses in mathematics, statistics, logic, languages, history, etc., students are being taught material that is fairly formalized. Why do we need to tie up the time of intelligent faculty in these more or less routine tasks when programed media are now available in increasing amounts?

If we set about to use these instructional media, is the design of their use to be construed as a housekeeping task? If it is, then one argues that it is possible to improve the instructional part of education without having to delve deeply into goals of the whole educational system.

But there is a good argument against considering the instruction process as a housekeeping task of educators: the change to any programed method is costly, in time, in inconvenience, in all the ways that worry people when radical change is contemplated. Furthermore, no one has yet made a convincing case that the returns will vastly exceed the costs. For example, it may be superficially true that programed learning reduces teacher time, but then will the teacher be required all the more to maintain student motivation? Lacking evidence of large savings, the proponents of the whole system point of view can claim that we should examine other radical alternatives. For example, abolishing or vastly modifying the instructional system might be far better.

From this example, one learns something more about the housekeeping principle. It is necessary to have some method, however tentative, of estimating the savings to the system that the effort will bring about. In other words, "If you see a mess, clean it up, unless the net return to the whole system seems too small!" Of course, no housewife would permit this outrageous modification of the principle, but most husbands and all boys will understand it immediately.

Cost and Benefit of Parts of Systems

This modified principle, whatever it may mean, does demand some method of examining the whole system. Are there any techniques for doing this adequately? There is one such technique that may prove very helpful; it is based on the idea that there are two fundamental design properties of any part of a system: its *benefit* to the whole and its *price* (or cost).

However, neither benefit nor price is what it appears to be on the surface. We have already seen how what appears to be a benefit to a part is a loss to the whole. We can also see that what appears to be a cost to a part may be a much larger cost to the whole, because the whole has had to sacrifice a great deal of its resources to sustain the part. The *true* price the part pays is the lost opportunity the whole pays. This is the idea behind the technique: to determine benefit and price in terms of the whole system.

Decomposition of Systems

Imagine a system with a number of parts, or subunits. Each part is assigned at the outset a specific measurable task. In order to perform its task, the part must make use of some of the system's scarce resources (teacher time, rooms, equipment, etc.). We could determine how well a part is performing if we could measure the value (benefit) of its output and the costs of its operations in the same units. The trouble is that its output may be number of students that passed, and its input may be teacher hours. As a first attempt to get around this difficulty, we might translate passed students into a certain proportion of an adjusted tuition fee (adjusted to take account of endowment funds and other types of support), and we might translate teacher's hours into an adjusted per hour salary (adjusted to take account of overhead, research, student contact hours, etc.).

With these figures in hand, we would have a first estimate of the worth of a course. The estimate, however, is quite obviously a bad one. Suppose, for example, that the course is a fundamental one, a prerequisite for many others. Its net return according to the above calculations may be very poor, and yet no one would argue on this basis alone that the course should be dropped. Or a course may use one teacher plus cheap assistants to lecture to a thousand, with a marvelous "net return." But the one teacher may be a very scarce item, needed for other purposes in the school's life, and the scarcity may not be reflected well at all in the teacher's salary. Or the course may be a snap for tired seniors, and the true gross return may be virtually nil.

Now if a school system could be organized as a competitive economy, these difficulties might be removed, in part at least. The students would have to "bid" for the privilege of signing up for each course, and the course manager would have to "bid" for the teacher's time. This, indeed, is somewhat the way in which the older continental universities were run.

The trouble is that a competitive market requires wide and accurate dissemination of information. If the students don't know what's good for them in the long run, they won't bid properly, nor will the course managers bid for a teacher unless they know all about his qualifications. If it were possible to centralize information, we might hope to run a school on a partially competitive basis. We would then permit the units to bid, but the central information unit would keep revising the bids in terms of its long range estimates, until some convergence to a correct solution seemed to emerge. This is essentially what is called the "decomposition model" of an organization. In its precise form, this model is simply a way of calculating an optimal strategy for a system with thousands of variables.

To define the model a little more precisely (the available literature will carry the interested reader still further), an example follows which is not necessarily adaptable to a school system. A large system is having a problem of allocating a scarce resource over thousands of places: e.g., books, teachers,

scientists, food, etc. Allocation problems often can be studied by linear programing techniques. In large problems, the method consists of "decomposing"
the problem. In the illustration, each place would work out its optimal plan of
operation, assuming certain costs and returns generated by its limited information. It then sends its requirement plan to the central unit, but instead of this
plan's being accepted or rejected, the central unit sends back a revised estimate
of the true prices and returns. For example, if a resource is very scarce, i.e.,
demanded by many places, the central unit increases its cost (the so-called
"shadow price"). In other cases, the central unit may decrease a price. The parts
then reestimate their optimal plans with the new information, and thus, under
certain conditions, the whole system approaches an optimal plan.

It should be emphasized that the shadow price of a teacher is not his
salary; it is the lost opportunity cost of his using his time for one type of
instruction rather than another.

It will be seen that the decomposition model tries to retain the advantages
of centralized planning and decentralized control. Whether or not the details of
this whole system imagery can be applied to educational systems, the idea is
an important one. In some sense it permits the entire system to think through a
plan before acting upon it. Each part competes for scarce resources, and each
part's proposed effort is priced out by the other parts. The central control
receives the plans of the parts and adjusts them in terms of its overall information. Of course, this is one way of describing current practices of large school
systems, but the current practice is often very ill-formulated, and no one has
tried to study the practice from a more precise and adequately controlled point
of view.

One rather obvious difficulty in becoming more precise is our inability
to assign even preliminary costs and returns to the parts of educational systems.
Lacking quantitative measures, we may nonetheless resort to computer simulation of school systems in order to apply judgment to the outcomes, that is,
the process of debate and deliberation concerning the human value of system
performance. Simulation permits the human observer to see how the system,
or a stripped-down version of it, actually performs. It should be understood,
however, that simulation is an expensive process and that the results are always
confusing unless some explicit model is being tested.

There are, of course, other ways of modeling systems besides the one just
discussed. But whatever method is used, the time and expense are large. We are
not discussing simple techniques that can be readily adapted to everyday
activities. A serious attempt to observe and redesign a school system requires
a long time and many different kinds of intellectual resources: educators,
systems scientists, political scientists, social psychologists, to name a few. It is
going to take a long time; *therefore*, the sooner we start, the better.

On Starting: Balanced View Required

To think of the principle of cost and benefit of the whole as *the* primary
principle of large system design is a serious mistake. It must be balanced against
the housekeeping principle already mentioned. There is unquestionably a good

case to be made for trying to understand the whole system, because a failure to do so will lead to overemphasis of one aspect to the detriment of the whole. But understanding the whole system is a long, expensive, tedious task. To wait until this task is even approximately completed is to delay action.

After all, very few of the large systems we humans inhabit are understood by anybody. And yet people act in them every day. They do this by studying a part and trying to redesign it so that it will work better, i.e., by housekeeping. This is our daily system living. If a class is not progressing as well as we should like, we try to do something about it, even though in the back of our minds there may be the haunting thought that the entire course is better left out of the curriculum. All our top administrators are system designers, trying to patch up the leaks and fix the broken parts, as best they can.

Now the pragmatic idea behind the housekeeping principle is not simply to act for action's sake; it is far deeper than that. The idea is that man can only think if he acts. In other words, in order to think about the whole system, one has to act within it. The only way to act within it is to start somewhere. But not anywhere. And here is the art of system design: to find those problems of the parts, the study of which enables us best to think most adequately about the whole.

The principles of system design proposed in this article are frankly dialectical. The housekeeping principle tells us to look at the parts and start where feasible research can be initiated modestly. The whole system principle tells us to look at the whole and consider whole costs and whole benefits. The good system designer is one who listens carefully to the debate between these two sound principles.

The Future: Much Still To Be Done

There is still much to be done in developing an adequate philosophy of system design. It has been assumed in this article that the designer can identify parts and wholes in a satisfactory manner, and a philosophy of parts and wholes has been suggested wherein neither takes precedence over the other. Perhaps the real strength of this philosophy lies in the fact that in some cases it can be made precise and indeed can become the basis of a computerized analysis. But the philosophy itself presupposes that the designer has a sound idea of how the system is constructed and what its boundaries are. That in many cases we don't know these things is almost too obvious to say. It is all very well to talk about an educational system "and its environment," but how do we set the boundaries? Is the school board a part of the system or of its environment? Or the PTA, or the city council, or the state legislature? All these parts or environments play a role in the development of the educational system. How should we regard them? The most obvious answer is that something is a part of a system if it can be redesigned, i.e., if it can be changed by the designer. This makes the boundaries of a system relative to the designer, which may be the proper way to look at the matter. But a great deal more research is required before we will have a good answer to such questions of system design.

A far more serious issue is raised in the question: what criteria should be used to judge the effectiveness of a change in a system? Although it would appear that through this article it has been assumed that true benefit can be measured, we have not come far enough to do any such thing. To put it simply, we don't know why we educate. Some will say, "to survive," feeling no obligation to prove that humans should survive, or should survive in their present form. Some will say, "to develop the human mind," feeling no obligation to state what better development might be. Some will say, "to create greater understanding," but understanding for what? Aristotle said, "in order to contemplate, i.e., in order to do that which makes a man a man." Whatever may be said of Aristotle's particular ethical principle, one must agree that the criteria of educational systems are based on an ethical theory. Ethics is not merely the output of personal feeling. It is, in addition, the object of study of system designers. We need to take very seriously Aristotle's concept: what we need to do is realize man as he ought by his nature to be realized. But this is a system science problem applied to man himself. Can we ever expect a system science capable of studying it?

References

1. Almon, C. "Central Planning without Complete Information at the Center." *Linear Programming and Extensions.* (By G. B. Dantzig.) Princeton, N.J.: Princeton University Press, 1962.

2. Arrow, K. J., and Hurwicz, L. "Decentralization and Computation in Resource Allocation." *Studies in Mathematical Econometrics.* (Edited by R. W. Phouts and others.) Chapel Hill: University of North Carolina Press, 1962.

3. Carr, C., and others. *Quantitative Decision Procedures.* New York: McGraw-Hill Book Co., 1964.

4. Churchman, C. W. *Prediction and Optimal Decision.* Englewood Cliffs, N.J.: Prentice-Hall, 1961.

5. ———. "The X of X." *Management Science* 9, 1963.

6. Churchman, C. W., and Eisenberg, H. "Deliberation and Judgment." *Human Judgments and Optimality.* (Edited by M. Shelly and others.) New York: John Wiley & Sons, 1964.

7. Churchman, C. W., and others. *Introduction to Operations Research.* New York: John Wiley & Sons, 1957. Chapter VI.

8. Dantzig, G., and Wolfe, P. "Decomposition Principle for Linear Programs." *Operations Research*, 8, 1960.

9. Dean, B. V., and others. *Mathematics for Management.* New York: John Wiley & Sons, 1963.

10. Hoggatt, A. C., and Balderston, F. E. *Symposium on Simulation Models.* Cincinnati: Southwestern Publishing Co., 1963.

11. Kaufmann, A. *Methods and Models of Operations Research.* Englewood Cliffs, N.J.: Prentice-Hall, 1963.

A Walk on the Altered Side

J. D. Finn

One thing that is new is the prevalence of newness, the changing scale and scope of change itself, so that the world alters as we walk in it, so that the years of man's life measure not some small growth or rearrangement or moderation of what he learned in childhood, but a great upheaval.

J. Robert Oppenheimer

As I write these lines, I am traveling 35,000 feet above the Grand Canyon of the Colorado River at a speed in excess of 600 miles per hour. A voice comes on the intercom—a mild technical miracle in itself. It is the voice of the pilot relaying, in a matter-of-fact way, one of the greatest stories of this generation. For above me—150 miles or so—a Marine colonel by the name of John Glenn is traveling in a space capsule at a speed of 17,000 miles per hour. While I have been reaching Arizona from Los Angeles, he has come halfway around the globe. Glenn has been twice around the world since his flight began; the decision has just been made to try for the third orbit.

Below me the Arizona desert—dimly seen through a covering of white clouds—sits ancient and quiet. Memories are buried here—of the conquistadores who explored it, of the Indians, and, before them, of geologic time. A contrast, heightened by the middle ground, the limbo, the partial ascent to the stars symbolized by the magnificent aircraft in which I ride—a contrast greater than man has ever known—exists in this relationship of ancient desert and the capsule called Friendship 7. Between them rides the jet, symbol of our generation. For we, truly, must be the midwives of the new era.

The conquistadores were inevitable after Columbus and Magellan; John Glenn was inevitable only after Newton, Einstein, Planck, Helmholtz, and generations of other scientists and unknown but dedicated engineers, technicians and inventors. The distance between the caveman and Magellan is as nothing compared to the distance between Magellan and Glenn. Most of us do

This article was delivered as a paper before a meeting of the John Dewey Society at Las Vegas, Nevada, March 3, 1962.

From: Finn, J. D. 1962. A walk on the altered side. *Phi delta kappan* 44(1):29–34. Reprinted with permission.

not live in the world of John Glenn; many of us cannot or will not; many of us do not take kindly to the role of midwifery in this birth of newness. Returning to the Oppenheimer metaphor, the world does, indeed, alter as we walk in it; the world of John Glenn, not our transitory world, is the world of our children. Their side is the altered side, where, as gap bridgers, as educators, we must learn to walk.

It is in this context that I should like to remark upon a relatively new relationship in the world of education. A new world, symbolized at least to a modest degree by the flight into space, seems to be forming within the educational society. This world is technological in nature. Men are seeking to solve some of the problems of education by technological means. Technology is not, as many of the technically illiterate seem to think, a collection of gadgets, of hardware, of instrumentation. It is, instead, best described as a way of thinking about certain classes of problems and their solutions.

This view of technology when applied to education becomes a legitimate object of concern for the educational philosopher. We are met here in the name of John Dewey, in the name of educational philosophy. I would like, in the short time at my disposal, to outline some of these philosophic concerns as I see them from the point of view of a student of instructional technology.

The Revolution's Potential

Perhaps it would be useful to indicate briefly some of the dimensions of this *potential* technological revolution in education. I emphasize potential because it has not yet happened; it may never happen; education may remain the only natural (primitive) sector of our culture, but I strongly doubt it.

Since about 1930 we have had a slow development of a group of tools for communication and teaching, and a program of research into their use. These instruments and materials include what today we call conventional audiovisual devices—the sound motion picture, various forms of projected still pictures, recordings, etc. Since 1950, this arsenal has expanded to include television, electronic learning laboratories, teaching machines of various kinds, and, recently, computers. Accompanying these devices and materials, again, has been a vigorous program of research into the nature of learning and communication, supported by a rapidly growing body of theory derived from experimental and social psychology and related disciplines such as linguistics, criticism and engineering.

In other sectors of the educational enterprise, other technological innovations are being tested. The work of Lloyd Trump and his associates in school organization, the various attempts at team teaching, and experimentation with new school environments are examples. I shall confine my remarks principally to the main line of instructional technology—audiovisual materials and the so-called newer media and their intellectual bases.

I mentioned a slow development of these approaches to instruction. More important, this development was almost discontinuous with any main lines of growth of American education during the past 30 years. It was so little connected with progressive education, for example, that I found the word *films* only in a footnote relating to Alice Keliher in Lawrence Cremin's book (Cremin, 1961, p. 257). It has not notably influenced the theory of school administration or the education of superintendents. In preparing this paper, I had occasion to examine a number of recent books on educational philosophy. With one or two exceptions, they are so little concerned with these developments that, using the philosophers as a source, one must conclude that a technology of instruction does not exist. The Association for Supervision and Curriculum Development, until very recently, also turned a blind (and horrified) eye in the direction of instructional technology.

Within the last five years this discontinuity has ended and the possibilities of a technology of instruction have suddenly thrust themselves into the educational mainstream. The philosophers have begun to cluck, if not in books, then in speeches, articles and conversations; the curriculum specialists have been seen running about throwing up barricades to protect the child from the machine monster; and educational statesmen have managed to raise the adrenaline of their constituents with speeches that sound as if they were ghostwritten by Ned Ludd or Jean Jacques Rousseau. We are urged to destroy the weaving machines and return to nature—all in the same breath.

I am not concerned here either with educational statesmen or curriculum specialists. I would like to concentrate on the philosophers. For I come not to defend instructional technology, as I am sure our chairman would like me to do, but instead, I come to indict. I feel that many educational philosophers have lost the way and that they have committed an even worse crime—they have failed to understand.

From Apathy through Antagonism

First, there is a generalized, nonspecific attitude that holds that instructional technology is both trivial and, at the same time, dangerous. This position is well stated in Van Til's excellent paper (Van Til, 1962) in which, on the one hand, he dismisses technology as mere tinkering when compared to the real concerns of education and, on the other, sees it as a threat for mind control of Orwellian proportions. In fact, I get the impression that in some philosophical and curriculum circles the attitude toward instructional technology runs all the way from apathy through antipathy to antagonism.

This negative approach is not surprising. The intellectual has, for the most part, always hated the city which makes his intellectuality possible. And a technological civilization is an urban civilization. Thoreau, of course, was the great prototype of the intellectual who hates the city. He refused to stay in the city and once said, "The only room in Boston which I visit with alacrity is the gentlemen's room at the Fitchburg depot, where I wait for cars, sometimes for two hours, in order to get out of town." There is something comically ironic—perhaps Freudian—about this. For it has always seemed to me that plumbing—and I assume they had plumbing in the gentlemen's room of the Fitchburg depot even in those days—is a rather appropriate symbol of a technological society.

Opposition to Scientism

Morton and Lucia White remind us that John Dewey himself, between 1899 and 1927, developed the same attitude toward the city and its industrialization. They said, "Instead of taking the city as the model *for* the progressive school, he almost speaks as though the urban community should be modeled *on* the progressive school…. At the end of his life Dewey seemed to conclude every speech with the words, "Divide the cities into settlement houses" (White and White, 1961, p. 176). And, a bit later, White and White summarize: "For functionalism, like pragmatism, is one of a complex of American ideas that could not exist in a nonurban society, and yet its greatest spokesmen seem to hate the American city" (White and White, 1961, p. 176). I suggest that educational philosophy has reached the stage when, in order to remedy what is a special case of the same general syndrome, it should cease hating the city.

Second, to this day there is in educational philosophy a distrust and a strong antagonism to what in the '30s was called *scientism* in education. Charters, Judd, and Bobbitt all felt the hot-tipped shafts of Dewey, Kilpatrick, Bode, and Childs. Kilpatrick was even spanked for too much attachment to Thorndike's connectionism, although, for the life of me, I could never see it in his project method.

Scientism in those days was Charters and educational engineering and activity analysis; scientism today is B. F. Skinner and pigeons and programmed learning. Charters was demolished for inventing a system of curriculum- making designed—so it was charged—to preserve the social status quo, and the measurement movement was subject to blast after blast. Today philosophers and curriculum specialists make jokes about pigeons not being people—neglecting, by the way, many other forms of learning research and programming theory.

For those of you who follow Dewey, Bode and Kilpatrick, whose god was the method of science, this is, indeed, a strange attitude. It was strange when they had it; it is stranger now.

Take only one facet of this scientism—Charters' theories of analysis. The philosophy group at Ohio State University ridiculed them. Yet, today, those theories are being used for identical problems by psychologists who never heard of Charters or of his contemporary in the industrial field, Allen. For analysis is needed in all sorts of programming, in the statement of objectives, and throughout the developing technology of instruction.

Analysis, in the sense that Charters used it and as it is being used today in a hundred ways, is, in part at least, the discrimination of details. As Gerard Piel points out, J. Bronowski, the British mathematician, in commenting on the contributions of Leonardo da Vinci, said, "[He] gave science what it most needed, the artist's sense that the detail of nature is significant. Until science had this sense, no one could care—or could think that it mattered—how fast two unequal masses fell or whether the orbits of planets are accurately circles or ellipses" (Piel, 1961, p. 208). I suggest that, because of a social bias characteristic of the '30s, the great exponents of the scientific method in education successfully struck down one of the great educational scientists of that generation and prevented a generalized scientific technique from becoming more effective in education. I suggest that the educational philosophers of this generation ought to avoid such a mistake. I can tell them this: Even if they do not, their strictures will not have the same effect.

The Question of Means and Ends

A third point on which I should like to offer advice is in the other direction. I think current educational philosophy should pay more instead of less attention to Dewey on the questions of means and ends in education. Mr. Van Til continually restates the point that until the question of aim is settled by philosophic reflection, it does absolutely no good to consider the means necessary to achieve those ends. The means in this case, of course, are the devices, materials and approaches of a technology of instruction. Bode made the same point somewhat more succinctly when he said many years ago, "Unless we know where we are going there is not much comfort in being assured that we are on the way and traveling fast" (Bode, 1921, p. 241).

There has probably been more confusion on ends and means, method and subject matter, than on any other point in educational theory these last 30 years. We need, first of all, clarification once again of this question; and clarification, I take it, is one of the jobs of the philosopher.

The confusion began with Dewey, who has to be read very critically in order to determine when he is talking about the method of science as such and educational method as such. Kilpatrick tossed in the notion of concomitant learnings, which introduced so many variables into the learning process that method, subject matter, student, and the school flagpole got mixed into a great ball of fuzz. When the curriculum specialists got through with it, curriculum was defined as no less than life, in which there was really no method except, perhaps, the pursuit of happiness. While all of these views had much to recommend them, and all had laid hold of a piece of the truth, the usefulness of these generalizations for intelligent action had been reduced, not only to zero, but into the negative.

On the other hand, a much more naive view about method also still prevails, fostered in such intellectual circles as the Council for Basic Education and the California State Legislature. This view holds that method is a mere manipulation of a few variables such as good enunciation on the part of the teacher—skills that can be learned in less time than it takes to learn to drive a car.

We Still Need Direction

The ultimate result of the development of the Dewey position through Kilpatrick to the ASCD was that method, on the one hand, reduced itself to a worship of group dynamics while pacifying the god of child-individuality; on the other hand, it was completely subordinated to something called aim, which was the result of a process of naval contemplation, either on the part of educational philosophers or of curriculum committees. In either case, we have received little help in doing our job from these statements of aim, most of which degenerate into generalized propositions from which no action may be deduced. The ultimate result of the other concept—that method is nothing but the manipulation of a few tricks—is, first of all, ignorance; and, secondly, a perilous bypassing of both individuals and values.

The suggested direction for clarification of this long-suffered problem is to return to Dewey and work from there. Because he believed in a unified, nondualistic universe, Dewey maintained that method could not, *when in use*, be separated from subject matter: that eating and food were inseparable, for example. However, for purposes of study and control, he was equally firm on the point that method had to be teased out of this universe, examined, analyzed and put to work in the most intelligent way possible.

Now, add to this idea the fact that, as early as the time of writing *School and Society*, Dewey suggested that we live in a technological, industrial culture and that technology was, in fact, the main determinant of its direction. The school, he felt, should reflect this. Such a view could be considered a special case of the general law of pragmatism—that ends and means are inseparable, that ends become means to further ends.

If you now consider technology from two perspectives—the entirety of technology that has transformed our society in about 200 years and the special application of technology to the instructional process—it is possible to indicate the direction the educational philosopher must go to clarify the problem of method in relation to aim.

First, as the perceptive students of general technology continually insist, technology in society is an organic process. This concept is central to Hannah Arendt's *The Human Condition*. In it she said, "As matters stand today, it has become as senseless to describe this world of machines in terms of means and ends as it has always been senseless to ask nature if she produced the seed to produce a tree or the tree to produce the seed" (Arendt, 1959, p. 133). Slightly later, she quotes Werner Heisenberg to the effect that general technology is no longer "the product of a conscious human effort to enlarge material power, but rather like a biological development of mankind in which the innate structures of the human organism are transplanted in an ever-increasing measure into the environment of man" (Arendt, 1959, p. 133).

The first obligation of the philosopher is to understand these concepts—a task that is not easy because the views they represent, as Kurt Marek has pointed out, are qualitatively and psychosomatically different from any ever held before. They do not fit into the tight, abstract, three-dimensional world of Euclid and the present educational philosopher. They would, strangely enough, fit into Dewey's world—a world of organic unity, although, as I indicated before, if his later work is a clue, he would probably not have been happy with the consequences of his own thought.

Taking technological development as the central organic process of our society, the implications, as this process invades education, are interesting indeed. The process does not destroy aim and its role, but it binds aim inevitably to technology. For technology is an aim-generator as much as purpose or philosophy is a technical direction-giver. Each conditions the other and is not, as Mr. Van Til maintains, arranged in a hierarchy with aim on top and method at the bottom.

An example might serve to throw some light on this relationship. In any number of technological approaches to instruction—programmed learning, the use of massed films, or in the developing instructional systems, for example—there is one unvarying requirement. That requirement is an absolutely clear statement of objectives. The general statements of the philosopher and the curriculum specialist are not good enough. Objectives must be developed from general aim statements as experiments and hypotheses are developed from general scientific laws. There is no guarantee in either case that the specific will correspond completely with the general. The specifics are conditioned by the instructional reality—a condition that philosophers abhor but that scientists, in the case of scientific laws, do not worry about.

At any rate, objectives can only be developed in this sense by a thorough analysis heretofore rarely applied in education. This is where a technology gets its direction. It is hard work to create such objectives and, if the philosophers resent everything else, they should see that such a procedure, in fact, brings philosophic thinking into practice—more than a hundred generations of philosophers have been able to do.

Further, I should like to remind you of my introductory point that technology is, fundamentally, a way of thinking. As such, it inevitably will play some role in the development of educational aims. Once a technology exists, certain aims dreamed of in philosophy may disappear. As Marek has said of technology in general:

> In our technological age, man can conceive of nothing that he might not invent. A magic carpet is no longer a scientific problem, but only a problem in construction. All the pipe dreams of the old high cultures can today be made to come true, but some of them are so primitive (like the magic carpet, for example) that it is no longer worth the trouble. The pipe dreams of the men of the old high cultures appear to have been consummated in the same historical period as the old high cultures themselves (Marek, 1961, p. 43).

Take care lest the educational philosophy you are preaching does not meet the same fate.

In discussing the hatred of the city, the attack on scientism, and the problem of ends and means, we have only scratched the surface of the great job of readjustment needed in educational philosophy as technology, reflecting the increasing technical complexity of our culture, invades the instructional process. In the space left, all that can be done is to list some other tasks which, I suggest, should occupy the attention of educational philosophers.

These include a thorough study of the process of technology in our culture as a whole. Outside of some indication in Phenix's new book (1961) and in Thelen (1960), I find little evidence that this is going on. What has gone on, incidentally, is inadequate; philosophers have presumed too much. They have presumed that they can study technology in a vacuum without, for example, the cooperation of engineers and without the mastery of certain languages and concepts. In order to look properly at the altered side, such multi-disciplined study is necessary. To give the philosophers something to think about, why is it that recently the greatest visions (in, it is true, a somewhat restricted sense) of what might be possible in education have come from Simon Ramo, a technologist (1960, p. 367–381)?

What Are the Myths About the Machine?

Educational philosophers should spend some time in examining current myths and destroying them. Many educators have demonized the machine in the manner of witch doctors. Concerning this practice generally, Marek said somewhat bitterly, "The machine is demonized only by those who feel helpless in its presence. Where such demonization occurs today, its authors are neither scientists, nor engineers, nor managers, nor workers, but only outdistanced philosophers and writers sulking in their historical corner." Shades of C. P. Snow! And there are other myths of our age of midwifery that must disappear under the hand of the philosopher.

Another challenging area opened up by the organic processes of technology includes both technical and practical problems. For example, who among you will follow Bode's great example and, continuing his work which stopped in 1940, relate concepts of mind in their newer sense to educational theory? To do this today you would have to consort with cyberneticians, electrical engineers, and neurologists. Related to this is the general problem of knowledge—its nature, its size, its structure. At the level of so-called practical problems, I *urge* you to face the economic and productivity problems inherent in an attempt to educate all Americans. These things have never concerned you centrally. They must now.

Finally, you must face the consequences of the generation in which you have been born and the world in which you live. You cannot deny technology on arbitrary, literary, uninformed grounds. If you deny the teaching machine, the computer, television, and the motion picture, if you deny new ways of teaching and learning, you cannot stop until you deny yourselves fire, the wheel, and even the very language which you speak. For, as Karl Jaspers so well put it, "A denial of technology's last step is equivalent to a denial of the first" (Jaspers, 1961, p. 192).

And, as Max Lerner reminds us, we Americans have not sold our souls to the devil of technology in a Faustian bargain. It is as true of education as of society as a whole that "truer than the Faustian bargain…is the image of Prometheus stealing fire from the gods in order to light a path of progress for men. The path is not yet clear, nor the meaning of progress, nor where it is leading: but the bold intent, the irreverence, and the secular daring have all become part of the American experience" (Lerner, 1957, p. 263). Does this not imply that, as midwives to the new era, as conductors to the altered side, the vista of educational philosophy is more exciting than ever? I think John Dewey would have liked that.

References

Arendt, Hannah. *The Human Condition.* Garden City, N.Y.: Doubleday Anchor Books, 1959.

Bode, Boyd H. *Fundamentals of Education.* New York: The Macmillan Company, 1921.

Cremin, Lawrence A. *The Transformation of the School: Progressivism in American Education, 1876–1957.* New York: Alfred A. Knopf, 1961.

Jaspers, Karl. *The Future of Mankind.* Trans. by E. B. Ashton. Chicago: The University of Chicago Press, 1961.

Lerner, Max. *America as a Civilization. Life and Thought in the United States Today.* New York: Simon and Schuster, 1957.

Marek, Kurt W. (C. W. Ceram). *Yestermorrow: Notes on Man's Progress.* Trans. by Ralph Manheim. New York: Alfred A. Knopf, 1961.

Phenix, Philip H. *Education and the Common Good: A Moral Philosophy of the Curriculum.* New York: Harper & Brothers Publishers, 1961.

Piel, Gerard. *Science in the Cause of Man.* New York: Alfred A. Knopf, 1961.

Ramo, Simon: "A New Technique of Education," in *Teaching Machines and Programmed Learning: A Source Book.* A. A. Lumsdaine and Robert Glaser (Eds.). Washington, D.C.: Department of Audiovisual Instruction, NEA, 1960.

Thelen, Herbert A. *Education and the Human Quest.* New York: Harper & Brothers, 1960.

Van Til, William. Presentation at March convention of ASCD in Las Vegas, N.M.

Van Til, William. "Is Progressive Education Obsolete?" *Saturday Review,* February 17, 1962, pp. 56–57+.

White, Lucia and Morton. "The American Intellectual versus the American City," *Daedalus,* Vol. 90, Winter 1961, pp. 166–179.

A Systems Approach to Audio-Visual Communications
The Okoboji 1956 Keynote Address

Charles F. Hoban

At the second Okoboji Conference in 1956, Charles F. Hoban, The Institute for Cooperative Research, University of Pennsylvania, Philadelphia, was asked to give the keynote address. He chose the topic, "A Systems Approach to Audio-Visual Communications," that was considered the first time a systems in communication had ever been presented.

In the fall of 1974, after the twentieth conference, he was asked to examine his 1956 statement, and to comment on the changes he has observed in the intervening nineteen years. Hoban's "Epilogue: 1975" follows his address.

For some time we have been attaching the word *communication* to the audio-visual field. Consequently it seems appropriate that we should examine audio-visual communication from a systems point of view, i.e., as a communications system. My talk this afternoon is a brief attempt at an exploratory analysis of the A-V communications system.

We have been handicapped to some extent in the continuing development of audio-visual communication by the disturbing fact that the field lacks a unique central or core concept. The hyphenated term, *audio-visual*, has been firmly established in our profession, and is fairly current in the vocabulary of the general public, thanks in part to the rapid growth of television. But, by no

---

Note: This was presented to the Conference as a talk, based on a series of transparencies. In writing up the talk, I have made some minor omissions, additions, and corrections, but I have tried to preserve intact, without elaboration, all the essential points and some of the flavor of the oral presentation. C. F. H.

From: Hoban, C. F. Jr. 1977. A systems approach to audiovisual communications. In *Okoboji: A 20 year review of leadership 1955–1974*, edited by L. W. Cochran, 67–72. Dubuque, Iowa: Kendall/Hunt. Reprinted with permission.

Figure 1

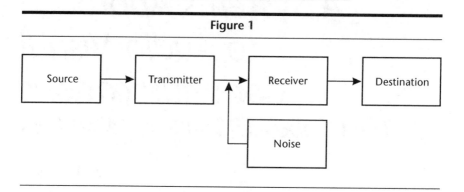

torture of imagination, can the term *audio-visual* be stretched conceptually so as to include all the communications media and equipment with which we deal—tapes, filmstrips, radio, field trips, and so forth. Furthermore, it seems unlikely that we can find a single term, or concept, which defines and limits the operations in which A-V specialists engage. This accounts somewhat for the unsolved riddle of a name for our interests and activities.

If we are to bring order into the picture, we had better attack the problem at some level beyond that of definition. To all practical purposes we can define the audio-visual field to mean whatever we decide it means. This, in fact, is what has happened in local situations. Duties, responsibilities, and activities of audio-visual specialists are, within reasonable limits, locally assigned.

A fruitful approach to better understanding and greater efficiency in the audio-visual field seems to lie in the concept of *communication*.

The classical definition of communication is generally stated as a question: "Who says what, to whom, over what network, with what effect?" This question is deceptively simple. It is easy to express, but complex in its implications.

Most, but not all of the structure of communication contained in this question can be represented in the standard communications schematic of figure 1.

For the purpose of this presentation, the ingredient of "noise" can be ignored, so we can concentrate on the basic functions of the system. The function of figure 1 that is likely to arouse conceptual difficulty is that of information "source." We seem to take it for granted that information is a common possession of "educated" people (like ourselves, for instance), or at least that it always exists and is universally available. The facts of the matter are that information is discovered or invented, that it is a human product, and that it is shared only through a storage and distribution system. In the context of our previous definition of communication, the information source is the "who says what."

Another aspect of figure 1 that should be noted is the direction of the information flow, from source to destination. As we will later modify this basic representation of a communications system so as to apply to audio-visual communication, it may be desirable to indicate interaction among the basic components of the system, but the uni-directional flow of information (   )

will be preserved throughout this discussion to indicate that the information, i.e., the subject-matter content, flows from the information source to the destination (the audience, the learner), and that this flow is not reversible. The explanation of this point is a sticky one, which we can safely pass by at this time. It may be illustrated by the thought that the function of the teacher is to teach and the function of the student is to learn. The roles are interchangeable, but the functions are not.

When I get into a discussion such as this, I begin to wonder whether I am really making a worthwhile point, or indulging in a sort of superlearnedness. So, let's move along toward a functional analysis of the audio-visual communications system. I probably should point out that I know I have used the term, *information*, without adequately defining it, but, again, I feel free to avoid this difficult task since definition is not essential to our purpose here, and none of the usual operational definitions of information in communications theory is entirely adequate to our purpose. As a matter of fact, this entire discussion of the functional analysis is intentionally loose. It is an opening rather than the closing word on the subject.

In figure 2, I will keep the information source, but substitute *producer* for *transmitter*, *distributor* for *receiver*, and *user* for *destination*. These are the essential functions of an audio-visual communications system. Under each of these functions I will list major operations. It is sometimes more convenient to express these as operators, e.g., writer, curriculum analyzer, etc., and at other times to express them as operations, e.g., selection, circulation, etc.

We see in figure 2 that as information sources in the audio-visual communications system we have the curriculum analyzer, the technical advisor, or subject matter specialist, and, in the case of sponsored materials, the sponsor. These are the people who decide the purpose of a film, book, TV program, etc., and select and authenticate its content.

The producer transforms this information into what we are now choosing to label as "instructional materials." The production function requires a programmer, who assigns production priorities, allocates the budget, sets up the time schedule, and keeps the production process going on a hopefully paying basis. The writer gets the "story" in acceptable and reproducible form. The production manager whips the show into shape, and puts it on the air or onto film; and the processor either transmits (broadcasts) it, prints it (on film), or records it (on tape or platter).

The distributor is the go-between. From the list of distribution operations shown in figure 2, it is evident that he is a busy fellow. He selects the films (recordings, etc.) for local use from the relatively large repertory available; he catalogs them and classifies them according to some criteria geared to the user's needs; he stores these materials, generally on racks so they are easily accessible; he puts them into circulation as requested by the user; he maintains these materials in good working order, and also maintains the equipment necessary to their use; and he continuously provides an advisory service to the user, not only on appropriate materials, but also on ways of getting best results from their use.

Historically, audio-visual specialists have been primarily distributors, i.e., they have concentrated on the distribution function of the audio-visual

Figure 2

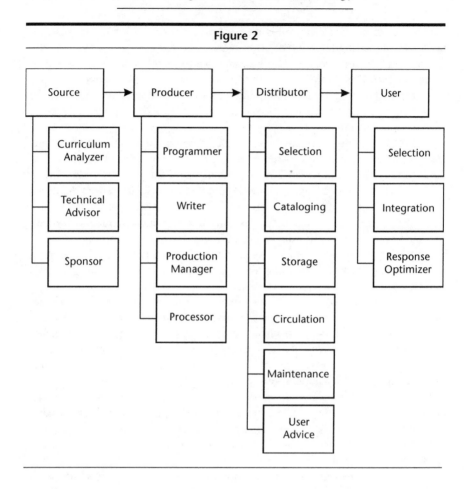

communications system. Inspection of the operations of the distributor makes it easy to understand why librarians have added audio-visual materials to their treasure. Each of the distribution operations listed in figure 2 is and has historically been performed by librarians. Library schools provide technical and professional training in exactly these operations. Inclusion of A-V materials as a commodity of library service extends the scope of informational materials distributed by libraries, but in no way alters the distribution function of the library.

On the other hand, radio and TV educational specialists have primarily concentrated on the production function. The appealing case for TV in education rests very heavily on the "master-teacher," brought instantaneously by ETV to student groups limited in number only by the size of the network.

With a functional analysis of a communications system such as that sketched out for us here, the sources of several of the problems of professional growth are relatively easy to identify.

Returning to figure 2, we can quickly sketch the operations of the user as selection and integration of (informational) materials into the instructional

Figure 3

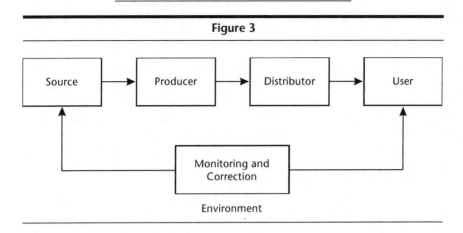

program, and optimizing student response to the information transmitted over the communications system. I realize that designation of a teacher (or group leader) as a response optimizer in figure 2 is indulging in the jargon of superlearnedness, but I know of no other way of expressing this essential operation without talking all around the subject and failing to make the point. There has it seems to me, been an undue emphasis, particularly in utilization research, on maximizing the response of a class to an audio-visual presentation. I think this unfortunate, for it tends to overemphasize the value of a particular informational presentation, and to limit the range of alternative activities of both teachers and pupils. By substituting the concept of optimization for that of maximization, activities directed to increasing response to a given informational presentation (e.g., a film, TV program, etc.) can be cut off at the point of diminishing returns, and we get out of the business of torturing lessons to the point of exhaustion of student interest.

We need figure 3 to close our communications system. So far, the information flows in one direction only, and with an "open system" such as indicated in figure 1, there is no way by which the source, the producer, or the distributor can determine whether the information flowing to the user is adequate to its intents and purposes. There is no feedback on the effectiveness of the information transmitted. To the four functions of an A-V communications system (or any communications system) we must add a fifth—monitoring and correction, or, in more familiar language, evaluation.

It would simplify matters to label this function as "evaluation," but what is intended here is the *observation of effects*, and the *feedback of these observations* to the distributor, the producer, and the information source for corrective action, as appropriate. In this case, the "user" of A-V materials is the teacher, and the effects are the reactions of the students to the film, filmstrip, radio program, etc.

Without observation of audience responses, there is no systematic way by which the effectiveness of specific teaching materials (films, filmstrips, charts, radio and TV programs, books, workbooks, etc.) can be improved. It is evident that some provision must be made for monitoring and correction if

advances are to be made in the *actual effectiveness* of A-V and other informational (instructional) materials.

One final item before bringing this analysis to a close. Our communications system exists in an environment in which there is competition for funds
and facilities, lack of appreciation of the importance of newer media of
communication in education, and resistance to mechanization of the teaching
process, or any part of it. All of these impediments are real, and cannot safely
be ignored, but it seems reasonable to assume that a genuine improvement of
the A-V communications system in all its functions is a necessary step toward
overcoming environmental obstacles and resistances.

Five steps in this direction that are increasingly apparent:

1. An orderly attack on the actual requirements for A-V materials for
   improved instruction.

2. A systematic program for determining and improving the effects of
   A-V materials in actual teaching.

3. An increase in the scope of materials with which A-V specialists
   associate themselves.

4. An increase, particularly on the local level, of production of materials adapted to local requirements.

5. An understanding of the general principles of electronics so as to
   anticipate and employ newer media of communication as their
   feasibility for educational use is demonstrated.

In closing this brief discussion, let me repeat that this has been an
exploratory attempt to analyze the functions of a communications system,
and to specify some of the operations necessary to carry out these functions
with reference to an audio-visual communications system. A good teacher
performs most, if not all these functions and operations in making and using,
for instance, a set of charts for teaching second-grade arithmetic. In an A-V
communications system, this is done on a grand scale for many teachers,
many subjects, and many purposes, so as to free the classroom teacher for
better planning and more individualized instruction. As "A-V specialists" or
"material specialists," "media specialists," our job is to increase the over-all
effectiveness of the system.

Epilogue: 1975

In the nearly twenty years since the above talk was given, the systems
approach has caught on and expanded beyond anything I then expected. It is
most visible to us in the new and important area known as instructional design
and development.

This latter concept (ID&D) transforms the functions of media and of
media specialists, making the latter much more than service managers, camera-
men, and supply officers. They think in broader terms, work more closely with
curriculum planners, teachers, and instructional supervisors. They view the
field of media as one of the several available means to a clearer end than the
vague, indeterminate "improvement and enrichment of instruction." ID&D

changes the media man from a technician to a teacher-educator, a planner and analyzer, who thinks big and can deal with bigness realistically and effectively. That is, it does when and if we are willing and able to grow with the systems concept and its ramifications.

I hasten to add that this is not easy—there is no easy way. Difficulties multiply when the systems concept has not penetrated the educational institutions with which we are associated, or if we are content with what we are doing as worthwhile in itself. Which, in a limited sense and under some present circumstances, it is.

It is my not-too-popular opinion that we have carried the rationalizing process of the systems approach about as far as we need to at this time. The rationalizing process consists largely of developing linear and circular flow charts, interconnecting boxes with abstract words in them, sequences and interactions of high abstractions, directions on where to begin and how to proceed—abstractly.

All this has Parkinsonian utility. It provides agenda to keep committees meeting. It generates articles for whole issues of professional journals. It yields impressive-looking graphics and windmills to tilt at. And visible busyness, of an Oh-boy! genre.

As I see it, what we need to do now is to focus our energies on the implementation at the practical level of the rationales already developed. Again, I hasten to add that this is quite easy for me to say, or write, since I am retiring from my faculty at the end of the 1975 Spring term. Let George do it!

Good beginnings have been made in various places in implementation but these places are relatively few and progress is slow. This is to be expected. The modus operandi of institutions with long traditions does not change overnight. You can become quite a nuisance if you try too hard at increasing the immediacy of future shock. I know. In advanced age, I have sheathed the sword and taken to pen and typewriter. While the printed product has little immediate effect, it won't go away. Sooner or later, some eager graduate student will read it, and start agitating all over again. There's nothing quite like rediscovering what was long since discovered. It works.

In any system, everything is related to everything else, sooner or later and in one way or another. This means that every essential element, factor, or component, and some seemingly inconsequential ones, can seriously affect the final product, outcome, or output of the system. What media people do or don't do not only affects other people in the system but the quality of the output of the entire system. This follows from general systems theory.

But large social systems are difficult to analyze, develop, change, or implement. School systems, colleges, and universities are large social systems. There are so many components in the educational system—so many individuals, roles, organized groups, prescriptive bureaucrats, legislative dictators, etc.—that they are difficult even to itemize. Furthermore, their importance, potency, and level of activity are difficult to predict at any given time, or over time. When component salience, potency, and interaction are unpredictable, then the broad systems approach is something of a dream; a dream, however, not without symbolic significance. At least we can recognize the broad outlines of an educational system and take this broad outline into account in our professional roles and activities.

Because of the difficulties of large systems analysis and development, a feasible approach is to deal with manageable subsystems. That is what we do when we design and develop individual units or courses of instruction. That is what I did in 1956 with the AV system. It was a good thing to do then, but perhaps not good enough in 1975.

We can do more and better in a way simple to prescribe but not always so easy to accomplish in practice. I have in mind the coordination and integration of our subsystems approaches into the mission(s) and operations of the larger system of which we are a part and play a role.

Four preconditions must be met, perhaps more, before substantial progress can be made in getting better. One, the mission(s) of the larger system of which we are a part must be cogently, clearly, and realistically defined—some job! Two, a broad consensus must exist on the defined mission(s)—also, some job! Three, other subsystems within the larger system must be willing to see themselves as parts of the larger system, and be willing to cooperate with each other in terms of the larger system goals and functions. And fourth, or perhaps first, all subsystems must have and take the opportunity to participate in the formulation of the mission(s) and policies of the larger system. Of course this is difficult; the blood of my own trying lies along the path of my personal history.

Two major obstacles to development of the systems approach are the departmentalization of instruction and the We-Know-What's-Best-for-Them attitudes of school boards, administrators, and teachers. Departmentalization begins early in the elementary school. It leads to specialization, and specialization leads to autonomy which is a divisive rather than a cohesive phenomenon.

The We-Know-Best philosophy is a gross misrepresentation of reality that leads to friction in the community, hostility toward the schools, and occasional violence. The classic case is that of the adopted textbooks and library readings in some West Virginia schools. Parents and community groups with strong belief and value systems regarded some of these texts and readings as subversive to their constitutionally guaranteed rights. Discord, bombing, and rifle fire followed after peaceful protest failed. There is only one possible outcome: the parents will win, but at a possible cost in excessive demands for educational restraints. After all, the children are theirs, not the school boards', or the administrators', or the teachers'. It is sad to think that were it not for the We-Know-Best attitude of educators, it might all have been averted. In too many cases, the "professional educators" simply do not know best; and worse, they don't know they don't know.

Examples of out-of-school components of the educational system and of the necessity of taking them into systematic account can be multiplied in even more sensitive areas, if there are more sensitive areas.

The point is that, in a systems approach to education and instruction, the school is not an independent entity, but the creation of the community. What the community can create it can destroy—if provoked beyond reasonable limits.

All the things I mentioned here, and more unmentioned, are parts of what makes the systems approach to education so difficult and so essential.

Educational Technology, Programed Learning, and Instructional Science

A. A. Lumsdaine[1]

Education and Technology

We have been hearing a good deal for the past few years about "educational technology," and likely we shall be hearing a great deal more about it in the coming years. The interaction of education and technology is a bidirectional one: technological advances in society not only pose new requirements for education but also offer new resources.

New Educational Requirements Posed by Technological Change

Advances in physical-science and biological-science technology, ranging from the microscope to the space capsule and from the control of disease to the impact of automation on the spectrum of required occupational skills, obviously change the requirements for the job that education must do. These changing requirements are an increasing source of concern to professional educators as well as to the lay public.[2] However, the changed educational *needs* imposed by technological developments in society have, as such, little direct implication for the *means* whereby these needs are to be met. Despite their importance, we shall, therefore, be relatively little concerned in this paper with implications of technological change, per se, for the requirements of education. However, the implications of educational technology as a source of new tools for improving instruction are central to our present concern.

The preparation of this paper was aided by research conducted with the support of the Cooperative-Research and Educational-Media Branches of the United States Office of Education, Department of Health, Education, and Welfare.

From: Lumsdaine, A. A. 1964. Educational technology, programed learning, and instructional science. In *Theories of learning and instruction: The sixty-third yearbook of the National Society for the Study of Education*, Part 1, edited by E. R. Hilgard, 371–401. Chicago: Univ. of Chicago Press. Reprinted with permission of the National Society for the Study of Education.

Technological Developments as Educational Resources

It seems to have gone largely unnoticed that the concept of technology as a resource for education is actually two quite distinct concepts. These need to be differentiated, even though the two are *de facto* often functionally interrelated. Both of these concepts of "educational technology" (or "instructional technology") have important relations to learning and behavior theory, on the one hand, and to educational practice on the other.

Educational technology[1]. The first meaning of educational technology refers to the application of physical-science and engineering technology to provide mechanical or electro-mechanical tools, instrumentation, or "hardware" which can be used for instructional purposes. This is the principal sense in which the term has been used by Finn and other spokesmen for the "audio-visual education" movement and by the electronic communications industry.[3] In this sense, the reference is generally to the use of equipment for presenting instructional materials, such as still and motion picture projectors (silent and sound), tape recorders (including the special arrangements employed as a "language laboratory"), television, "teaching machines," and, most recently, computer-based teaching systems.

Educational technology[2]. In the second sense, educational technology does not concern hardware, as such, but refers rather to a "technology" in a generic sense, as a derivative or application of an underlying science—somewhat as the technology of engineering relates to the science of physics or the technology of medical practice to the underlying biological sciences.[4] The focus of the present yearbook suggests the status of the science of behavior, especially learning theory, as a primary "underlying science" from which applications to a technology of instruction might be anticipated. However, potential contributions of other kinds of theorization to instructional practice also have been discussed—for example, theories of communication and cybernetics,[5] perceptual theories,[6] and branches of logistics or economics concerned with the utilization of instructional personnel and equipment.[7]

These two basic kinds of educational technology can interact in the design and use of instrumentation to provide better control over the learning situation, by providing a richer array of stimulus material (for example, through motion pictures), and also by providing for interaction between the responses of the learner and the presentation of instructional material.

Other technological contributions to education. The second kind of educational technology ("technology[2]") might also be considered as one aspect of a broader concept of "psychotechnology," referring to application of the science of psychology to practical human affairs. Not all such applications, of course, are primarily concerned with education: psychotherapy, personnel selection, and "human engineering" are obvious examples. Furthermore, there are aspects of psychotechnology not deriving from learning and behavior theory which have important educational applications. Examples are the application of psychometrics to aptitude and achievement testing and of statistical method and experimental design—deriving basically from the mathematics of measurement and probability theory—to the analysis of educational data. A further illustration is the application of "task-analysis" concepts to the design of curricula (see chaps. ii and vii).[8]

Technological Contributions to Instruction

Applications of Physical Science and Engineering Arts to Instructional Resources

Among the contributions which physical-science technology has contributed to teaching, one should not overlook the fundamental importance of the early advances represented by the invention of paper and, later, of movable type. These basic technological "breakthroughs" made feasible the use of printed materials as instruments of teaching, thus removing the need for dependence on the individual teacher's oral discourse with a student or group of students as a sole channel of education. Further major technological advances were the invention of photography and lithography, adding pictorialization to the economically mass-producible resources of instruction. These advances were augmented by the capability for using projected pictures (based on developments in optics and illumination, as well as photography) through the development of various forms of slide or transparency projectors, the camera lucida, and the opaque projector; later, sound recording, silent and sound-synchronized motion pictures; and, quite recently, the electronic audio-visual transmission apparatus of television.[9] Figure 1 is a diagrammatic representation of some interrelations between contributions from physical and behavioral science and educational technology.

Motion pictures and, later, television not only "brought the world to the classroom" in the sense of providing otherwise unavailable visual resources but also made feasible the multiplication of the audience that might profit from the talents of the superior teacher. They also provided special presentation techniques (e.g., animation, overlay, and photomontage) and permitted close-up views to give each student a "front seat" or "over-the-shoulder" view of a process which an instructor is demonstrating.[10]

Development of Equipment and Materials Related to Educational Needs and Psychological Theory

To what extent have developments in instructional hardware and materials for their use (technology$_1$) been influenced by educational requirements and, particularly, by behavioral-science research and learning theory (technology$_2$)?

Audio-visual devices and materials. The development of motion-picture projection equipment and of television transmission and receiving equipment occurred almost entirely without reference to education (much less to learning theory). This is particularly evident in the case of television; for motion pictures the situation is historically a bit less clear, since Edison evidently conceived the motion-picture projector initially as an educational

Figure 1. Some of the interrelationships among developments in physical and behavioral sciences related to educational technology.

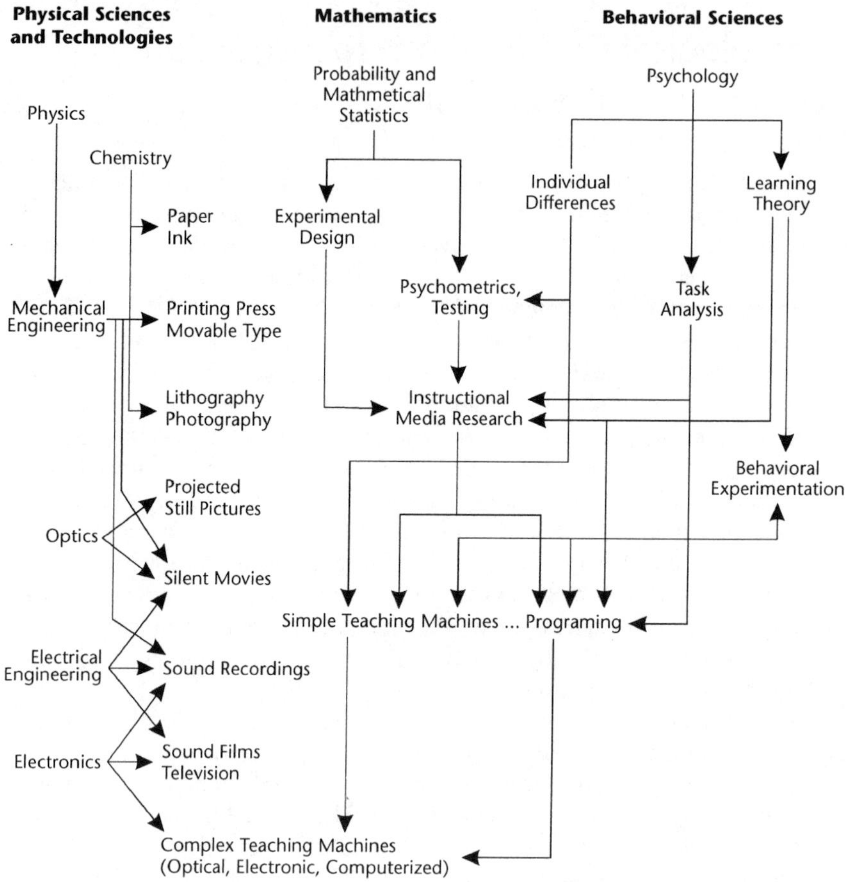

tool.[11] However, its major development and technical perfection were conducted primarily by and for the benefit of the entertainment industry; only when technically perfected was much use made of the motion picture as an instructional instrument. Even the development of 16-mm. and, later, 8-mm. equipment was only partly stimulated by classroom-instruction possibilities, being largely aimed also at amateur application or "home movies."

Historically, the audio-visual media have been used primarily for group or "mass" presentation, without explicit regard to individual differences in learning ability. Their use is by no means so limited, as we shall see, but is related to the fact that development of projection equipment appears to have been carried out largely in terms of imitating, on a reduced scale, the properties of the theatrical projector. Only quite recently has a beginning been made to incorporate features in projection equipment that facilitate more flexible use by teachers and students.

Guidelines for the use of instructional films have stressed their roles as *aids* to teaching rather than as self-contained sequences of instruction. However, there has been an increasing tendency of late to construct films designed to stand alone as independent instructional media.[12] On the other hand, concurrent with this later trend is the recent increase in the feasibility of using film sequences as aids for the classroom teacher and as study materials for individual students—application made more practical by the development of such devices as self-threading 8-mm. cartridge-loading projectors. These developments go hand in hand with an increase in the number of very short films which range from a few seconds to a few minutes in length and which are suitable for instructional purposes. Additional features making film more effective for individual instruction include provision for stopping a filmed demonstration to provide a still image at full illumination before proceeding to the next sequence.[13]

Rationale and uses of A-V media. Another noteworthy characteristic of audio-visual media, as they customarily have been employed, is that they are almost exclusively used as vehicles for presenting stimulus materials, with little explicit attention to the response aspect of the stimulus-response paradigm of learning. Porter[14] has noted this limitation in contrasting such stimulus devices with stimulus-*response* devices like the memory drum and the teaching machine. However, this limitation is not a necessary one and, at least at the research level, combinations of the audio-visual media with various forms of response-registering devices have recently been given increasing attention for both group and individual instruction.[15]

A great impetus to the use of motion pictures for instruction was given by the extensive employment of training films during World War II. The development of films for military instruction on a large scale during the war and, subsequently, for general education was based in large part on the concepts of the value of mass presentation of demonstrational material and of using such techniques as animation and dramatic or story-telling devices for expository purposes. This development occurred almost exclusively without reference to express inputs from theories of learning as developed by psychologists. Indeed, it could be argued that most of the development of audio-visual materials was relatively little influenced by *any* very precise theoretical notions. While such concepts as that of getting closer to the reality base of Dale's "cone of experience"[16] may have influenced the *acceptance* of audio-visual aids, they seem to have had less effect on film design and to have led to relatively little experimental research. It is also difficult to find ways in which other forms of communication models or related theory have been explicitly made a basis for empirical research or for determining the directions along which audio-visual materials have developed.[17] In the main, such theorization seems to have been introduced more as a *post hoc* rationalization for audio-visual instruction than as a direct contribution to the design of instructional materials or hardware.

Teaching machines and programed instruction. The history of the development of audio-visual hardware, primarily independent of educational requirements, and of group-instruction media, largely independent of psychological theory, contrasts strikingly with the situation in more recent developments of

teaching machines and programed-instruction sequences. The initial developments by Pressey in the late 1920's illustrate this change toward greater
dependence on theory as do also the more recent developments which followed
the impact of Skinner's work at Harvard and military research on response
factors in the use of films.[18] Even though Pressey's devices initially emphasized
the automation of testing rather than of instruction, it was evident that they
incorporated principles of learning enunciated by psychologists—the major
emphases being on active participation, immediate confirmation, and individual progression adapted to the capabilities of individual learners. The development of programed-learning sequences during the past few years illustrates a
practical development representing a large investment, directed toward a major
change in educational practice[19] which has, to a large extent, grown directly
out of the concern of psychologists with theory and experimentation on
learning.

     Early in the development of programed-learning materials for individual
student use, there appeared a number of specific attempts to provide rules for
constructing such materials.[20] Thus far it is difficult, by contrast, to find such
precepts being used to guide the construction of the more traditional kinds of
instructional materials except in the *research* literature.[21] The main development of instructional films and televised programs also has thus far largely
ignored the use of empirical data for testing and improving the effectiveness
of program sequences. Quite the contrary has been true of the development of
individual learning programs, where very considerable (even though as yet far
from optimal) use of empirical data as a basis for revision has been a conspicuous feature of the practical development almost from the very outset.[22] However, it seems likely that empirically verifiable programing rules will
increasingly be developed in the future for film and TV instruction, and that
provision will be made for greater use of test data for improving program
effectiveness.[23] This could help greatly to increase the potential of these media
for group instruction up to the inherent limits set by a fixed rate and sequence
in group presentation.

Experimental Research on Instructional Media

     Prior to the recent concern with programed instruction, by far the largest
amount of experimental research on instructional media was conducted in the
context of instructional films which, because of their reproducible character,
have important potentialities both as objects of research and as vehicles for
research on instructional variables.[24] In most respects, however, this research
has only scratched the surface of prevailing ignorance concerning the operation
of variables which govern the effectiveness of instruction. Much of the research, up to the past five years or so, was conducted under a few major
programs or projects, mostly with federal support from military agencies.[25]
Perhaps the most concerted single series of inquiries made thus far was pursued
in the context of a basically stimulus-response orientation, with special reference to factors which control student response during learning.[26] The extent to
which such research programs have influenced the production of films for

classroom teaching is difficult to assess. Doubtless there has been some influence, but most of the research was not closely integrated with the activities of production agencies, and to a considerable extent the main stream of instructional-film and TV production has continued without much direct influence from the results of experimental research.[27]

Research on variables influencing the effects of instructional media has been stimulated greatly during the past four or five years by the impetus of concern with programed instruction which resulted from the influence of Skinner's 1954 and 1958 papers and, to a lesser extent, from military research programs, particularly that of the Air Force Personnel and Training Center. The expansion of such research on instructional media has been facilitated in recent years by the considerable amount of financial support made available by major foundations and from federal sources, especially the United States Office of Education's Cooperative Research and Educational-Media programs.

The sponsorship of the Lumsdaine and Glaser sourcebook on teaching machines and programed learning by the National Education Association's Department of Audio-visual Instruction in 1960 made possible the presentation to large segments of the educational world the papers of Skinner and his associates as well as the early studies of Pressey and some of the military research on training. Together with a number of popular articles on teaching machines, this publication may have marked a real turning point in the concern of the professional education community for the applicability of the theory and experimental science of learning to practical problems of instruction. However, it is likely that these sources of information would have had much less influence had there not been a growing volume of instructional materials in the form of programs, developed initially by psychologists and later by educators, available for commercial sale to schools. As the writer has previously noted, "We should not expect the conclusions and principles derived from ... research to find their way into educational and training practice unless we make the translation ourselves or develop a systematic technology through which such translation may be effected."[28] The actual construction and experimental tryout of programed-learning materials applicable to school curricula provide a very direct bridge between learning theory and application in the classroom.[29]

"Programed Learning" and "Programed Instruction"[30]

Some major concepts underlying these two terms seem likely to represent a truly revolutionary development in educational history.[31] They also constitute a crucial interface between learning theory and the development of educational practice. However, the terms are not easy to define, and such definitions as have been offered are sometimes inconsistent or overly restrictive. A source of confusion is the tendency to identify some particular kind of program as synonymous with the term "program" or to fasten on some particular feature of current programs as a principal identifying characteristic.[32]

Skinner's Influence; The Concept of Programing

Historically, the term "program," as applied to a sequence of instruction presented by a teaching machine, derives from the 1954 and 1958 papers of Skinner, whose influence has, directly or indirectly, guided the mainstream of developments in programed instruction during the later 1950's and early 1960's.[33]

Skinner's work stimulated many experimental psychologists to become interested in applying S-R theory and experimental techniques to practical problems of instruction. The nature of his influence can be indicated by noting some important characteristics implied in the concept of programing. To begin with, Skinner and most others associated with programing developments emphasized the three characteristics also exemplified in Pressey's devices—namely, frequent response, immediate correction or confirmation, and progression at an individual rate. A crucial, new concept introduced by Skinner was the idea that any educational subject matter could be regarded as an accumulative repertoire of behavior which could be analyzed logically and behaviorally into a number of small "steps" representing increments of successive approximation to final mastery. Another basic concept was that an optimal sequence of steps could be developed and refined on the basis of detailed records of the responses made by typical students to a preliminary version of an instructional program.

This concept of empirically developed programs meant not only that the progress of any one student through a program could be regarded a successive approximation to mastery of the subject but also that successive revisions of the program, based on feedback from students to the programer, could be regarded as successive approximations to an ideal learning sequence. A corollary was that the size and sequencing of the steps could be such that the student need seldom make an error, since potential errors could be anticipated and headed off before they were reached. Another implicit corollary is that optimal sequencing, applicable to many students, can often be better determined through psychological analysis of the stimulus and response features of the learning task, together with empirical development based on responses of typical students, than by the efforts of any one student to sequence his own activities.[34]

Essential Versus Secondary Aspects of the Programed-Learning Concept

In the writer's opinion, the afore-mentioned concepts are more central to the importance of programing than are the differences between Pressey and Skinner on the importance of students composing their own answers rather than depending on transfer from multiple-choice responding.[35] It is easy to lose sight of fundamental aspects of the rationale of programed learning, which emerge from the general orientation to which Skinner has given the most impetus, because of the tendency to identify certain aspects of theory or format as definitive of this major trend in programing.

Some of the numerous aspects with respect to which different conceptions of programed instruction vary include: (*a*) stress on the notion of reproducibility or control of learner behavior; (*b*) degree of individualization of rate and/or sequence of instruction in accordance with the responses of the learner; (*c*) theoretical *vs.* empirical bases for program development; (*d*) the need for, and feasibility of, specifying instructional objectives in behaviorally stated terms; (*e*) the extent to which a program purports to take responsibility for managing the attainment of specified objectives *vs.* leaving it largely up to the student to manage his own learning activities; and (*f*) stress on instrumentation *vs.* stress on program content. Some of these differences stem from historical trends identified in Figure 2.

Generic definition of "program." How can we most usefully define what we mean, in essence, by a "program"? Perhaps the most satisfactory general definition is as follows: *An instructional program is a vehicle which generates an essentially reproducible sequence of instructional events and accepts responsibility for efficiently accomplishing a specified change from a given range of initial competences or behavioral tendencies to a specified terminal range of competences or behavioral tendencies.* Such a definition has a minimum of restrictive connotations and can encompass most of the forms of programs that have been proposed. It makes no particular theoretical presuppositions and does not even require individual progress or overt response by the learner as part of the definition (though these characteristics may turn out to be theoretically or experimentally deducible as consequences of the general definition). Thus, a variety of program types and styles is admitted, which may differ in terms of using larger or smaller steps, varying amounts and kinds of student response, and any number of forms or combinations of "linear" paths or types of contingent alternative or "branching" sequences. However, it is evident that, in some sense at least, the definition implies a programed sequence of learner *behavior*, not merely a reproducible set of stimulus materials.[36]

A program is presequenced and implies a *presentation* to the student, not just a source of material to which the student may expose himself. A program thus has a beginning and an end; to borrow a phrase from computer programing, it has a start order and a stop order. The crucial aspect of this conception of programing is expressed by the "programer's credo" that if the student doesn't learn, the programer hasn't taught. This is the fundamental acceptance of responsibility for the management of learning—for trying to see to it that the student does learn and taking the blame for his failures. In an ideal program, the "stop order" occurs only when the student shows either that he has mastered the capabilities which are the program's objectives or that he is basically incapable of doing so.

Empirical guidance of programing. If we consider programs in the generic sense proposed above and do not limit our attention to particular features which are the focus of Pressey's objections, a strong argument for programing is that it leads to the study of stimulus-sequence conditions that promote effective learning. Since the existing state of the art does not permit predicting an optimal sequence on the basis of theory, an essential aspect of any program is some form of self-correction through feedback to the program,

Figure 2. Converging streams of influence affecting present concepts and practices in programed instruction.

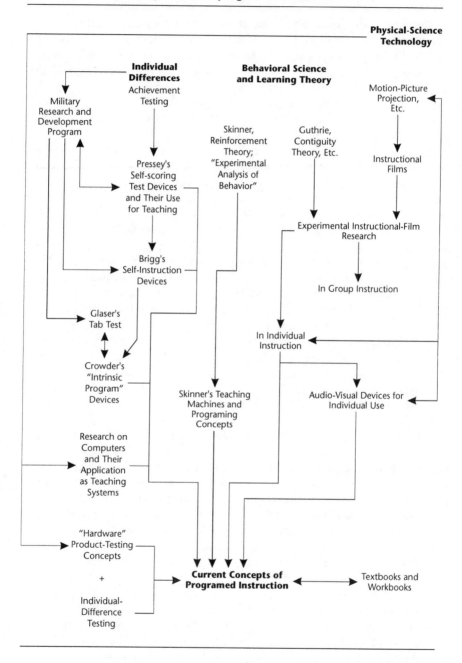

leading to cumulative revision based on programing errors revealed by students' responses to preliminary forms of a program. These responses include students' errors made on the individual "frames" of a program as well as later test data that may be correlated point by point with specific portions of the program. (This form of self-correction should be distinguished from that provided by a "branching" program in which decision points, based on errors of individual students but not made by other students, are used as the occasion for altering the sequence for a particular student.)

A sense in which progressive improvement may be conceived in the development of the art of programing (as distinct from the development of a single program) is successive approximation, through cumulative experience and research on programing variables, to the ability to write an initially very effective program sequence. It seems apparent that thus far we have taken only a few steps toward this goal, but it is the belief of many that the goal may ultimately be a realizable one. This belief is based on the reproducibility and control provided by instructional programs, particularly when used with suitable "teaching-machine" instrumentation, which make them very effective vehicles for experimental research leading to validation of instructional programing principles that can eventually comprise a science of instruction. (Such validation ultimately implies experiments in which the "subjects" in an experiment are a sample of programers—rather than just samples of students—and the experimental variable is instruction in the use of one or more programing principles.) Some illustrative experimental results relevant in the development of programing principles are discussed in a later section.

It should be emphasized that existing programs at best only approximate the potentiality for the kind of control over learning which could realize a goal of guaranteed mastery for all qualified students; many current programs are likely to be no more effective than alternative kinds of material. Indeed, some current "programs" merely follow the general superficial format implied by a particular rationale of programing, without meeting either the theoretical assumptions or empirical requirements which are supposed to be exemplified. A conspicuous shortcoming is the lack of sufficient try-out and revision, but there are also many other obvious failings in some existing programs, including inadequate analysis of the subject matter and inept use of what seem at present to be the more promising techniques of prompting, "vanishing", and feedback to the learner.

Variations in Conceptions of Individual Learning Programs

Individual learning programs are being produced in a wide variety of forms, and an increasing number of styles are emerging, employing various novel techniques. The fact that these initially tended to cluster around two or three main types should not blind us to the possibilities of almost infinite variation. An advantage of the definition proposed is that the *means* whereby educational ends are sought are not restricted to any particular form, provided we satisfy the condition of reproducibility and accept responsibility for trying to effect a specifiable change in behavior.

"Branching" variations. Programs that are being experimented with depart, in varying degrees, from conventionalized "Skinner" or "Crowder" patterns of programing. Thus, there is an increasing tendency to combine "small-step" constructed-response programs with various forms of "branching," to employ mixed modes of response (e.g., both written and multiple-choice), to use a variety of auxiliary displays, and so on.[37] Numerous forms of branching have been experimented with, including complex computer-mediated branching sequences.[38] Thus, the tendency to erroneously limit "branching" to the particular style of "intrinsic" programing with branching after every frame, originated by Crowder,[39] seems to be declining.[40]

"Adjunct" and "module" programs. The general concept of programing, which implies learning through behavioral control by a program, readily encompasses "adjunct" (supplementary) programs that follow other forms of instruction, as recommended by Pressey in chapter xv. The question is not one of either-or but of degree. In some cases it may be hard to draw the line between "small-step" programs with extensive auxiliary "panel" material[41] and relatively free-study situations with autoinstructional materials serving as a frequent review. The basic question really is this: At what points is what degree of specifiable control over the student's learning to be provided—by the teacher, by the program, by the device that presents the program, and by the student himself?

"Module" or short-segment programs which can be interspersed between other forms of instruction to cover limited, specific units rather than entire courses are likewise compatible with the given definition of a program, provided the initial and terminal capabilities of the student are determined by suitable measurement. In applying this definition to a program which is *supplementary* (following other instruction), we need not specify fully the nature of the prior instruction if we specify the student's competence at the end of the prior instruction and, hence, his initial competence at the beginning of the program sequence. However, even the quite broad definition of a program that has been proposed is not compatible with the use of programs as *complementary* to concurrent instruction *of an unspecified sort.* In such use, there is the problem of knowing what accounted for the terminal behavior, at least unless this behavior is isolated by means of a controlled experiment to make possible the identification of the effective contribution of the program itself. Even with such experimentation, the results may be of little use for prediction unless the nature of the "other" instruction is also so fully specified that, in effect, it also acquires the properties of a parallel "program" (as it has been defined in this chapter).

Programed learning as a set of events. We may even include the reading of a conventional textbook passage, *under specified conditions,* as a form of "program" if we are willing to submit such a "program" as accepting responsibility for teaching. However, in order to do so, the *use* of the text must be in some sense "programed," so that the vehicle of instruction is a specifiable set of events rather than remaining as an inert "thing" to be used in some unreproducible, uncontrolled manner. The same consideration applies logically also to the use of "programs" in the commonly more restricted sense of the term:

Except to the extent that the conditions of a program's use may be "built in" through some kind of instrumentation, we need a specification of how the program is assigned and used, not merely an identification of the program *material* itself. A program needs to be thought of as generating a set of *events*, from which we can predict learning; a concept of programed learning that implies a specification of behavioral events on the part of the learner is more powerful than a concept of programed instruction that connotes only a set of materials or stimuli.

S-R Orientation in Programing

A basic emphasis in the programed-learning orientation is on theorization conceived in terms of what the student *does,* reflecting Dewey's emphasis on learning by doing as well as the S-R orientation of the behavioral laboratory. This response-oriented point of view contrasts with conceptions of teaching or communication which concentrate primarily on the stimulus properties of a "message" which students "receive," and which tend to assume that what the student is told he then knows.[42] Emphasis on the study of student behavior, particularly as applied in the testing of programs and their cumulative revision, would make it seem likely, a priori, that thoroughgoing application could scarcely fail to produce, eventually, learning materials of superior effectiveness—both in the case of individually paced programs and of fixed-pace presentations, such as films and television.

Roles of student response. In connection with this response-oriented point of view, attention should be given to several quite different functions of students' overt responses. In addition to the use of response data for revising a program, these functions include: (*a*) identifying a response which can be explicitly reinforced; (*b*) giving practice in making the response—most clearly important where response learning rather than merely association of an already learned response to new stimuli is required; (*c*) providing a basis for regulation of the sequence of the program—that is, to mediate "branching," either step by step or by longer segments; and (*d*) controlling the student's reading or observing through the selection of response requirements[43] so that the student must read or observe effectively in order to make an acceptable response. The best selection of those responses which are to be performed overtly in a program may differ considerably, depending on which of these functions the response is meant to serve.

Implicit responses. An S-R model can apply theoretically not only to overt response but also to implicit or "covert" responses, such as those involved in reading or in "thinking an answer" required by a program. An extreme position sometimes expressed is that the student will learn only the responses which he overtly performs. Literally interpreted, this seems indefensible, since it is obvious that individuals do learn from silent reading and listening. However, making the provisional assumption that the student should respond explicitly to everything which he is to learn may be a useful heuristic in writing a program. Experimental inquiry concerned with the effectiveness of overt and covert responding calls attention to the importance of a better understanding of implicit responses and of theorization, such as Sheffield's[44] on perceptual responding in serial tasks and Cook and Kendler's[45] on mediating responses in the learning of paired-associate material.[46]

Applicability of S-R reinforcement and contiguity principles. A dualism between points of view stressing reinforcement following the to-be-learned response as against a Guthrian contiguity paradigm has been noted by Hill. The latter viewpoint, leading to stress on prompting and the manipulation of cues preceding a response, appears to the writer to be more closely related *de facto* to programing operations and to "rules" of pro-graming that have been enunciated,[47] even though an operant-conditioning paradigm, stressing reinforcement following the response, is often pointed to as the principal theoretical model for programed learning.

The writer has argued elsewhere[48] for more attention to a contiguity theory of the type generally advocated by Guthrie and pointed to a need for more of the kind of theorizing done by Sheffield.[49] The practical service of such theory in relation to programing is that it keeps attention focused on the learner's responses in relation to the controllable conditions of stimulation. As Hill has noted in chapter ii, contiguity theory makes the assumption that the necessary and sufficient condition for any learning to occur is temporal contiguity of cue and response. This position has been assumed from the outset by such theorists as Guthrie and Sheffield, and more recently a similar view has been adopted by Spence and by Estes. The writer also adheres to this view; however, as noted in a previous discussion,[50] there are some crucial classes of responses needed in education for which it is difficult to identify cues that can be used to elicit the responses consistently. Especially important here is the class of responses involved in "paying attention" or "keeping at" the task of studying. It is for such classes of behavior that one might expect the manipulation of reinforcement schedules to be practically most useful. From this point of view, the difference in applicability of operant and elicited-response paradigms lies not per se in the kind of response to be learned but, rather, in the practical availability of an antecedent stimulus for eliciting the response that it is desired to condition.[51] Another possible way of saying this is that the important difference between emphasis on reinforcement schedules and a contiguity-theory emphasis on prompting conditions is a difference in the kind of instructional control over learning that is practicable in various situations, rather than per se a difference in basic requirements for learning.

Some Research Evidence Bearing on a Science of Instruction

Interrelations among theory, research, and practice are complex, as indicated in many parts of this yearbook. The practical relevance of a theory of learning lies in its efficacy for guiding the preparation of learning programs so as to reduce the amount of sheer trial and error (and hence cost) needed to arrive at an effective instructional product. In this sense the statement applies that "nothing is as practical as a good theory." However, general theories applicable to all forms of learning will probably need to be supplemented by intermediate-level principles based on theorization dealing with specific kinds of learning situations in order to provide more specific guidelines for particular programing decisions.[52] Not only do such principles need to be validated through experiment but the programing decisions to which they lead will generally have to be further verified through empirical tryout of specific programs, as has been emphasized, just as do similar theory-based decisions in, say, aeronautical engineering or preventive medicine.[53]

In this section, a few illustrative empirical results relating to principles at an intermediate level will be considered. Such experimental evidence as we thus far can marshal bearing on theoretical factors in instruction seems to come primarily from experiments on instructional media, conducted under controlled yet realistic conditions, rather than from less structured "naturalistic" experimentation with classroom-teaching "methods" or, on the other hand, from experiments conducted in highly artificial psychological-laboratory learning situations. This fact seems relevant to the question of whether a science of instructional programing, dealing with intermediate-level principles, needs to be developed as such—or whether implications of more general learning and behavior theory can ultimately suffice as a foundation from which a technology of practical programing principles can be directly derived.[54]

Contingent Generalizations and a Science of Instruction

The need for and probable character of such intermediate-level principles in the development of a science of instruction rests in part on the proposition that, in view of the complexity of human learning and the diversity of human learning tasks, we can expect to find relatively few universal generalizations that hold for all classes of instructional objectives, all classes of learners, and all conditions of instruction. Rather, what is likely to be most needed is a series of *contingent* generalizations that take account of the interactions of variables. Experimentally, this position argues for factorial experiments in which two or more variables are studied in combination, so that qualifications on a generalization can be determined, and we may validate contingent generalizations of the form: "Under condition A, result one is obtained, whereas under condition B, result two is obtained."[55] However, this stress on contingent generalizations does not imply the use of large, multifactor "shot-gun" experiments; on the contrary, the writer has argued[56] that relatively simple, more sharply focused experiments seem likely to be more productive.

A good example of contingent generalizations based on a simple factorial experiment is found in the differential results obtained in an experiment by Sheffield on the effects of a "one-sided" persuasive communication (which omitted arguments favoring the opposite conclusion) and a "two-sided" argument (which drew the same conclusion but nevertheless mentioned the opposing arguments).[57] The one-sided presentation was more effective in changing the opinions of those listeners who were favorably predisposed at the outset toward the conclusion being advocated, whereas the two-sided argument was the more effective in the case of those who were initially negative toward the advocated point of view. A similar differential conclusion was drawn from an instructional experiment reported by Maccoby, Michael, and Levine.[58] They were concerned with the question of whether effects of practice exercises interpolated between segments of a film were confined to the material practiced or also had a motivational carry-over to other, unrelated material contained in the same program. Such motivational carryover was found when the learners' extrinsic level of motivation was low but not when it was increased by the incentive of the students being told they would be tested at the end of the film.[59]

Prompting, "Small Steps," and "Vanishing"

Emphasis on prompting has been supported on the basis of results obtained by Cook[60] and collaborators, showing consistent superiority in paired-associates tasks for "prompting" over "confirmation" conditions.[61] Results obtained by Angell and Lumsdaine[62] showed, however, that a *mixture* of prompted and unprompted trials was more effective than complete prompting throughout—a finding consonant with the basic rationale for vanishing of cues as well as with the more general argument that we must somehow prepare the learner to cope with an unprompted criterion situation.[63] It seems likely that a fruitful field for further experimental inquiry on principles of programing will concern gradients for the vanishing or withdrawal of prompts.[64]

The notion of introducing suitable prompts wherever needed, followed by their gradual withdrawal ("vanishing"), is closely related to the notion of using small (in the sense of easy) steps in an instructional program; however, possible confusion in conceptualization may arise owing to the use of several different meanings of the term "small steps."[65] A related fact is that some experiments have tended to confound "size of step" (in one or more senses) with number of steps, or total length of program.[66] The most direct independent variation of step size thus far has been in the case of procedural learning, notably in the studies reported by Maccoby and Sheffield.[67] In their studies, length of demonstrational segments (and hence temporal proximity *vs.* remoteness of prompts for the imitative performance of each succeeding step in a serial task) was systematically varied without altering the length or content of the total instructional material. Short steps were found to be generally more effective than long steps for initial learning, with some evidence also supporting the theoretical expectation, in line with the concept of vanishing, that initial use of short steps followed by progressive lengthening of steps would lead to the best performance in a later test situation.

Retention as Related to Programing Theory and Assessment

Theoretical as well as practical interest in delayed-retention measures goes beyond a concern with merely determining whether differences produced by programs persist after an interval of time. For example, analysis of another experiment by Sheffield showed that in some instances effects of an indoctrination program on attitudes showed an actual increase, or "sleeper effect," with the passage of time, whereas in other cases the decrease consonant with expected forgetting was found.[68] Similarly, in a recent experiment by Rothkopf,[69] differences in the effects of program variations which showed up only after a considerable retention interval were found for identification learning (basically, paired-associates) in a technical subject matter (electrical resistor codes). He compared rote drill on paired associates, similar drill using mnemonics, and programed instructional materials that employed "vanishing" (as implemented by a so-called "Ruleg" pattern[70]). Rothkopf failed to find any evidence of appreciable differences in immediate retention but found marked differences favoring the programed over rote instruction when retention was measured after a number of weeks.

A somewhat analogous result concerning the value of "vanishing" has been reported by Angell and Lumsdaine[71] in comparing the effects of two forms of a program to teach a short-cut method for squaring two-digit numbers.[72] In one form of the program, vanishing of prompts was used in accordance with current practices that prevail in much linear-style programing. The other program was substantially identical, except that prompts were deliberately continued throughout the program. The results failed to show evidence of any significant differences in terms of immediate testing, but the vanishing program was significantly superior when retention was measured a week or so later. (An instructive, if perhaps only analogical, parallel may be noted between these results and those obtained in laboratory-learning experiments, with both humans and lower animals, on "partial" or intermittent reinforcement. Like vanishing, this involves omission of the unconditional or reinforcing stimulus on some of the trials, and it is in general superior to 100 percent reinforcement primarily with respect to rate of extinction rather than with respect to rate of acquisition.) It is evident that such results are not only of interest in relation to theory but also can affect decisions concerning suitable time intervals between instruction and testing in the conduct of applied research studies for assessing the effectiveness of specific programs.

Task Variables

The emphasis on contingent generalizations that has been noted suggests a possible basis for reconciliation between Gagne's contention that the most applicable principles for the design of training programs are to be found in principles of task analysis as against the position of those who would seek the main basis for instructional programing in principles deriving from learning theory. The writer would suggest that these two kinds of orientation can be reconciled in terms of theorization which states relationships among stimulus and response variables as contingent principles that take explicit account of the characteristics of specific learning tasks. Thus, the importance of an analysis of task characteristics can figure not only in the identification of what it is that has to be learned, but also as a basis for relating the cue-discrimination characteristics and response requirements of a particular task to the program sequences needed to teach it most effectively.

This approach is exemplified in the theoretical analysis presented by Sheffield[73] based on contiguity learning principles, and investigated experimentally in studies by Sheffield, Maccoby, and collaborators dealing with the phasing of practice in relation to the size and placement of demonstration sequences in teaching procedural tasks.[74] These were analyzed as a function of task-organization features, such as contextually similar "natural units," and testing of differential predictions was possible with respect to, for example, several aspects of the whole-learning, part-learning problem as affected by particular characteristics of a given task. One such contingent generalization was that both the identification of optimum practice units and the temporal arrangements in which such units are utilized will depend on the degree and kind of inherent task organization. This was shown by Sheffield[75] to follow from the consideration that the arrangement of practice and demonstrational segments needs to reconcile the potentially competing requirements of reducing intraserial interference and of integrating subsequences into total-task performance.

On the other hand, it may also be profitable to seek for generalizations that have considerable invariance regardless of superficial differences of subject matter or type of instructional objective. For example, the general principle of anticipating undesired response tendencies has been noted as a common problem in effective persuasion and in heading off incipient error tendencies in teaching perceptual-motor or symbolic skills.[76] Similarly, theorization may extend to variables which apply in common to more than one class of tasks as ordinarily defined in terms of such gross characteristics as manual versus verbal tasks. For example, Sheffield and Maccoby[77] have noted that the principles of task organization encountered in the serial learning of mechanical-assembly tasks would appear to be much the same as those which may apply to the organization of a lecture.

Concluding Comments: A Science and Technology of Programed Learning

The potential for both empirical and theory-guided improvability inherent in the concept of programed learning suggests that the limits for its attainment are far from having been reached as yet. One of the important influences of Skinner's work has been to foster a shift away from experimental studies which merely observe conditions under which learning and forgetting take place, and toward a greater emphasis on the management of efficient learning conditions designed to bring about desired forms of behavior.

The attempt to develop instructional materials not only to serve as a vehicle for testing hypotheses but also to attain a high degree of instructional effectiveness tends to generate provisional "rules" for effective programing of instruction, which can be implemented in experimental materials even though these rules are not tested directly within the confines of a given programing project.[78] Such working guidelines need to be translated into hypotheses that can be subjected to experimental test if a genuine science of instruction is to evolve.

Such a science of instruction can help to undergird not only an educational technology of programing principles but also the development of better specifications for the design of instructional hardware, ranging from simple teaching-machine components to complex computerized systems. It seems likely that this development will generally require the formulation of theory-oriented contingent generalizations, with task and learner characteristics as modifying parameters in terms of which hypothesized cue-response relationships are differentially predicted. It also seems likely that these relationships must, in considerable part, both be based on and lead to an improved knowledge of the functioning of implicit responses in human learning from instructional programs. In addition, the fruitfulness of S-R contiguity theory and reinforcement-manipulation paradigms needs to be further delineated in terms of classes of learning tasks which differ with respect to the initial degree to which desired responses can be predictably elicited by available cues.

Finally, it may well be re-emphasized that differences in present conceptions and forms of programing, as well as their current theoretical rationales, are less important than the basic conviction that instruction is amenable to systematic description and improvement through experimental inquiry.[79] Such inquiry needs to be directed both to the development of a theory and science of instruction, as a long-range goal and as a shorter-range goal, to the development of an improved technology for perfecting and describing the performance characteristics of particular programs in contributing to behaviorally specified instructional outcomes.

Notes

1. The preparation of this paper was aided by research conducted with the support of the Cooperative-Research and Educational-Media Branches of the United States Office of Education, Department of Health, Education, and Welfare.

2. For implications of automation for educational *needs* and of technological tools as *means* for education, see respectively: G. E. Arnstein, *Automation: The New Industrial Revolution* (Washington: National Education Association, October, 1962, mimeographed); James D. Finn, Donald G. Perrin, and Lee E. Campion, *Studies in the Growth of Instructional Technology*, I, *Audio-visual Instrumentation for Instruction in the Public Schools, 1930–1960* (Technological Development Project, Occasional Paper No. 6. Washington: National Education Association, 1962).

3. James D. Finn, "Automation and Education, II, Automatizing the Classroom," *Audio-Visual Communication Review*, V (Spring, 1957), 451–67; James D. Finn, "Automation and Education, III: Technology and the Instructional Process," *Audio-Visual Communication Review*, VIII (Winter, 1960), 5–26; Finn, Perrin, and Campion, *op. cit.*

4. Arthur W. Melton, "The Science of Learning and the Technology of Educational Methods," *Harvard Educational Review*, XXIX (Spring, 1959), 96–106. (Abstracted in *Teaching Machines and Programmed Learning*, pp. 658–60. Edited by A. A. Lumsdaine and Robert Glaser. Washington: National Education Association, 1960.)

5. George Gerbner, "Toward a General Model of Communication," *Audio-Visual Communication Review*, IV (Summer, 1956), 171–99; Wilbur Schramm, "Procedures and Effects of Mass Communication," in *Mass Media and Education*, pp. 113–38 (Fifty-third Yearbook of the National Society for the Study of Education, Part II. Chicago: University of Chicago Press, 1954).

6. "Perception Theory and AV Education," *Audio-Visual Communication Review*, X (September–October, 1962), Supplement No. 5 (Edited by Kenneth Norberg).

7. J. Lloyd Trump, *Images of the Future: A New Approach to the Secondary School*. Urbana, Illinois: Commission on the Experimental Study of the Utilization of the Staff in the Secondary School, 1959.

8. References herein to numbered chapters not otherwise designated are to chapters in this yearbook. [These references have been deleted.—Ed.]

9. L. Paul Saettler, *History of Instructional Technology*, Vol. II, *The Technical Development of the New Media*. Technological Development Project, Occasional Paper No. 2. Washington: National Educational Association, 1961 (mimeographed).

10. Some experimental evidence on such factors is presented in Sol M. Roshal, "Film-mediated Learning with Varying Representations of the Task: Viewing Angle, Portrayal of Demonstration, Motion, and Student Participation," in *Student Response in Programmed Instruction*, pp. 155–75. Edited by A. A. Lumsdaine. Washington: National Academy of Sciences, National Research Council, 1961 (Distributed by Office of Technical Services, U.S. Department of Commerce; Publication No. AD281936).

11. Saettler, *op. cit.*

12. For example, Harvey E. White, Introductory Physics. Wilmette, Illinois: Encyclopaedia Britannica Films, Inc., 1957. (Comprises 162 half-hour 16-mm. sound films.)

13. See A. A. Lumsdaine, "Partial and More Complete Automation of Teaching in Group and Individual Learning Situations," in Automatic Teaching: The State of the Art, pp. 147–66 (Edited by Eugene H. Galanter. New York: John Wiley & Sons, Inc., 1959); A. A. Lumsdaine, "Teaching Machines and Self-Instructional Materials," *Audio-Visual Communications Review*, VII (Summer, 1959), 163–81. (Reprinted under title, "Teaching Machines: An Introductory Overview," in *Teaching Machines and Programmed Learning, op. cit.*, pp. 5–22.

14. Douglas Porter, "A Critical Review of a Portion of the Literature on Teaching Devices," *Harvard Educational Review*, XXVII (1957), 126–47. (Reprinted in *Teaching Machines and Programmed Learning, op. cit.*, pp. 114–32.)

15. Lumsdaine, "Partial and More Complete Automation of Teaching in Group and Individual Learning Situations," *op. cit.*, pp. 149–52; *Student Response in Programmed Instruction, op. cit.*, pp. 1–3; George L. Gropper and A. A. Lumsdaine, *The Use of Student Response To Improve Televised Instruction: An Overview* (Studies in Televised Instruction, Report No. 7. Pittsburgh: American Institute for Research, 1961).

16. Edgar Dale, *Audio-Visual Methods in Teaching*, p. 43. New York: Dryden Press, 1954 (revised).

17. For discussion of such models, see Schramm, *op. cit.*; Gerbner, *op cit.*; and "The Changing Role of the Audiovisual Process in Education: A Definition and a Glossary of Related Terms," TDP Monograph No. I, *Audio-Visual Communication Review*, XI (January–February, 1963), Supplement No. 6 (Edited by D. P. Ely). Concerning the need for audio-visual theory, see Charles F. Schuller,

"AV Theory Is Essential: How Do We Build It?" *Audiovisual Instruction*, VII (September, 1962), 436–37. Growing recognition of the relevance of psychological learning theories for the design of audio-visual media of instruction is evidenced by such publications as Neal E. Miller *et al.*, "Graphic Communication and the Crisis in Education," *Audio-Visual Communication Review*, V, No. 3 (1957), Special Issue; and "Learning Theory and AV Utilization," *Audio-Visual Communication Review*, IX (January–February, 1961), Supplement 4 (Edited by Wesley C. Meierhenry).

18. Concerning convergence of influence of Skinner's work and that of the military programs, see Wilbur Schramm, *Programed Instruction*, pp. 44–45 (New York: Fund for the Advancement of Education, 1962); also, *Teaching Machines and Programmed Learning, op. cit.*, pp. 257–64.

19. Schramm, *Programed Instruction, op. cit.*, pp. 5–11.

20. For examples of such rules, see: David J. Klaus, "The Art of Auto-Instructional Programming," *Audio-Visual Communication Review*, IX (March–April, 1961), 130–42; B. F. Skinner and James G. Holland, *The Use of Teaching Machines in College Instruction: Final Report* (New York: Fund for the Advancement of Education, 1958; also in *Teaching Machines and Programmed Learning, op. cit.*, pp. 159–72); Lloyd E. Homme and Robert Glaser, "Problems in Programming Verbal Learning Sequences" (Paper read at American Psychological Association Convention, 1959; in *Teaching Machines and Programmed Learning, op. cit.*, pp. 486–96).

21. For example, see M. A. May, "Verbal Responses to Demonstrational Films," in *Learning from Films*, pp. 168–80 (Edited by Mark A. May and Arthur A. Lumsdaine. New Haven, Connecticut: Yale University Press, 1958); Fred D. Sheffield and Nathan Maccoby, "Summary and Interpretation of Research on Organizational Principles in Constructing Filmed Demonstrations," in *Student Response in Programmed Instruction, op. cit.*, pp. 117–31.

22. For example, see James G. Holland, "A Teaching Machine Program in Psychology," in *Automatic Teaching: The State of the Art, op. cit.*, pp. 69–82; James G. Holland, "Teaching Machines: An Application of Principles from the Laboratory," in *Teaching Machines and Programmed Learning, op. cit.*, pp. 215–28; and Susan R. Meyer, "Report on the Initial Test of a Junior High-School Vocabulary Program," in *Teaching Machines and Programmed Learning, op. cit.*, pp. 229–46.

23. See Gropper and Lumsdaine, *op. cit.*

24. The most recent and comprehensive survey is that by A. A. Lumsdaine, "Instruments and Media of Instruction," in *Handbook of Research on Teaching*, pp. 609–54 (Edited by N. L. Gage. Chicago: Rand McNally & Co., 1963). Prior summaries include: Charles F. Hoban, Jr., and E. B. Van Ormer, *Instructional Film Research, 1918–1950* (Pennsylvania State University Instructional Film Research Program. Port Washington, New York: U.S. Naval Training Device Center, 1950; Technical Report No. SDC 269-7-19); Miller *et al., op. cit.*; W. H. Allen, "Audio-Visual Communication Research," in *Encyclopedia of Educational Research*, pp. 115–37 (Edited by C. W. Harris. New York: Macmillan Co., 1960).

25. These programs are described in Lumsdaine, "Instruments and Media of Instruction," *op. cit.*, pp. 605–9.

26. See *Student Response in Programmed Instruction, op. cit.*, especially the studies by Sheffield, Maccoby, and co-workers (chaps. ii–ix, pp. 13–131).

27. Much the same statement can be made about the development of "hardware" training devices by military agencies and industry, where systematic research by psychologists began only as a sort of small sideshow following massive and costly programs of device development.

28. Lumsdaine, "Instruments and Media of Instruction," *op. cit.*, p. 670.

29. See Melton, *op. cit.*; also, Lumsdaine, "Instruments and Media of Instruction," *op. cit.*, pp. 586–87, 670.

30. For a commentary on the prevailing inconsistency in spelling of these terms, see editorial note in *Contemporary Psychology*, VII (1962), 354.

31. Schramm, *Programed Instruction, op, cit.*

32. See the characterization given by Pressey, which is more restrictive than the definition here proposed.

33. B. F. Skinner, "The Science of Learning and the Art of Teaching," *Harvard Educational Review*, XXIV (1954), 86–97; "Teaching Machines," *Science*, CXXVIII (October 24, 1958), 969–77 (Reprinted in *Teaching Machines and Programmed Learning, op. cit.*, pp. 99–113 and 137–58); "Why We Need Teaching Machines," in *Cumulative Record*, pp. 182.01–182.02 (Edited by B. F. Skinner. New York: Appleton-Century-Crofts, 1961).

34. That such effective management of learning is not necessarily easy to achieve is suggested by such studies as: J. Jepson Wulff and David L. Emeson, "The Relationship between 'What Is Learned' and 'How It's Taught,'" in *Student Response in Programmed Instruction, op. cit.*, pp. 457–70; Slater E. Newman, "Student *vs.* Instructor Design of Study Method," *Journal of Educational Psychology*, XLVIII (October, 1957), 328–33; see also chapter xv.

35. See chapter xv; Skinner, "Teaching Machines," *op. cit.*, p. 140.

36. Cf. a similar definition by Susan M. Markle in "The Changing Role of the Audiovisual Process in Education," *op. cit.*, p. 64, and the somewhat more restrictive characterization of programs by Schramm, *Programed Instruction, op. cit.*, pp. 1–3.

37. E.g., H. H. Shettel, D. Angell, and A. A. Lumsdaine, *Final Report: Self-Instructional Programs for SAGE System Operators.* Pittsburgh: American Institute for Research (Report No. AIR-C11-61-FR-2252), 1961.

38. Some such branching programs use, on occasion, the preference of the student as a basis for choosing among alternative pathways. See, for example: J. C. R. Licklider, "Preliminary Experiments in Computer-aided Teaching," in *Programmed Learning and Computer-based Instruction*, pp. 217–39 (Edited by John E. Coulson. New York: John Wiley & Sons, Inc., 1962); and William R. Uttal, "On Conversational Interaction," in *Programmed Learning and Computer-based Instruction, ibid.*, pp. 171–90.

39. Norman A. Crowder, "Automatic Tutoring by Intrinsic Programming," in *Teaching Machines and Programmed Learning, op. cit.*, pp. 286–98.

40. Actually, in the original programs for Skinner's disc machine (Skinner, "Teaching Machines," *op. cit.*) at least two kinds of "branching" were employed, namely drop-out of mastered items and use of instructions for selective review of discs. Pressey's second machine [S. L. Pressey, "A Machine for Automatic

Teaching of Drill Material," *School and Society*, XXV (May 7, 1927), 549–52]
also dropped out mastered items. For further discussion of similarities and
differences between Skinner-type and Crowder-type programs, see A. A.
Lumsdaine, "The Development of Teaching Machines and Programmed Self-
Instruction," in *New Teaching Aids for the American Classroom*, pp. 136–73
[Stanford University, California: The Institute for Communication Research,
1960. (Abstract in *Teaching Machines and Programmed Learning, op. cit.*, pp.
653–54.)]. Allowing the student the "branching" option of calling for additional
prompts has been employed experimentally by D. Angell and A. A. Lumsdaine,
A Study of Subject-controlled Partial Cueing in Paired-Associate Learning
[Palo Alto, California: American Institute for Research, 1961. (Report No.
AIR-C14-9/61-SR4.)] and is incorporated in the "Didak" machine described in
Skinner, "Why We Need Teaching Machines," *op. cit.*

41. A "panel" means an auxiliary display used with, and referred to in, a program.
See Skinner and Holland, *op. cit.*, pp. 161–62; "The Changing Role of the
Audiovisual Process in Education," *op. cit.*, p. 62. For an example, see Susan
M. Markle, L. D. Eigen, P. K. Komoski, *A Programed Primer on Programing*
(New York: Center for Programed Instruction, 1961).

42. Skinner, "Why We Need Teaching Machines," *op. cit.*

43. Skinner and Holland, *op. cit.*, p. 163.

44. Fred D. Sheffield, "Theoretical Considerations in Learning of Complex Sequential Tasks from Demonstration and Practice," in *Student Response in
Programmed Instruction, op. cit.*, pp. 13–32.

45. John Oliver Cook and Tracy S. Kendler, "A Theoretical Model to Explain Some
Paired-Associate Learning Data," in *Symposium on Air Force Human Engineering, Personnel, and Training Research,* pp. 90–98. Edited by Glen Finch
and Frank Cameron. Washington: National Academy of Sciences, National
Research Council, 1956.

46. See also John Oliver Cook, "From Audience Participation to Paired-Associates
Learning," in *Student Response in Programmed Instruction, op. cit.*, pp. 351–
66.

47. Lumsdaine, "Some Theoretical and Practical Problems in Programmed Instruction, *op. cit.*, pp. 136–41. See, also, David Zeaman, "Skinner's Theory of
Teaching Machines," in *Automatic Teaching: The State of the Art, op. cit.*, pp.
167–76.

48. *Ibid.*, pp. 137–43.

49. Sheffield, *op. cit.*

50. Lumsdaine, "Some Theoretical and Practical Problems in Programmed Instruction," *op. cit.*, p. 139.

51. This contrasts with the position taken by Mowrer, reported by Hill.

52. See Lumsdaine, *Student Response in Programmed Instruction.*

53. The need for empirical data as a basis for assessing programs has been stressed
by Rothkopf on the basis of what he has termed the "immature" status of
theories of programing, and is reflected in the conclusion by the Joint Committee on Programed Instruction of the American Education Research Association,
American Psychological Association, and the Department of Audiovisual Instruction of the National Education Association that the only defensible standards for assessing the effectiveness of specific programs at the present time

must be on the basis of data from empirical tryouts. (This does not, of course, preclude adherence to principles of programing as rules of thumb in the construction of any particular program.) See Ernst Z. Rothkopf, "Criteria for the Acceptance of Self-Instructional Programs," in *Improving the Efficiency and Quality of Learning*, pp. 30–38 (Edited by Arthur E. Traxler. Washington: Educational Records Bureau and American Council on Education, 1961); and "Criteria for Assessing Programed Instructional Materials" (1962 Report of the Joint Committee on Programed Instruction and Teaching Machines, American Educational Research Association, American Psychological Association, and Department of Audiovisual Instruction, National Education Association), *Audiovisual Instruction*, VIII (February, 1963), 84–89.

54. Melton, *op. cit.*; *Student Response in Programmed Instruction, op. cit.*, pp. 497–500.

55. This view was advocated in Carl I. Hovland, Arthur A. Lumsdaine, and Fred D. Sheffield, *Experiments on Mass Communication*, pp. 8–9. Princeton, New Jersey: Princeton University Press, 1949. See also, Lumsdaine, "Instruments and Media of Instruction," *op. cit.*, pp. 602–3.

56. Lumsdaine, *Student Response in Programmed Instruction. op. cit.*, p. 500; "Instruments and Media of Instruction," *op. cit.*, p. 604.

57. This experiment was reported by Hovland, Lumsdaine and Sheffield, *op. cit.*, pp. 201–27.

58. Nathan Maccoby, Donald N. Michael, and Seymour Levine, "Further Studies of Student Participation Procedures in Film Instruction: Review and Preview, Covert Practice, and Motivational Interactions," in *Student Response in Programmed Instruction. op. cit.*, pp. 295–325.

59. An often-overlooked formal requirement for establishing a contingent generalization of this general character is that the *difference* in the incidence of the phenomenon be shown to be reliably greater under condition A than under condition B, rather than merely that the phenomenon be found under condition A and not demonstrated under condition B. (This condition was met in the above-cited experiment by Sheffield but was not fully met in the experiment reported by Maccoby, Michael, and Levine, *ibid.*, see esp. pp. 321–22.)

60. Cook, *op. cit.*

61. The term "prompting" is used here in a generic sense, referring to any initially adequate stimulus for eliciting the desired response; this is distinguished from Skinner's more restricted usage (B. F. Skinner, *Verbal Behavior*, pp. 255–58. New York: Appleton-Century-Crofts, 1957), which excludes direct copying. The terminology adopted by Briggs (Leslie J. Briggs, *A Survey of Cueing Methods in Education and in Automatic Programs*, p. 4. Pittsburgh: American Institute for Research, May, 1960. Report No. AIR-314-60-IR-106) is exactly the opposite of Skinner's, restricting prompting—as distinguished from "cueing"—to direct copying. The term "vanishing" (cf. Skinner, "Teaching Machines," in *Teaching Machines and Programmed Learning, op. cit.*, p. 146) is used here as synonymous with "fading." See Markle's definitions of these terms in "The Changing Role of the Audiovisual Process in Education: A Definition and a Glossary of Related Terms," *op. cit.*, pp. 131–35.

62. David Angell and A. A. Lumsdaine, "Prompted and Unprompted Trials versus Prompted Trials Only in Paired-Associate Learning," in *Student Response in Programmed Instruction, op. cit.*, pp. 389–98.

63. For further discussion, see *Student Response in Programmed Instruction, op. cit.*, pp. 479–83; Angell and Lumsdaine, "Prompted and Unprompted Trials Only in Paired-Associates Learning," *op. cit.*; David Angell and A. A. Lumsdaine, *Retention of Material Presented by Autoinstructional Programs Which Vanish and Which Do Not Vanish Verbal Cues* [Palo Alto, California: American Institute for Research, 1962. (Report No. AIR-C14-8/62-TR)].

64. A. A. Lumsdaine, "Response Cueing and 'Size-of-Step' in Automated Learning Programs." Paper read at the American Psychological Association Convention, 1959. (Printed in *Teaching Machines and Programmed Learning, op. cit.*, pp. 517–39, under the title "Some Issues Concerning Devices and Programs for Automated Learning.")

65. *Ibid.*, p. 532.

66. Examples are found in J. E. Coulson and H. F. Silberman, *Results of an Initial Experiment in Automated Teaching* (Santa Monica, California: System Development Corp., 1959; also in *Teaching Machines and Programmed Learning, op. cit.*, pp. 452–68); and J. L. Evans, R. Glaser, and L. E. Homme, "A Preliminary Investigation of Variation in the Properties of Verbal Learning Sequences of the 'Teaching Machine' Type," in *Teaching Machines and Programmed Learning, op. cit.*, pp. 446–51.

67. Nathan Maccoby and Fred D. Sheffield, "Theory and Experimental Research on the Teaching of Complex Sequential Procedures by Alternate Demonstration and Practice," in *Symposium on Air Force Human Engineering, Personnel, and Training Research, op. cit.*, pp. 99–107; Nathan Maccoby and Fred D. Sheffield, "Combining Practice with Demonstration in Teaching Complex Sequences: Summary and Interpretation," in *Student Responses in Programmed Instruction, op. cit.*, pp. 77–85.

68. Which of these would occur was, further, found to be partly predictable on the basis of individuals' intellectual characteristics and their initial opinions; see Hovland, Lumsdaine, and Sheffield, *op. cit.*, pp. 182–200.

69. Ernst Z. Rothkopf, "Programed Self-Instructional Booklets, Mnemonic Phrases, and Unguided Study in the Acquisition of Equivalences," in *Journal of Programed Instruction*, I (1962), 19–28.

70. The "Ruleg" (rule-example) concept involves sequences in which, typically, a rule plus an example is used as the basis for prompting the student's completing a further, incomplete example; in later frames, these prompts are withdrawn one at a time until the student is able to respond appropriately without prompting. See Evans, Glaser, and Homme, *op. cit.* (Abstracted in *Teaching Machines and Programmed Learning, op. cit.*, 619–20.)

71. Angell and Lumsdaine, "Retention of Material Presented by Autoinstructional Programs Which Vanish and Which Do Not Vanish Verbal Cues," *op. cit.*

72. These were experimental modifications of a program by James L. Evans, "Squaring Two-digit Numbers Ending in 5," in *Programmed Learning: Evolving Principles and Industrial Applications*, pp. 85–87. Edited by Jerome P. Lysaught. Ann Arbor, Michigan: Foundation for Research on Human Behavior, 1961.

73. Sheffield, *op. cit.*
74. Summaries by Sheffield and Maccoby in *Student Response in Programmed Instruction, op. cit.*, 117–31; more detailed reports by Sheffield, Maccoby, Margolis, and others on pp. 87–116 of the same volume; see also the learning-task analysis in experiments by Wulff and Emeson, *op. cit.*
75. Sheffield, *op. cit.*
76. Concerning error probabilities in skill learning, see Abram Amsel, "Error Responses and Reinforcement Schedules in Self-Instructional Devices," in *Teaching Machines and Programmed Learning, op. cit.*, pp. 506–16. Concerning anticipation of undesired response tendencies in designing a persuasive communication, see Hovland, Lumsdaine, and Sheffield, *op. cit.*, p. 203.
77. Sheffield and Maccoby, *op. cit.*
78. Examples of such rules are to be found in May, *op. cit.*, pp. 176–78, and in Sheffield and Maccoby, *op. cit.*, pp. 129–31.
79. This conviction reflects the position expressed in Lumsdaine and Glaser in *Teaching Machines and Programmed Learning, op. cit.*, p. 564.

Design and Development

Learning
Hierarchies

R. M. Gagné

A few years ago, in the course of studies of the learning of tasks resembling those learned in schools (Gagné, 1962), I used the term "learning hierarchy" to refer to a set of specified intellectual capabilities having, according to theoretical considerations, an ordered relationship to each other. It was possible, I stated, beginning with a clear statement of some terminal objective of instruction, to analyze this final capability into subordinate skills in an order such that lower-level ones could be predicted to generate positive transfer to higher-order ones. The entire set of ordered intellectual skills formed a hierarchy which was considered to bear some relation to a plan for effective instruction.

An example of a hierarchy, pertaining to the addition of integers, is shown in figure 1. In the framework of instruction in "modern math," children learn two distinguishable terminal capabilities: one of these, shown on the right, is simply finding sums of positive and negative numbers; a second, shown on the left, constitutes a demonstration of the logical validity of adding any pair of integers, using the properties of the number system to effect this demonstration. For both these tasks, an analysis revealed a set of subordinate capabilities shown in the figure, some in common and some not in common, ranging down to some relatively simple skills which the children were presumed to possess at the beginning of their instruction.

What I should like to do at this point is to tell you some things I have learned about learning hierarchies in the last couple of years. In part, these things have been learned by additional research, both mine and other people's; and in part, from the various reactions I have received about them from many sources. I need to say, surely, that critical comments have most certainly caused me to rethink and clarify, at least in my own mind, what the nature, characteristics, and uses of learning hierarchies may be. Since such hierarchies contain elements of theory, I am most eager to alter or augment these elements to provide improved prediction, if that is possible. What I am likely to be most

Presidential address given by retiring president of Division 15 at the Annual Meeting of the American Psychological Association, San Francisco, California, August 31, 1968.

Figure 1   A learning hierarchy on the addition of integers.

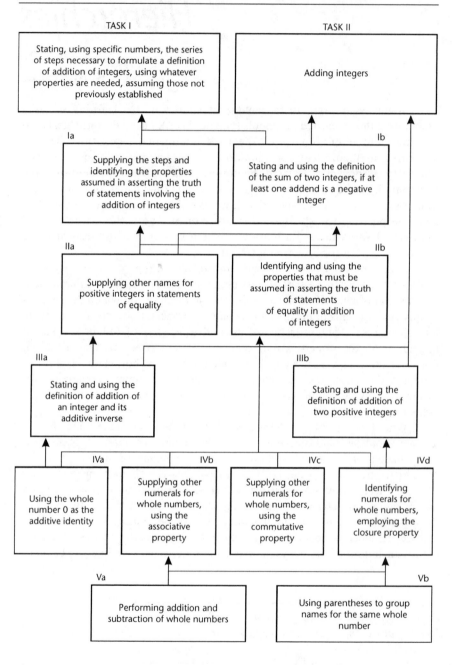

(From Gagné, R. M., Mayor, J. R., Garstens, H. L., and Paradise, N. E. (1962). Factors in acquiring knowledge of a mathematical task. *Psychological Monographs*, 76, No. 526.)

obstinate about changing, however, is the basic idea of the feasibility of predicting optimal sequences of learning events.

Characteristics of Learning Hierarchies

What are the characteristics of a learning hierarchy? How does one know when he has one, and what precisely can be predicted from it?

To find initial answers to such questions, one can review the kind of study which first gave rise to the idea. This was a study derived from an investigation of the learning of a task of constructing formulas for the sums of number series (Gagné, 1962). In the original study using programmed instruction (Gagné and Brown, 1961), individual differences in learning from the program were of course highly evident. One could have attributed them to differences in "intelligence," and let it go at that. But it seemed to me these differences in learning performance were more likely attributable to certain identifiable skills which were not directly represented in the program itself, but which were needed along the way in doing what the program demanded. They were activities that the learners could or could not do, and which the program was accordingly more or less successful in teaching them to do.

The next step was to figure out what these "subordinate skills" might be. Beginning with the final task, I found it was possible to identify nine subordinate capabilities, related to each other in an ordered way, by successively asking the question concerning each task, "What would the individual already have to know how to do in order to learn this new capability simply by being given verbal instructions?" It is probably of some importance to note that the kinds of capabilities identified in this manner did not directly pertain to number series, but rather included such skills as the following:

a. identifying the location of numerals in a tabular array by means of letters giving their row and column location;

b. completing statements of equality by supplying missing numbers in equations containing mixed arithmetic operations;

c. identifying the numbers or letters in a tabular array which formed certain spatial patterns represented by lines connecting at 90 degrees and 45 degrees.

I emphasize that the subordinate skills so identified are not related to number series in a logical sense; what they are related to, psychologically, is the kind of behavior the learner has to engage in if he is going to be successful at *figuring out* from a tabular array of number series properties, how to formulate an equation for their sum.

Having identified a hierarchy of capabilities in this way, the next step was to test its validity. First, a test was made on a number of subjects to determine which of these subordinate tasks they already knew how to do. Two subjects could do all of the subordinate tasks but not the final one; two could do all but two; one all but three; and two all but four. Each of these learners was then taught to do whichever subordinate tasks he couldn't initially perform. Then, having completed this learning, each was given verbal directions about how to do the final task, without any practice on it. Six out of these seven subjects then proceeded to execute the final task of making a formula for four number series which he hadn't seen before. Additional evidence showed that a similarly marked change in capability was brought about in these learners at each "level" of the hierarchy for which instruction had been given.

Certain patterns of responding to the tests of subordinate tasks also were revealed in this study. Specifically, those who got subordinate skill number 1 correct, also got all the skills lower in the hierarchy correct. Those who got number 2 correct, and missed number 1, got all the skills lower than number 2 correct also. In other words, in these seven learners, there was in fact an ordered relationship (similar to that displayed in a Guttman-type scale) among the subordinate capabilities measured.

On the basis of this brief review, I should like to consider the question of what a learning hierarchy is. What properties of the learning hierarchy were either postulated or revealed in this study?

First, the question by means of which the analysis is begun, namely, "What would the individual have to know how to do ... etc.," implies that one is searching for subordinate tasks which will transfer positively to the learning of the task in question. The criterion for such transfer is a stringent one—it is desired that the subordinate skill or skills facilitate the learning to such an extent that it will occur when only verbal instructions, and no further trials of practice, are given. It is evident that choices are being made here, since there are perhaps a number of kinds of subordinate skills which would, under suitable conditions, exhibit some degree of transfer to a given learning task. The method doesn't imply that all of these are searched for, but only those that will meet this stringent criterion. It is fair to say, therefore, that a subordinate capability identified by this method is a skill which is hypothesized to exhibit a substantial amount of positive transfer to the learning of the skill in question.

Second, how does one know if the order assigned to the skills in the hierarchy is correct? To specify this order, one depends first of all on the application of knowledge about transfer of learning, which comes from a great number of sources. A general guide to such ordering is the one I have described (Gagné, 1965), in which simple responses are subordinate to chains or multiple discriminations, which in turn are subordinate to classifying, which in turn is subordinate to using principles or rules. But this of course is rather general guidance, and does not begin to account adequately for the specific choices that must be made in any particular instance. Sometimes one is not sure about the location of a subordinate capability, particularly as to whether it is truly subordinate or merely at the same level.

Empirical tryout of the series of hypotheses represented by a hierarchy seems to be a reasonable approach to this problem. On the basis of such a tryout, one can in effect determine whether a particular skill transfers positively to another, or whether they are independent, or whether perhaps they covary in their transfer effects. I have in one paper made some suggestions about how these determinations might be made (Gagné, 1967), but I perceive these to be very unsophisticated compared with procedures I can only dimly imagine. An example of a successful tryout of this sort is in a study by Cox and Graham

(1966), using a task of elementary mathematics. They were able to show that an initially hypothesized order was incorrect, according to their results. When the hierarchy was rearranged, the existence of an order of subordinate skills was confirmed. Thus it seems to me reasonable to suppose that many individual hypotheses about transfer represented in a hierarchy may have to be checked by some empirical means. If they turn out to be wrong, the conservative conclusion surely is that something is wrong with the specific hierarchy proposed. To the contrary, however, it does not seem reasonable to conclude on the basis of such evidence that *all* hierarchies are wrong.

A third characteristic of hierarchies seems to be of considerable interest. Do they represent a sole learning route to the learning of the final task, or perhaps even a most efficient learning route? Must each individual learner necessarily proceed to acquire each subordinate skill in order to enable him ultimately to learn the final task? By reference again to the method of analysis by means of which the hierarchy is generated, it is quite apparent that the answer to this question is no. Nothing in the method of analysis tells us about the capabilities of the individual learner. A given individual may be able to "skip" one or more of the subordinate tasks, just as a given learner may be able to "skip" parts of an adaptive program of instruction. Another individual may be able to bring to bear on the learning of any given skills some capability which comes from quite a different domain of knowledge, which is not even represented in the hierarchy.

A learning hierarchy, then, in the present state of our knowledge, cannot represent a unique or most efficient route for any given learner. Instead, what it represents is the most probably expectation of greatest positive transfer for an entire sample of learners concerning whom we know nothing more than what specifically relevant skills they start with.

A related point needs to be made about what a learning hierarchy represents, and what it does not represent. Perhaps the best way to say this is that a learning hierarchy does not represent everything that can be learned, nor even everything that *is* learned, within the domain it attempts to describe. In particular, a diagram of a hierarchy does not represent what is perhaps the most important result of learning, the potentiality for transfer which is generated. I have spoken of the events reflected in a learning hierarchy as *cumulative learning* (Gagné, 1968). The cumulative effects of such learning show themselves, in a minimal fashion, by the occurrence of positive transfer from one level of skill to another. But beyond this, there is the fact that each new capability that is learned may generalize to many other situations and domains which cannot possibly be represented on a single chart. In considering, for example, how a child who has learned the skill of volume conservation in rectangular containers, and the skill of conservation in cylindrical containers, may then learn to "conserve" volume in irregularly shaped containers (Gagné, 1968, p. 187), I have pointed out a number of particular subordinate skills from which positive transfer may be expected. The new task can be learned much more quickly than the old, not because the latter is subordinate to it, but because there are many common subordinate skills from which positive transfer may be expected.

Figure 2   The latent consequences of cumulative learning, indicated by sources of positive transfer to the learning of advanced capabilities.

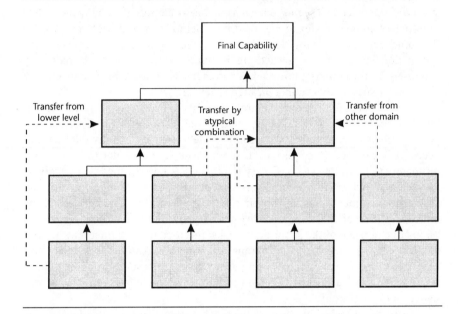

According to this reasoning, there are latent consequences of cumulative learning, which are not directly represented on a diagram of a learning hierarchy. Were they to be represented, one would have to draw lines of transfer, somewhat as indicated in figure 2. Depending on particular circumstances in the individual learner, there may be transfer from a lower level, in other words, "skipping." As another possibility, transfer may occur from quite a different domain of knowledge, as when one uses a skill at identifying number series patterns to solve a problem in classifying patterns of letters. Still a third possibility, which should not be overlooked, is the atypical combination of subordinate skills which, while they may seem conceptually very different, may in the case of an individual learner be able to combine to yield a rather unexpected source of learning transfer. A learning hierarchy cannot, in any practical sense, represent all of these possibilities. Yet to deny their existence would be wrong, and in fact quite contrary to the basic conception of what cumulative learning is supposed to accomplish.

Intellectual Skills

I turn now to one of the most important characteristics of learning hierarchies, and one concerning which I myself have been inconsistent in past writings. The question is, what exactly are these entities, sometimes called capabilities, that make up a learning hierarchy? The answer I would now give is the following. They are *intellectual skills*, which some writers would perhaps call *cognitive strategies*. What they are not is just as important. They are not entities of verbalizable knowledge. I have found that when deriving them, one must carefully record statements of "what the individual can do," and just as carefully avoid statements about "what the individual knows."

I believe that my previous formulation of these entities is misleading, when it deals with what are called "concepts" and "principles." I should prefer to substitute for these, words emphasizing capabilities for action, such as "classifying," and "rule-following." This is more than a nominal change, however. I mean that what learning hierarchies describe is, in computer language, subroutines of a program; what they do not describe is the facts or propositions retrievable from memory as verbalizable statements.

Why do I emphasize this distinction, and what has led me to make it? First, it is surely noteworthy that the original hierarchies were developed in connection with mathematics tasks. If one stops to think about it, the substance of mathematics is largely a set of skills for manipulating numbers. They differ in complexity, of course, and also in specificity. But they are always intellectual skills, and they are not (and probably should not be) verbalizable knowledge. In the original study using number series (Gagné, 1962), for example, what was being learned was not "knowledge" about number series, but a set of particular *skills* of forming relationships among sets of numbers displayed in a systematic array.

You may recall that I incautiously attempted to generalize the ideas of learning hierarchies to such subject matter fields as the social sciences (cf. Gagné, 1967). In doing this, it is quite easy to fall into the trap of describing "knowledge" entities rather than skill entities. For example, some time ago one of my students worked out a learning hierarchy on weather prediction, with my help and acquiescence. The idea was to teach fourth graders how to predict weather from a weather chart superimposed on a map showing terrain features. The subordinate entities of this hierarchy had a high degree of plausibility, and appeared to describe what the child needed to *know* if he was going to predict the weather. When a teaching program based upon this chart was tried out, with much good will and persistence, the results can most succinctly be described by saying that it didn't work. The children did not learn much when a sequence of instruction based upon this chart was followed. Under these circumstances, little or no evidence could be seen in the data that positive transfer was occurring from one level of the hierarchy to the next.

I believe that the fundamental reason for this lack of success was that this was not a learning hierarchy for the task of predicting weather. It did not represent the intellectual skills the child needs to possess in tackling the job of figuring out from the "weather chart" how to make a forecast of the weather. I haven't yet made an analysis that satisfies me, but I suspect the intellectual skills which should be included are such things as these: (1) from general descriptions, formulating relevant propositions in syllogistic form; (2) making a systematic review of the effects of specific factors on an air mass; and (3) constructing specific statements describing weather at designated future times. What should be noted is that such skills as these were not represented in the original formulation. They represent intellectual operations that the child can *do*. But they are not descriptions of what he *knows* (that is, of what he can recall in the sense of non-verbatim verbal propositions).

Then there is the evidence about the effectiveness of certain kinds of sequences in instruction, or in instructional programs. First I should say that I am not sure that a learning hierarchy is supposed to represent a *presentation sequence* for instruction in an entirely uncomplicated way. Presumably, there should be some relation between an ordered set of intellectual skills and an ordering of a sequence of presentation of a set of frames or topics in an instructional program. Results like those of Payne, Krathwohl, and Gordon (1967), however, surely serve to give added emphasis to the distinction between verbalizable knowledge and intellectual skills. The painstaking study conducted by these investigators showed in a most convincing way that sequence of presentation, so far as reasonably mature adult learners are concerned, does not affect what is learned. The authors of this study suggest that, even when frames or topics are presented in scrambled order, the adult learner is able to make them into a coherent and meaningful internal arrangement, and to learn from them. Accordingly, one is led to believe from this study, and others like it, that a learner may acquire certain intellectual skills from a presentation that is quite disorganized when viewed as a sequence of verbalizable knowledge.

It is conceivable that this line of reasoning also applies to the study of Merrill (1965), who found no advantage to review and correction following each topic of an instructional program on imaginary science, as opposed to a condition of no review and correction. While I am by no means highly confident of this interpretation, I believe it might be examined within this general context. To summarize the point, it is that learners can acquire verbalizable knowledge, and even intellectual skills, from sequences of presentation that are altered in various ways from what may be considered "highly organized." The hypothesis I should like to reaffirm, however, is that regardless of presentation sequence, if one is able to identify the intellectual skills that are learned, he will find them to generate positive transfer in an ordered fashion.

Another line of thinking which I believe reinforces the distinction between intellectual skills and verbalizable knowledge comes from an analysis of the kinds of tasks described by Guilford (1967). While I have not undertaken an analysis of all the tasks Guilford describes, I have done some of them, and enough to lead me to believe that in most cases they are sampling both these kinds of entities. The performance being measured, in other words, typically samples the stored verbalizable knowledge the individual has available; and it also samples the intellectual skills that can be brought to bear upon the task. Consider a rather simple example, shown in figure 3. "Which of these letter combinations does not belong with the rest?" The answer is 3, because it contains two vowels.

What kinds of intellectual skills does the individual bring to bear on such a task? I have suggested what I think they might be, in the hierarchy on the right. They include such things as (1) making hypotheses which are tried and discarded, without repetition; and (2) distinguishing various features of letter combinations, such as vowels and consonants, location of letters in the alphabet, symbol repetition, and so forth. But it is equally apparent, is it not, that the

Figure 3   A learning hierarchy for a task of letter combinations, indicating the contribution of intellectual skills and verbal knowledge.

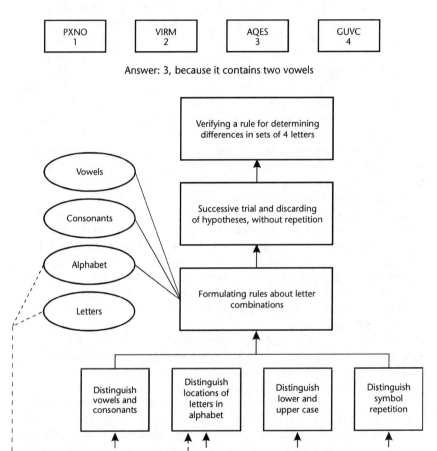

(Example is from Guilford, J. 1967. *The Nature of Human Intelligence.* New York: McGraw-Hill.)

individual who can solve this task also brings to bear some stored verbal entities: he must know what the vowels are, what the consonants are, what the alphabet is, and what the letters are. Both intellectual skills and an elementary kind of verbalizable knowledge are required in performing the task. But my hypothesis is that they are learned in different ways. The skills have an ordered relation to each other, such that subordinate ones contribute positive transfer to superordinate ones. But I do not suppose that the verbalizable entities necessarily have this relationship to each other. Stated in overly simple fashion, one does *not* have to learn consonants and vowels first in order to insure greatest transfer to learning the entire set of letters; and one does *not* have to learn the letters first before learning their position in the alphabet.

This example is admittedly an elementary one, and I should not want that fact to obscure what I think to be the generalizability of this distinction. Consider another task, that of solving five-letter anagrams. The work of Mayzner and Tresselt (1965) and others has shown that such a task derives positive transfer from an identifiable set of intellectual skills, pertaining to the formulation of hypotheses regarding probabilities of letter combinations, probabilities of initial letter occurrences, and others. But it is equally evident that an individual learner who is successful at solving anagrams must have a store of verbalizable knowledge to call upon, which in this case is words. In solving a set of anagrams, the individual will show greater success if he knows a large number of words, besides having mastered the intellectual skills involved.

These are the major reasons, then, why I am led to think that learning hierarchies are descriptions of the relationships of positive transfer among intellectual skills, but that they are not descriptions of how one acquires verbalizable knowledge. Obviously, in solving any given problem, both kinds of retained entities must be brought to bear. And it seems equally true that, when a new intellectual skill is being acquired, knowledge must be available to the learner, since the skill cannot be learned "in a vacuum." I do not, in other words, wish to say that either kind of entity is the more important for learning. Both are essential. What seems to me most evident is that they need to be distinguished, and that the conditions governing positive transfer to them are probably very different.

To complete this account of the distinction between intellectual skills and verbalizable knowledge, it is of some importance to point out that this matter has possibly profound implications in its relation to the curriculum. Most educational psychologists, to be sure, recognize the distinction and clearly state that both intellectual skills and verbalizable knowledge must be learned in the schools. Ausubel (1968), for example, acknowledges the difference early in his text on educational psychology. Skinner (1968) draws a distinction between behaviors to be learned for dealing with particular classes of events, and precurrent self-management behaviors, which are more general in their applicability. Rothkopf (1968) distinguishes mathemagenic behaviors from the substance of what is learned. But the importance of each of these types of learned capability for curriculum design and planning would doubtless be estimated differently by these theorists, and probably still differently by me.

I should be inclined to entertain the notion that the most important things learned in school are intellectual skills, and not verbalizable knowledge. The major reason is, very simply, that one can always look up the knowledge, but the skills have to become "built-in." I can obviously not do justice to this very weighty question at this time. The curriculum implications are such as to lead to a heavy emphasis on what is often referred to as "process," in contrast to content. In elementary science, for example (cf. AAAS Commission on Science Education, 1967), this line of thinking leads one to prefer teaching children the intellectual skills involved in classifying, measuring, and predicting, rather than the verbalizable knowledge of the accomplishments of science.

Now I must return to the major theme of learning hierarchies. To characterize them briefly, they represent an ordered set of intellectual skills, such that each entity generates a substantial amount of positive transfer to the learning of a not-previously-acquired higher-order capability. The learning of each entity also requires the recall of relevant verbalizable knowledge, which, however, is not itself represented in the hierarchy.

What kinds of evidence should be sought in the attempt to verify the hypotheses represented in a learning hierarchy, and what are the sources of such evidence? First of all, I should be inclined to seek evidence about the transfer of learning from one class of intellectual skill to another—in other words, from studies dealing with two successive levels of a hierarchy, rather than with all the levels at once. The reason for this is a fairly simple one involving consideration of the usual controls of an experiment. If one measures transfer from task A to task B, there will usually be certain proportions of success for task B. But one cannot then take the same groups of subjects, varying in their success with task B, and go on to measure transfer to task C, without violating certain principles of random selection. Thus, the basic experimental method remains one of measuring positive transfer from task A to task B; or alternatively, from task B to task C.

There is quite a good deal of evidence concerning positive transfer from one class of intellectual skill to another. For example, in the verbal paired-associate learning field, the evidence reviewed by Battig (1968) is to the effect that the learning of paired associates is typically facilitated by prior discrimination learning on stimulus-terms and response-terms, as well as by prior learning of stimulus coding responses. When one looks at categorizing skills (or concepts) like those exhibited by children in performing reversal-shift tasks, recent investigations such as those of Tighe (1965), Smiley and Weir (1966), and Johnson and White (1967) clearly demonstrate the importance of relevant prior learning of dimensional discriminations for transfer to the reversal task. Similarly, the different sort of classifying required in transposition tasks is shown to derive positive transfer from prior discrimination learning in the studies of Beaty and Weir (1966) and Caron (1966).

The importance of prior classification learning for positive transfer to rule learning is shown in a number of studies dealing with conservation tasks of a type derived from the work of Piaget. Beilin, Kagan and Rabinowitz (1966), for example, found prior classification training to transfer to the task of water-level representation in children, to a greater extent than verbal training. In this field of interest, a study of particular relevance to the present discussion is that of Kingsley and Hall (1967). These investigators made a specific analysis to derive a hierarchy of subordinate skills in conservation tasks. They then tested each child to determine which of the subordinate skills he knew, and proceeded to train each of the missing ones. The method, in other words, resembled that employed in "The acquisition of knowledge" (Gagné, 1962), and substantial amounts of positive transfer to the final conservation tasks were obtained.

There are also a number of recent studies verifying the general idea of positive transfer to problem-solving situations from prior learning on subordinate relevant rules. DiVesta and Walls (1967), for example, demonstrated positive transfer from relevant "pre-utilization" training to the Maier two-string problem. Davis (1967) showed the effectiveness for transfer of previously learned verbal rules to switch-light problems, and a similar theme is developed by Overing and Travers (1966, 1967) in their studies of the problem of hitting an underwater target. In problems concerning mathematical groups and combinatorial topology, Scandura and Wells (1967) demonstrated positive transfer effects from prior learning in concrete situations involving relevant rules.

In this brief sampling of relatively recent studies, one can see repeated many times the general affirmation of the hypothesis that the learning of each particular category of intellectual skill depends substantially, in a positive transfer sense, on the previous learning of another particular category of intellectual skill. In brief, problem-solving draws positive transfer from prior rule learning, which is contributed to in the same sense by prior classification learning, which is in turn strongly affected by prior discrimination learning, and so on. I should say, therefore, that I look for verification of the learning hierarchy idea in studies of positive transfer from one intellectual skill to another. In studies of this sort over the past few years, there is a good deal of confirming evidence.

The other major type of study from which evidence about learning hierarchies may be derived is one which attempts to try out a total hierarchy, applicable perhaps to a limited topic, but in which the various levels of intellectual skill are to be learned in a single instructional sequence. The collaborative studies I did on the learning of algebraic equation-solving and adding integers (Gagné and Paradise, 1961; Gagné, Mayor, Garstens, and Paradise, 1962), for example, are of this sort. The results one first obtains from such studies may indicate that some incorrect hypotheses were made concerning predictions about positive transfer. Specifically, a capability thought to be subordinate to another may turn out to be superordinate, or even coordinate. Such a finding calls for the rearrangement of the hierarchy, as was done, for example, in the previously mentioned study by Cox and Graham (1966) dealing with the addition of two-place numbers. Following such a step, the new hierarchy can then be tried out, in order to seek evidence of positive transfer from one "level" to the next.

I need to mention that methods of analyzing data from such a study are not at all clear. Various possibilities have been tried beginning with Guttman scaling techniques, but none seem entirely satisfactory as yet. It is highly encouraging to know, however, that the measurement techniques needed for such analyses are apparently being worked on by a number of highly competent people. Hopefully, these will contrast with the rather crude methods used in the study from which Figure 1 was taken. Just to remind you what these were, by reference to Figure 1, what we attempted to do was to find the probability of achieving Task 1 for those learners who had learned an immediately subordinate capability, Ia, and to contrast this probability with that for learners who had *not* learned the same subordinate capability. The findings were 73% for the first set of learners, and only 9% for the second set. In other words, there was indeed substantial positive transfer. Similar confirming findings were reported for all of the comparisons possible within the learning hierarchy.

My present estimate is, then, that there are two major kinds of study which are likely to provide evidence concerning learning hierarchies. One investigates only two "levels" of a hierarchy at a time, and in effect becomes a more-or-less traditional study of positive transfer between categories of intellectual skill. The other type attempts to construct a hierarchy which applies to longer sequences of instruction, and which after first establishing a suitable order for the capabilities to be learned, seeks a measure of the dependence (in the positive transfer sense) of one learned entity on another.

Concluding Statement

It will surely be apparent from this restatement and possible clarification of a theoretical view, that in one sense the notion of a learning hierarchy reduces itself to the notion of positive transfer. The question remains, what transfers to what? My answer has been, and still is, that the "what" of this question can be answered in terms of different varieties of learned capabilities. In particular, specific responses transfer to discriminations, which transfer to classifications, which transfer to rules, which in turn may transfer to more complex forms of rule-governed behavior, such as that exhibited in problem solving.

The entities that are affected by positive transfer in this manner deserve to be called intellectual skills or strategies. But it seems important to distinguish these from verbalizable knowledges. While the learning and retention of the latter entities must surely have a theoretical rationale of its own, as for example, Ausubel's (1968), it seems to me to differ in respect to the properties of positive transfer which are applicable to intellectual skills.

When one says, therefore, as I am inclined to say, that we need more evidence about learning hierarchies, he may simply be repeating something that has surely been said before: we need more evidence about positive transfer. Despite the encouraging signs from recent studies I have mentioned, it appears that there is an enormous amount still to be known about this subject. Perhaps reducing "learning hierarchies" to such familiar terms will encourage more investigation and more systematic thinking about this phenomenon, which is so obviously of central importance to education.

References

AAAS Commission on Science Education. (1967). *Science—A Process Approach, Purposes, Accomplishments, Expectations*. Washington, D.C.: American Association for the Advancement of Science.

Ausubel, D. P. (1968). *Educational Psychology: A Cognitive View*. New York: Holt, Rinehart & Winston.

Battig, W. F. (1968). Paired-associate learning. In T. R. Dixon and D. L. Horton (Eds.), *Verbal Behavior and General Behavior Theory*, pp. 149–171. Englewood Cliffs, N.J.: Prentice-Hall.

Beaty, W. E., and Weir, M. W. (1966). Children's performance on the intermediate-size transposition problem as a function of two different training procedures. *Journal of Experimental Child Psychology*, 4: 332–340.

Beilin, H., Kagan, J., and Rabinowitz, R. (1966). Effects of verbal and perceptual training on water level representation. *Child Development*, 37: 317–330.

Caron, A. J. (1966). Far transposition of intermediate-size in preverbal children. *Journal of Experimental Child Psychology*, 3: 296–311.

Cox, R. C., and Graham, G. T. (1966). The development of a sequentially scaled achievement test. Paper read at Annual Meeting, American Educational Research Association, Chicago.

Davis, G. A. (1967). Detrimental effects of distraction, additional response alternatives, and longer response chains in solving switch-light problems. *Journal of Experimental Psychology*, 73: 45–55.

DiVesta, F. J. and Walls, R. T. (1967). Transfer of object-function in problem solving. *American Educational Research Journal*, 4: 207–216.

Gagné, R. M. (1962). The acquisition of knowledge. *Psychological Review*, 69: 355–365.

Gagné, R. M. (1965). *The Conditions of Learning*. New York: Holt, Rinehart & Winston.

Gagné, R. M. (1967). Curriculum research and the promotion of learning. In *Perspectives of Curriculum Evaluation*, AERA Monograph Series on Curriculum Evaluation, No. 1, 19–38. Chicago: Rand-McNally.

Gagné, R. M. (1968). Contributions of learning to human development. *Psychological Review*, 75: 177–191.

Gagné, R. M., and Brown, L. T. (1961). Some factors in the programming of conceptual learning. *Journal of Experimental Psychology*, 62: 313–321.

Gagné, R. M., Major, J. R., Garstens, H. L., and Paradise, N. E. (1962). Factors in acquiring knowledge of a mathematical task. *Psychological Monographs*, 76, No. 526.

Gagné, R. M., and Paradise, N. E. (1961). Abilities and learning sets in knowledge acquisition. *Psychological Monographs*, 75, No. 518.

Guilford, J. P. (1968). *The Nature of Human Intelligence*. New York: McGraw-Hill.

Johnson, P. J., and White, P. M., Jr. (1967). Concept of dimensionality and reversal shift performance in children. *Journal of Experimental Child Psychology*, 5: 223–227.

Kingsley, R. C., and Hall, V. C. (1967). Training conservation through the use of learning sets. *Child Development*, 38: 1111–1126.

Mayzner, M. S., and Tresselt, M. E. (1965). Solving words as anagrams: An issue reexamined. *Psychonomic Science*, 3: 363–364.

Merrill, M. D. (1965). Correction and review on successive parts in learning a hierarchical task. *Journal of Educational Psychology*, 56: 225–234.

Overing, R. L. R., and Travers, R. M. W. (1966). Effect upon transfer of variations in training conditions. *Journal of Educational Psychology*, 57: 179–188.

Overing, R. L. R., and Travers, R. M. W. (1967). Variation in the amount of irrelevant cues in training and test conditions and the effect upon transfer. *Journal of Educational Psychology*, 58: 62–68.

Payne, D. A., Krathwohl, D. R., and Gordon, J. (1967). The effect of sequence on programmed instruction. *American Educational Research Journal*, 4: 125–132.

Rothkopf, E. Z. (1968). Two scientific approaches to the management of instruction. In R. M. Gagné and W. J. Gephart (Eds.), *Learning Research and School Subjects*. Itasca, Ill.: Peacock.

Scandura, J. M., and Wells, J. N. (1967). Advance organizers in learning abstract mathematics. *American Educational Research Journal*, 4: 295–301.

Skinner, B. F. (1968). *The Technology of Teaching*. New York: Appleton-Century-Crofts.

Smiley, S. S., and Weir, M. W. (1966). Role of dimensional dominance in reversal and non-reversal shift behavior. *Journal of Experimental Child Psychology*, 4: 296–307.

Tighe, L. S. (1965). Effect of perceptual pretraining on reversal and non-reversal shifts. *Journal of Experimental Psychology*, 70: 379–385.

Evaluation

Needs Assessments: Internal and External

Roger Kaufman

In recent work, it was suggested (Kaufman, 1977) that there were at least six varieties of needs assessment, one for each of the six steps of a "system approach" model (Kaufman, 1972). Based upon the starting assumptions or the actual data on hand, one could start a needs assessment at any one of the six steps.

One could start with an "alpha" needs assessment, for instance, which had no "givens" or sacred cows, and thus could look at any presenting set of problems or any situation and not have to assume much about currently operating organizations or existing policies or regulations.

A "beta" type needs assessment starts at the second system approach step, and usually assumes the validity and usefulness of the organizations which frequently sponsor or initiate needs assessments.

Four more possible varieties of needs assessments were identified; one for each of the remainder of the six steps of the generic system approach problem identification and problem resolution process. It was intended that this taxonomy of needs assessments would allow educators and other would-be problem solvers to know that different varieties and possibilities for conducting needs assessment were available, and the choice of one over others would be based upon knowledge of the possible array and thus be most responsive to the problems and organizations being addressed.

This paper deals with a possible way of separating these six modes of needs assessments into two "bundles" or types: internal and external.

Internal View of Education: The Way It Is

Most educators are hired, fired, and nurtured by an organization; a school, a district, or an agency which monitors or oversees these others. Thus any

At the time this paper was published, Roger Kaufman was with the Instructional Systems Development Center, Florida State University, Tallahassee. This paper was presented at the 1977 meeting of the Association for Educational Communications and Technology, Miami Beach, April 27, 1977, A Symposium on "Excellence in Instructional Development" (DID/RTD).

From: Kaufman, R. 1977. Needs assessments: internal and external. *Journal of instructional development* 1(1):5–8. Reprinted with permission of Association for Educational Communications and Technology.

changes and problems which arise naturally tend to be viewed from the perspective of that organization. From this perspective, any presenting problem, if we are part of a school district, is seen as an educational problem within the context of that district. If we were in a state educational agency for instance, that educational agency along with its policies, procedures, and history would become the frame of reference for thinking and doing. This might be best viewed as an "inside" view of a problem or problem context, and this perspective assumes that the organization in which the individual finds oneself is the proper starting point for planning, changing, or doing. This further assumes that the organization is basic, unyielding, and is the bedrock for change.

And why not? They pay the salaries, make the promotions, assign the offices, determine success and failure—why should not that organization and those bosses and opinion leaders be the beginning and end for all activity? The value placed upon personal and organizational survival seems to "drive" this perceptual frame.

External View of Education: The Way It Should Start

The simple truth is that what the schools do and what the schools accomplish is of concern to those who depend upon the schools, those who pay the bills and those who pass the legislation. We are not in a vacuum, and our results are seen and judged by those outside of the schools—those who are external to it. If educators are unthreatened by the concept, we will admit that the schools are a process, a means to an end for survival and contribution outside of the schools, upon legal exit from the education agency. Graduates and those legally leaving our schools might well be minimally (not maximally) judged by the extent to which they are able to exhibit behaviors and attitudes which result in their being able to survive and hopefully contribute in the world of work, world of play, world of families, and world of relationships—an external view of our education and our results (Kaufman, 1972).

This "external" referent should be the starting place for functional and useful educational planning, design, implementation, and evaluation—if education does not allow learners to live better and contribute better, it probably is not worth doing, and will probably end up being attacked and decimated by taxpayers and legislators.

Needs Assessment: Starting off Right

There are many models, varieties and concepts of needs assessment (cf. Gagné, 1977) as pointed out in the previously noted taxonomy suggestion; none are either correct or incorrect, the only question concerns which one is most appropriate for any given application.

The most basic (and useful) form of a needs assessment determines the gaps between current outcomes and required or desired outcomes based upon external survival and contribution. It reconciles differences among the educational partners of learners, educators and society, and places the needs (outcome gaps) in priority order for intended action. This is an "alpha" mode of needs assessment—the mode which takes an "external" view of the world in order to determine needs and their utility.

It is a gap analysis which determines the discrepancies between current results and required results, places these gaps in priority order, and selects those gaps of highest priority for action—for closure.

Since it looks at gaps in outcomes, not in processes[1], an alpha-type needs assessment is critical if one wants to identify problems before they try to solve them. It is a vital starting place for achieving educational success.

The central point is that an outcome gap analysis, which best starts at the first step in a system approach is a way of determining the problem to be addressed. The starting place, or the assumptions inherent in a selected starting place (e.g. assuming that the organization is the proper context for understanding and solving the problem or assuming that a teaching method is correct and trying to plan its implementation, etc.) is important in determining which problem will be addressed, and thus what the solution will look like and eventually accomplish (or not accomplish)[2].

Much has been written on Needs Assessment, and the interested reader is directed to many of the writings listed in this bibliography and elsewhere.

Internal Needs Assessment: The Way It Is Usually Done

When most educational agencies embark upon a needs assessment, they usually start with an analysis of the discrepancies between current student behaviors and accomplishments and goals and objectives for that accomplishment. The current goals, objectives, policies, laws, rules, regulations, and procedures are thus seen as "given", fixed, and generally unchangeable.

Gaps (needs) thus harvested are in relation to the goals and objectives of the organization, and these goals and objectives are *assumed* to be valid, valuable, and having utility and worth.

In the earlier taxonomy context, this mode of needs assessment is "beta", since it starts with the "givens" of the organizations which sponsor it.

Gamma, Delta, Epsilon, and Zeta needs assessments, in similar fashion, are also seen as "internal" needs assessments since they also operate within the context of existing organizations.

While these modes of needs assessments are necessary to the accomplishment of the system problem-solving approach, and indeed will eventually be performed when using the system approach to problem solving—it should be carefully noted and understood that they begin with the acceptance and understanding of all of the assumptions associated with starting analysis and planning with preconceived goals, objectives, policies and rules of an organization already in place and operating. This reduces and limits the degrees of freedom for revision and renewal to the borders of that organization or starting referent. For instance, consider the problems of trying to use needs assessment data to convince the management of a now-defunct railroad that they were not in the correct business in the first place—that they should be moving cargo and people, not running railcars from here to there! Being "locked-in" to an organization usually means that you can only change within that organization, and usually cannot redirect that organization's goals and purposes.

So acute is this problem that Reusch (1975) warned that in our society deviations in means are considered to be only misbehaviors, while deviations in goals are considered to be subversion!

Changes to the organization other than "tinkering" with the means, the how-to-do-its, have serious consequences. The implementation of an external needs assessment, then, is a serious proposition which should be undertaken knowing that there is a distinct possibility that the people in power might not look kindly toward the results, or the major changes it might suggest.

External Needs Assessment: The Rational Starting Place

As we noted earlier, the external view of education starts with looking outside of educational agencies for the "payoffs" of the education enterprise and endeavors. Do children learn anything which they can use when they go to the outside world? Do learners have anything which is worthwhile when they leave the school? Does the educational intervention have any utility when the halls of education are passed through and life outside begins? It is to this life outside, now and in the future, that an external needs assessment is addressed. Do the results outside of education have validity as well as utility?[3]

In an external needs assessment, criteria from actual performance (now and in the future) is used as a template for designing the goals and objectives of education (to form the basis for internal needs assessment and thus internal criteria for validity and utility) and for then selecting the best methods and means for achieving these outcomes.

Thus there seems to be a natural, logical, even rational progression for design and accomplishment which would lead us, in the planning, design, implementation, evaluation and revision of education in this manner:

Seen in this way, the starting point for educational planning and accomplishment are the realities outside of schools and school districts (and this concept is equally important in business and industry, the military, and government in order that the effort does more than seek its own continuance and makes a contribution, and in the case of business and industry, shows a proper return on investment).

Some Arguments Against an External Needs Assessment

Most people feel that they can only do what they were directed to do within the confines of good sense and judgment within their organization. This is good sense in a world which, as Reusch (1975) pointed out, tends to reinforce the status quo, and to look at even deviations in means as misbehaviors. Survival, some argue, requires that we do not "rock the boat." If one does rock the boat, then one risks, so that argument goes, losing the job.

Others feel that the world will not understand basic and major shifts and redirections, that changes should be made piece-by-piece (cf. Kaufman, 1976b), rather than a dramatic, all-at-once shift which could result in what Festinger called "cognitive dissonance".

A third argument goes "we cannot safely and completely predict the future, so it is very risky, perhaps even wrong to go ahead and change the world and the goals and objectives of those social agencies which are now operating." Lack of predictability is seen as reason for not changing.

There is some merit to these positions: it is not fun to get fired, and making errors, especially with large numbers of people, can be tragic. Change is usually more successful if it is seen by those affected as appropriate and at a pace they can "handle". Let's look at these briefly.

Is a job which is destructive, wrong or even unproductive, worth having? What are the individual job-holders' value systems relative to contributing to their fellow citizens and getting a regular paycheck? This unwillingness to recommend change, no matter how critical the change, is one which is often observed, but not often admired when seen in this light.

Moving slowly has much more merit than moving quickly and failing—if that is the choice. We do not want to change so quickly that the change attempt is abortive, and the changes never get accomplished. But an external needs assessment, if done with skill and objectivity, will yield information relative to change requirements, including the discovery of possible blocks to change so that the change, whenever required and necessary (but never for its own sake) may be phased and "gentled" in order for it to be valid, have utility, and be accepted.

The most troublesome argument is the one relating to the lack of predictability of the future. There are no crystal balls which seem to work well. Is this reason, however, not to try to predict and control the future so that future change will not be destructive? We make some predictions every day (how to drive, where to drive, what to eat and not eat—all based upon predictions of the future) and we must in order to survive. Change in our world is inevitable, the only question is whether we will be the masters or the victims of change. If we have a responsive and responsible method of planning, doing and revising, then we can see where our predictions are becoming incorrect and change in mid-course. Because we cannot completely predict the future is not a rational reason for the maintenance of the status quo. It would seem to make more sense to try to predict the requirements for survival and contribution in the future, and with sensitivity and analysis be willing to, and when required, shift what we are doing as well as how we are doing the job. As things stand now, not using an external needs assessment referent (and thus not obtaining external validity and utility criteria) means that we will just continue that which is now going on, or only find more efficient ways and means to do what it is we are already accomplishing.[4]

The arguments against an external needs assessment might be looked into in terms of resistance to change resulting from a shift from the known and comfortable to the unknown and the possible discomfort which comes with change. The arguments are not without merit, and one tempted to conduct an external needs assessment should attend carefully to the risks before proceeding.

Summary

There are two possible overarching referents for needs assessment: one which looks at needs from the point of view outside of the organization doing the study, and one which looks at needs from within that organization. The external view is here called, unsurprisingly, "external needs assessment" and the other is termed "internal needs assessment". Most current activities in needs assessment are of the internal variety.

The external needs assessment is suggested as a rational and logical starting place for organizational effort (including learning design) in that it studies and identifies the skills, knowledges and attitudes which are important outside of the school (or organization) and uses that information as the basis for educational design and effort. The internal needs assessment goes from that point forward to identify internally useful and worthy goals, objectives, methods and means to meet those required and desired outcomes. Most current effort in needs assessment is of the internal variety, and it is strongly urged that this referent be augmented with the external needs assessment data and information.

Notes

1   The word "need" in this context is only used as a noun to note a gap in outcomes and never a gap in process or how-to-do-its, when the word need is used as a verb or in a verb sense.

2   The system approach model, as a generic process for identifying as well as solving problems (Kaufman, 1972) is the underlying referent here. Those not familiar with this model are encouraged to review it.

3   It is tempting to form a new word "ulidity" to identify the dual components of validity (accomplishing stated outcomes) and utility (having recognized worth). Thus, outcomes having internal ulidity would be prized within an educational agency, while outcomes having external ulidity would be valued in the society and community within which the schools operate in terms of making a contribution to that external community. Most educational efforts today are striving for internal ulidity while this presentation intends to encourage the addition of external ulidity to the efforts and accomplishments.

4   In earlier works, this distinction has been referred to as one between a "system approach" (which takes the external view before progressing with the internal), and the "systems approach" which starts with the internal view (cf. Kaufman, 1972).

References

Gagné, R. M. "Discovering Educational Goals." A Paper delivered at AERA Annual Meeting, New York, N.Y., April 4–8, 1977.

Kaufman, R. A. *Educational System Planning.* Englewood Cliffs, N.J.: Prentice-Hall, 1972.

Kaufman, R. *Needs Assessment.* San Diego, California: University Consortium for Instructional Technology and Development, 1976.

Kaufman, R. *Identifying and Solving Problems: A System Approach.* La Jolla, California: University Associates Publishers, 1976a.

Kaufman, R. "Organizational Improvement: A Review of Models and an Attempted Synthesis." *Group and Organization Studies,* December, 1976b.

Kaufman, R. "Toward a Possible Taxonomy of Needs Assessments." *Educational Technology* (Special Issue on Needs Assessment). In Press. 1977.

Knight, Michael R., Breivogel, W., Pyatte, J. *Needs Assessment Materials: An Annotated Bibliography.* Gainesville, Florida: Florida Educational Research and Development Council, 1976.

New Jersey Department of Education. *Modelog.* Trenton, New Jersey: Division of Research, Planning and Evaluation, New Jersey Department of Education, 1975.

Reusch, J. *Knowledge in Action.* New York: J. Arronsen Publishers, 1975.

Witkin, Belle Ruth. *An Analysis of Needs Assessment Techniques for Educational Planning at State, Intermediate, and District Levels.* Hayward, California: Alameda County School Department, 1975.

Techniques for Evaluating Training Programs

Donald L. Kirkpatrick

This series of articles is based on the following assumption: That *one training director cannot borrow evaluation results* from another; *he/she can, however, borrow* evaluation *techniques*. Therefore, the techniques used by various trainers will be described without detailing the findings. Each of these four articles will discuss one of the evaluation steps which can be summarized as follows:

Step 1—REACTION

Step 2—LEARNING

Step 3—BEHAVIOR

Step 4—RESULTS

These articles are designed to stimulate training directors to increase their efforts in evaluating training programs. It is hoped that the specific suggestions will prove helpful in these evaluation attempts.

The following quotation from Daniel M. Goodacre III is most appropriate as an Introduction:

> Managers, needless to say, expect their manufacturing and sales departments to yield a good return and will go to great lengths to find out whether they have done so. When it comes to training, however, they may expect the return—but rarely do they make a like effort to measure the actual results. Fortunately for those in charge of training programs, this philanthropic attitude has come to be taken for granted. There is certainly no guarantee, however, that it will continue, and training directors might be well-advised to take the initiative and evaluate their programs before the day of reckoning arrives.

Donald L. Kirkpatrick is professor of management development at the University of Wisconsin-Extension, Milwaukee. A past national president of ASTD (1975), he has authored numerous articles and books.

From: Kirkpatrick, D. L. 1979. Techniques for evaluating training programs. *Training and development journal* (June 1979):178–192. Copyright June 1979, *Training & Development*, American Society for Training and Development.

Part 1—Reaction

Reaction may best be defined as how well the trainees liked a particular training program. Evaluating in terms of reaction is the same as measuring the feelings of the conferees. It is important to emphasize that it does not include a measurement of any learning that takes place. Because reaction is so easy to measure, nearly all training directors do it.

However, in this writer's opinion many of these attempts do not meet the standards listed below:

1. Determine what you want to find out.
2. Use a written comment sheet covering those items determined in step one above.
3. Design the form so that the reactions can be tabulated and quantified.
4. Obtain honest reactions by making the forms anonymous.
5. Encourage the conferees to write in additional comments not covered by the questions that were designed to be tabulated and quantified.

The comment sheet shown in figure 1 was used to measure reaction at an ASTD Summer Institute that was planned and coordinated by the staff of the Management Institute of the University of Wisconsin.

Those who planned this ASTD program were interested in reactions to: subject, technique (lecture vs. discussion), and the performance of the conference leader. Therefore, the form was designed accordingly. So the reactions could be readily tabulated and quantified, the conferees were asked to place a check in the appropriate spaces.

In question 3 concerning the leader, it was felt that a more meaningful rating would be given the leader if the conferees considered items A through G before checking the "overall rating." This question was designed to prevent a conference leader's personality from dominating group reaction.

Question 4 allowed the conferees to suggest any improvements that came to mind. The optional signature was used so that follow-up discussions with conferees could be done. About half of the conferees signed their names. With this type of group, the optional signature did not affect the honesty of their answers, in all probability. It is strongly suggested that unsigned sheets be used in most meetings, however.

This ASTD reaction sheet was used at the conclusion of every session in the institute program. Therefore, the conferees rated each conference leader for his contribution to the program. In many internal training programs, a series of meetings will be held and the reaction sheet will not be used until the end of the last session. This is especially true when one conference leader conducts the entire program. In this case, a comment sheet like the ASTD one might be adapted to the situation and modifications made.

How to Supplement the Evaluation of the Conferees

In doing research on the subject of evaluation, this writer received a very practical suggestion from Richard Johnson, past president of the New York

Figure 1 Rating chart.

Leader   Subject

                                Date

1. Was the Subject Pertinent to Your Needs and Interests?
    ☐ No   ☐ To Some Extent   ☐ Very Much So
2. How Was the Ratio of Lecture to Discussion?
    ☐ Too Much Lecture   ☐ O.K.   ☐ Too Much Discussion
3. How About the Leader?

	Excellent	Very Good	Good	Fair	Poor
A. How well did he/she state objectives?					
B. How well did he/she keep the session alive and interesting?					
C. How well did he/she use the blackboard, charts, and other aids?					
D. How well did he/she summarize during the session?					
E. How well did he/she maintain a friendly and helpful manner?					
F. How well did he/she illustrate and clarify the points?					
G. How was his/her summary at the close of the session?					

What Is Your Overall Rating of the Leader?
    ☐ Excellent   ☐ Very Good   ☐ Good   ☐ Fair   ☐ Poor
4. What Would Have Made the Session More Effective?

_____
_____
_____
_____
_____
_____

Signature_____

chapter of ASTD. Mr. Johnson suggested that the comment sheets be given to the enrollees before the program is over so that the suggestions can be used in improving the last section of the training program. For example, where a training program consists of a series of nine sessions, the comment sheet should be given to conferees at the end of the third session. Their comments and suggestions should be taken into consideration to make the last six sessions more effective.

So far in this article, the techniques for measuring the reactions of the enrollees have been discussed. It has been emphasized that the form should be designed so that tabulations can be readily made. In this writer's opinion, too many comment sheets are still being used in which the conferees are asked to write in their answers to questions. Using a form of this kind, it becomes very difficult to summarize comments and to determine patterns of reaction.

At the Management Institute of the University of Wisconsin, every session is evaluated in terms of the reactions of the conferees. This has been done for more than 10 years. Many times, the coordinator of the program felt that the group reaction was not a fair evaluation of the effectiveness of the program. Sometimes the staff men felt that the conference leader's personality made such an impression on the group that he received a very high rating. In other sessions, the coordinator felt that the conference leader received a low rating because he did not have a dynamic personality. Frequently, in the opinion of the coordinator, the latter type of conference leader presented much more practical and helpful material than the former. Therefore, The Management Institute adopted a procedure by which every conference leader is rated by the coordinator as well as by the group. The form in figure 2 is used for the coordinator's evaluation.

This procedure in which the coordinator of the program also evaluates each conference leader was used in the 1959 ASTD Summer Institute. It was found that a coordinator's rating was usually close to the group's rating, but in some instances it varied considerably. A combination of the two ratings was used by the Management Institute staff in evaluating the effectiveness of each conference leader. In selecting and orienting future conference leaders for ASTD Institutes, both of the evaluations will be taken into consideration.

It is suggested that the training director in each company consider this approach. A trained observer such as the Training Director [or] another qualified person would fill out an evaluation form independent of the group's reactions. A comparison of the two would give the best indication of the effectiveness of the program.

Measuring Reactions to Outside Training Programs

The forms and suggestions that have been described above will apply best to an internal training program. Since many companies send their management people to outside training programs at universities, American Management Association, National Industrial Conference Board, etc., it is suggested that the reaction of each person attending such a program be measured. Lowell Reed, Training Director of the Oscar Mayer & Company of Madison, Wisconsin, uses

Figure 2　Leader rating sheet.

Rating_____　Date _____　Rater's Initial_____

Name of Leader_____　Subject_____

	Very Much So	To Some Extent	No
A. PREPARATION			
1. Did he/she prepare for the meeting?			
2. Was his/her preparation geared to the group?			
B. CONDUCTING			
1. Did he/she read the material?			
2. Did he/she hold the interest of the group?			
3. Was he/she enthusiastic/dynamic?			
4. Did he/she use visual aids? If yes, what aids?			
5. Did he/she present the material clearly?			
6. Did he/she help the group apply the material?			
7. Did he/she adequately cover the subject?			
8. Did he/she summarize during conference and at end?			
9. Did he/she involve the group? If yes, how?			

C. CONSTRUCTIVE COMMENTS

   1. What would you suggest to improve future sessions?

D. POTENTIAL

   1. With proper coaching what would be the highest rating he/she could achieve?

E. ADDITIONAL COMMENTS

Figure 3   Oscar Mayer & Co. evaluation form.

Key	Programs
A	Modern Leadership for Middle Management
B	Supervisors' Leadership in Cost Control
C	Developing Supervisory Skills
D	Human Relations for Foremen & Supervisors
E	Leadership and Growth
F	Creative Thinking for Supervisors
G	Human Relations for New Foremen
T	Totals

	A	B	C	D	E	F	G	T
Questionnaires returned:	3	3	5	11	5	1	1	29
1. I thought the program was:								
A. Very well organized and helpful	3	3	5	11	5	1	1	29
B. It was of some value								
C. It was poorly organized and a waste of time								
2. In reference to the subject content:								
A. It was all theory and of little practical value								
B. It was both theory and practical	3	2	2	3	1			11
C. It was very practical and useful	0	1	3	9	4	1	1	19
3. Concerning the quality of the instruction:								
A. The instruction was excellent	2	3	4	11	4	1	1	26
B. I would consider the instruction average			1		1			2
C. The instruction was of poor quality								

the form in figure 3 for evaluating the reaction to the University of Wisconsin Management Institute program.

In this situation, Oscar Mayer & Company is not interested in the reaction to specific leaders. They are interested in reaction to the overall program to determine whether or not to send other foremen and supervisors. In other words, this particular questionnaire was designed to fit the need of the Oscar Mayer & Company. In addition to the tabulated responses described above, an opportunity was given each person to write in additional comments.

Another company uses the form in figure 4 to evaluate the reaction of their managers who attend an outside program.

The first step in the evaluation process is to measure the reactions to training programs. It is important to determine how people feel about the programs they attend. Decisions by top management are frequently made on the basis of one or two comments they receive from people who have attended. A supervisory training program may be cancelled because one superintendent told the plant manager that "this program is for the birds."

Also, people must like most of the program to obtain maximum benefit from it. According to Spencer for example, "for maximum learning you must have interest and enthusiasm." In a talk given by Cloyd Steinmetz, past

Figure 4 Supervisory Institute Program evaluation form.

IN GENERAL

1. How worthwhile was the Institute(s) for you?
   - ☐ Very worthwhile ☐ Not very worthwhile
   - ☐ Fairly worthwhile ☐ A waste of time

2. Did the Institute have:
   - ☐ Too much theory and not enough of the practical
   - ☐ Too much of the practical and not enough theory
   - ☐ About the right combination of theory and practice

HOW THE INSTITUTE WAS CONDUCTED

3. On the whole, the course was conducted
   - ☐ Very well ☐ Poorly
   - ☐ Fairly well ☐ Very poorly

4. Lecture and discussion
   - ☐ Too much lecture
   - ☐ Too much discussion
   - ☐ About the right amount of each

5. Discussion leaders
   - ☐ Too many from the University
   - ☐ Too many from business and industry
   - ☐ O.K.

6. Visual aids
   - ☐ Not enough movies, charts, etc.
   - ☐ Too much use of demonstrations, blackboards, movies, charts, etc.
   - ☐ O.K.

APPLICATION OF THE COURSE

7. Did the Institute apply to your particular operations?
   - ☐ Yes ☐ Partly ☐ No

FOLLOW-UP

8. Would you like to attend another Institute?
   - ☐ Yes ☐ No

COMMENT

9. Should these Institutes run for ☐ 5 days ☐ 4 days ☐ 3 days.

10. Please list 3 of your main problems:

    1. _____

    2. _____

    3. _____

11. Comments or suggestions

    _____

    _____

    _____

    _____

president of ASTD, "It is not enough to say, 'boys, here is the information, take it!' We must make it interesting and motivate them to want to take it."

To evaluate effectively, training directors should begin by doing a good job of measuring reactions and feelings of people who participate. It is important to do so in an organized fashion using written comment sheets which have been designed to obtain the desired reactions. It is also strongly suggested that the form be so designed that the comments can be tabulated and quantified. In the experience of the staff of The Management Institute, it is also desirable to have the coordinator, training director, or another trained observer make his or her own appraisal of the session in order to supplement the reactions of enrollees. The combination of these two evaluations is more meaningful than either one by itself.

Companies who send their people to attend outside institutes and conferences should make an effort to evaluate the reactions to these programs. Several suggested forms have been described.

When a training director has effectively measured the *reactions* of conferees and finds them to be very favorable, he/she can feel very proud. However, the trainer should also feel humble because the evaluation measurement has only begun.

Even though he/she has done a masterful job of measuring the reaction of the group, there is still no assurance that any learning has taken place. Neither is there any indication that the behavior of the participants will change because of the training program. And still farther away is any indication of the results that can be attributed to the training program. These three steps in the evaluation process—learning, behavior, and results will be discussed in detail in the next three articles of this series on Evaluation.

Part 2—Learning

We have emphasized in the first article that the reaction of the conferees is important in evaluating the training program. From an analysis of reactions, a training director can determine how well the program was accepted. He/she can also obtain comments and suggestions which will be helpful in improving future programs. It is important to obtain favorable reaction because:

1. Decisions on future training activities are frequently based on the reactions of one or more key persons.

2. The more favorable the reaction to the program, the more likely the conferees are to pay attention and learn the principles, facts, and techniques that are discussed.

However, it is important to recognize that favorable reaction to a program *does not assure* learning. All of us have attended meetings in which the conference leader or speaker used enthusiasm, showmanship, visual aids and illustrations to make his presentation well accepted by the group. A careful analysis of the subject content would reveal that the speaker said practically nothing of value—but did it very well. At our Management Institute at the University of Wisconsin, for example, this has been true on a number of cases. (Less and less, I hasten to add.)

Therefore, it is important to determine objectively the amount of learning that takes place. This article is aimed at suggesting ways and means for measuring this learning.

Learning Defined

There are several definitions for learning. For the purpose of this article, learning is defined in a rather limited way as follows: What principles, facts and techniques were understood and absorbed by the conferees? In other words, we are not concerned with the on-the-job use of these principles, facts, and techniques. This application will be discussed in a third article dealing with "Behavior."

Guideposts for Evaluating in Terms of Learning

Several guideposts should be used in establishing a procedure for measuring the amount of learning that takes place.

1. The learning of *each conferee* should be measured so that quantitative results can be determined.
2. A before-and-after approach should be used so that any learning can be related to the program.
3. As far as practical, the learning should be measured on an *objective* basis.
4. Where practical, a control group (not receiving the training) should be used to compare with the experimental group which receives the training.
5. Where practical, the evaluation results should be analyzed statistically so that learning can be proven in terms of correlation or level of confidence.

These guideposts indicate that evaluation in terms of learning is much more difficult than evaluation in terms of reaction as described in the first article. A knowledge of statistics, for example, is necessary. In many cases, the training department will have to call on the assistance of a statistician to plan the evaluation procedures, analyze the data, and interpret the results.

Suggested Methods

Classroom Performance: It is relatively easy to measure the learning that takes place in training programs that are teaching skills. The following programs would fall under this category: Job Instruction Training; Work Simplification; Interviewing Skills; Induction Techniques; Reading Improvement; Effective Speaking; and Effective Writing. Classroom activities such as demonstrations, individual performance of the skill being taught, and discussions following a role playing situation can be used as evaluation techniques. The training director can organize these in such a way that he/she will obtain a fairly objective evaluation of the learning that is taking place.

For example, in a course that is teaching Job Instruction Training to foremen, each foreman will demonstrate in front of the class the skills of JIT. From their performance, the training director can tell whether or not they have learned the principles of JIT and can use them, at least in a classroom situation. In a Work Simplification program, conferees can be required to fill out a "flow-process chart" and the training director can determine whether or not they know how to do it. In a Reading Improvement program, the reading speed and comprehension of each participant can be readily determined by their classroom performance. In an Effective Speaking program, each conferee is normally required to give a number of talks and an alert training director can measure to some extent the amount of learning that is taking place by observing a person's successive performances.

So in these kinds of situations, an evaluation of the learning can be built into the program. If it is organized and implemented properly, the training director can obtain a fairly objective measure of the amount of learning that has taken place. Directors can set up before-and-after situations in which each conferee demonstrates whether or not they know the principles and techniques being taught.

In every program, therefore, where skills of some kind are being taught, the training director should plan systematic classroom evaluation to measure the learning.

Paper-and-Pencil Tests: Where principles and facts are taught rather than techniques, it is more difficult to evaluate learning. The most common technique is the paper-and-pencil test. In some cases, standardized tests can be purchased to measure learning. In other cases, training directors must construct their own.

To measure the learning in human relations programs, two standardized tests are quite widely used in business and industry. The first is *How Supervised* by Hile and Remmers. This is published by The Psychological Corporation of New York and has been used by a number of companies on a before-and-after basis to measure the learning that takes place. A newer test is the *Supervisory Inventory on Human Relations* by Kirkpatrick and Planty. Sample test items from the latter are listed on the next page (answered by circling "A" for agree or "DA" for disagree).

There are also standardized tests available in such areas as Creativity and Economics. In following the guideposts that were suggested in the beginning of this article, this kind of a standardized test should be used in the following manner:

1. The tests should be given to all conferees prior to the program.

2. If possible, it should also be given to a control group which is comparable to the experimental group.

3. These pretests should be analyzed in terms of two approaches: In the first place, the total score of each person should be tabulated. Secondly, the responses to each item of the inventory should be tabulated in terms of right and wrong answers. This second tabulation not only enables a training person to evaluate the program but also gives some tips on the knowledge and understanding of the group prior to the program. This means that in the classroom, the trainer can stress those items most frequently misunderstood.

PLEASE ANSWER ALL STATEMENTS EVEN IF YOU ARE NOT SURE
Copyright © 1978 by D. L. Kirkpatrick

---

1. Anyone is able to do almost any job if he/she tries hard enough.	A DA
2. Intelligence consists of what we've leaned since we were born.	A DA
3. If a supervisor knows all about the work to be done, he/she is therefore qualified to teach others how to do it.	A DA
4. We are born with certain attitudes and there is little we can do to change them.	A DA
5. A supervisor should not praise members of the department when they do a good job because they will ask for a raise.	A DA
6. A well trained working force is a result of maintaining a large training department.	A DA
7. A supervisor would lose respect if he/she asked employees to help solve problems that concern them.	A DA
8. In making a decision, a good supervisor is concerned with his/her employees' feelings about the decision.	A DA
9. The supervisor is closer to his/her employees than to management.	A DA
10. The best way to train a new employee is to have him/her watch a good employee at the job.	A DA
11. Before deciding on the solution to a problem, a list of possible solutions should be made and compared.	A DA
12. A supervisor should be willing to listen to almost anything the employees want to tell him/her.	A DA

---

4. After the program is over, the same test or its equivalent should be given to the conferees and also to the control group. A comparison of pretest and posttest scores and responses to individual items can then be made. A statistical analysis of this data will reveal the effectiveness of the program in terms of learning.

One important word of caution must be made. Unless the test or inventory accurately covers the material presented, it will not be a valid measure of the effectiveness of the learning. Frequently a standardized test will cover only part of the material presented in the course. Therefore, only that part of the course covered in the inventory is being evaluated. Likewise, if certain items on the inventory are not being covered, no change in these items can be expected.

There are also many examples where training directors and others responsible for programs have developed their own paper-and-pencil tests to measure learning in their programs. For example, the American Telephone and Telegraph Company has incorporated into their "Personal Factors in Management" program, a short test measuring the sensitivity and empathy. First, each individual is asked to rank in order of importance, 10 items dealing with human relations. They are then assigned to a group which is asked to work 15 minutes at the task of arriving at a group ranking of the 10 statements. Following this 15-minute "heated discussion," each individual is asked to complete a short inventory which includes the following questions:

1. **A.** Are you satisfied with the performance of the group?

    Yes ☐   No ☐

   B. How many will say that they were satisfied with the performance of the group? _____

2. **A.** Do you feel that the discussion was dominated by two or three members?

    Yes ☐   No ☐

   B. How many will say that they thought the discussion was dominated by two or three members? _____

3. **A.** Did you have any feelings about the items being ranked that, for some reason, you felt it wise not to express during the discussion?

    Yes ☐   No ☐

   B. How many will say that they had such feelings? _____

4. **A.** Did you talk as often as you wished to during the discussion?

    Yes ☐   No ☐

   B. How many will say that they talked as often as they wished to? _____ .

The successive class sessions then attempt to teach each conferee to be more sensitive to the feelings and ideas of other people. Later in the course, another "empathy" test is given to see whether there is an increase in sensitivity.

At an ASTD Summer Institute in Madison, Wisconsin, Dr. Earl Planty of the University of Illinois introduced a test on decision making.[2] Several items from that test follow:

1. If my boss handed to me a well done piece of work and asked me to make changes on it, I would

    ☐ prove to him/her that the job is better without changes.

    ☐ do what he/she says and point out where he/she is wrong.

    ☐ complete the changes without comment.

    ☐ request a transfer from his/her department.

2. If I were office manager and one of the best clerks kept complaining about working conditions, I would

- ☐ try to determine the basis for the complaints.
- ☐ transfer the person to some other section.
- ☐ point out to the person that complaints are bad for morale.
- ☐ ask the person to write out the complaints for your superior.

3. If my supervisor criticized my work, I would

- ☐ compare my record with coworkers for him/her.
- ☐ explain the reason for poor performance to him/her.
- ☐ ask the supervisor why he/she selected me for criticism.
- ☐ ask him/her for suggestions on how to improve.

4. If I were setting up a new procedure in an office, I would

- ☐ do it on my own without enlisting anyone's aid.
- ☐ ask my superiors for suggestions.
- ☐ ask the people who work under me for suggestions.
- ☐ discuss it with my friends who are outside of the company.

This test or one like it can be given before and after a program on decision making to determine whether or not the participants learned the principles and procedures taught in the course.

In Morris A. Savitt's article called "Is Management Training Worthwhile?"[3] he described a program that he evaluated. He devised a questionnaire which was given at the beginning of the program "to determine how much knowledge of management principles and practices the conferees had at the beginning." At the end of the 10-week program, the same questionnaire was administered to test the progress made during the course. This is an example of a questionnaire tailored to a specific program.

Daniel M. Goodacre III, formerly of the B. F. Goodrich Company, has done a great deal of work in this area. He has developed and used achievement tests which are given before and after training programs to determine the amount of learning.

And so we see that the paper-and-pencil test can be used effectively in measuring the learning that takes place in a training program. It should be emphasized again that the approach to this kind of evaluation should be systematic and statistically oriented. A comparison of before-and-after scores and responses can then be made to prove how much learning has taken place.

Nile Soik of the Allen Bradley Company described an additional evaluation procedure in an article in the *Training and Development Journal*. Not only did he use the *Supervisory Inventory on Human Relations* before and after the program, but he also administered it six months later. He was measuring the forgetting that took place in the period following the program.

Summary

It is easy to see, then, that it is much more difficult to measure *learning* than it is to measure *reaction* to a program. A great deal of work is required in planning the evaluation procedure, in analyzing the data that is obtained, and interpreting the results. Wherever possible, it is suggested that training directors devise their own methods and techniques. As has been pointed out in this article, it is relatively easy to plan classroom demonstrations and presentations to measure learning where the program is aimed at the teaching of skills.

Where principles and facts are the objectives of the training program, it is advisable to use a paper-and-pencil test. Where suitable standardized tests can be found, it is easier to use them. In many programs, however, it is not possible to find a standardized test and the training person must use their skill and ingenuity in devising their own measuring instrument.

If training directors can prove that a program has been effective in terms of learning as well as in terms of reaction, they have objective data to use in selling future programs and in increasing their status and position in the company.

Part 3—Behavior

In the two previous articles in this series, we talked about techniques for evaluating training programs in terms of (1) REACTION and (2) LEARNING. It was emphasized that in our evaluations, we can borrow techniques but we cannot borrow results.

A personal experience may be the best way of starting this third article dealing with changes in behavior. When I joined The Management Institute of the University of Wisconsin in 1949, one of my first assignments was to sit through a one-week course on "Human Relations for Foremen and Supervisors." During the week I was particularly impressed by a foreman named Herman from a Milwaukee company. Whenever a conference leader asked a question requiring a good understanding of human relations principles and techniques, Herman was the first one who raised his hand. He had all the answers in terms of good human relations approaches. I was very much impressed and I said to myself "If I were in industry, I would like to work for a man like Herman."

It so happened that I had a first cousin who was working for that company. And oddly enough, Herman was his boss. At my first opportunity, I talked with my cousin, Jim, and asked him about Herman. Jim told me that Herman may know all the principles and techniques of human relations, but he certainly does not practice them on the job. He performed as the typical "bull-of-the-woods" who had little consideration for the feelings and ideas of his subordinates.

At this time I began to realize there may be a big difference between knowing principles and techniques and using them on the job.

Robert Katz, Professor at Dartmouth, wrote an article in the July-August 1956 issue of the *Harvard Business Review*. The article was called "Human

Relations Skills Can Be Sharpened." And he said: "If a person is going to change their job behavior, five basic requirements must exist":

1. They must want to improve.
2. They must recognize their own weaknesses.
3. They must work in a permissive climate.
4. They must have some help from someone who is interested and skilled.
5. They must have an opportunity to try out the new ideas.

It seems that Katz has put his finger on the problems that exist in a transition between learning and changes in behavior on the job.

Evaluation of training programs in terms of on-the-job behavior is more difficult than the reaction and learning evaluations described in the two previous articles. A more scientific approach is needed and many factors must be considered. During the last few years a number of attempts have been made and more and more effort is being put in this direction.

Several guideposts are to be followed in evaluating training programs in terms of behavioral changes:

1. A *systematic* appraisal should be made of on-the-job performance on a *before-and-after* basis.
2. The appraisal of performance should be made by one or more of the following groups (the more the better):
   A. The person receiving the training
   B. Their superior or superiors
   C. Their subordinates
   D. Their peers or other people thoroughly familiar with their performance.
3. A statistical analysis should be made to compare before-and-after performance and relate changes to the training program.
4. The post-training appraisal should be made three months or more after the training so that the trainers have an opportunity to put into practice what they have learned. Subsequent appraisals may add to the validity of the study.
5. A control group (not receiving the training) should be used.

Some of the best evaluation studies are briefly described below.

The Fleishman-Harris Studies [4]

To evaluate a training program that had been conducted at the Central School of The International Harvester Company, Fleishman developed a study design and a battery of research instruments for measuring the effectiveness of the training. Seven paper-and-pencil questionnaires were used and the trainees, their superiors, and their subordinates were all surveyed.

To supplement the data that Fleishman had discovered, Harris conducted a follow-up study in the same organization. He used a before-and-after measure of job performance and worked with experimental and control groups. He obtained information from the trainees themselves as well as from their subordinates.

Survey Research Center Studies [5]

The Survey Research Center of the University of Michigan has contributed much to evaluation of training programs in terms of on-the-job behavior. To measure the effectiveness of a human relations program conducted by Dr. Norman Maier at the Detroit Edison Co., and to measure the results of an experimental program called "feedback," a scientific approach to evaluation was used. A basic design was to use a before-and-after measure of on-the-job performance with experimental as well as control groups. The supervisors receiving the training as well as their subordinates were surveyed in order to compare the results of the research. The instrument used for measuring these changes was an attitude and opinion survey designed and developed by the Survey Research Center.

The Lindholm Study [6]

This study was carried out in the home office of a small insurance company during the period of October, 1950 to May, 1951. A questionnaire developed as part of the research program of the Industrial Relations Center of the University of Minnesota was used. It was given on a before-and-after basis to the subordinates of those who took the training. No control group was used. A statistical analysis of the before-and-after results of the attitude survey determined the effectiveness of the program in terms of on-the-job behavior.

The Blocker Study [7]

A different approach was used in the study conducted in an insurance company having approximately 600 employees. Fifteen supervisors who took a course on "Democratic Leadership" were analyzed during the three-month period following the course. Eight of the supervisors were classified as democratic and seven were classified as authoritarian based on their behavior prior to the program.

During the three-month period immediately following the program, the changes in behavior of the supervisors were analyzed through a study of their interview records. They used standard printed forms which made provision for recording the reason for the interview, attitude of the employee, comments of the supervisor, and action taken, if any. Each supervisor was required to make a complete record of each interview. They did not know that these records were to be used for an evaluation study. There were a total of 376 interviews with 186 employees.

The interview records were classified as authoritarian or democratic. The changes in interview approach and techniques were studied during the three-month period following the course to determine if on-the-job behavior of the supervisors changed.

The Tarnopol Approach [8]

In his article called "Evaluate Your Training Program," Tarnopol suggests the approach to use as well as a specific example of an evaluation experiment. He believes in the employee attitude survey given on a before-and-after basis using control as well as experimental groups. He stresses that "in our experience, five employees is a good minimum for measuring the behavior of their supervisor." He also stresses that "although canned questionnaires are available, it is advisable to use measuring instruments that are specifically suited to the requirements of both your company and your training program."

In his employee attitude approach, Tarnopol has suggested inserting some neutral questions which do not relate to the training being given. This is an added factor in interpreting the results of the research.

The Moon-Hariton Study [9]

Their study was made in an Engineering Section of a department of the General Electric Company in 1956. The staff of the General Electric Company was assisted by a representative of the Psychological Corporation.

In the spring of 1958, two years after the adoption of a new appraisal and training program, a decision was made to attempt to evaluate its effectiveness. It was felt that the opinion of the subordinates about changes in the managers' attitudes and behavior would provide a better measure than what the managers themselves thought about the benefits of the program. Thus a questionnaire was designed to obtain the subordinates' views about changes in their managers. Nevertheless, it was felt that the opinions of the manager would add to the picture. Accordingly, they were also surveyed.

The questionnaire asked the respondents to compare present conditions with what they were two years ago. In other words, instead of measuring the attitudes before and after the program, the subordinates and the managers were asked to indicate what changes had taken place during the last two years.

Buchanan-Brunstetter Study [10]

At the Republic Aviation Corporation, an attempt was made to measure the results of a training program. The questionnaire was used and an experimental and a control group were measured. The experimental group had received the training program during the past year while the control group was going to receive it during the following year. The subordinates of the supervisors in each one of these groups were asked to complete a questionnaire which related to the on-the-job behavior of their supervisor. After answering the questionnaire in which they described the job behavior of their supervisor, they were asked to go over the questionnaire again and to place a check opposite any items: "(1) which you think are *more* effectively done now than a year ago; (2) which you think are *less* effectively done now than a year ago."

In this experiment as well as in the Moon-Hariton approach, the subordinates were asked to indicate what changes in behavior had taken place during the last year. This was done because a before measure of their behavior had not been made.

The Stroud Study[11]

A new training program called "Personal Factors in Management" was evaluated at the Bell Telephone Company of Pennsylvania by Peggy Stroud. Several different approaches were used to compare the results and obtain a more valid indication of on-the-job behavioral changes that resulted from the program. The first step was the formulation of a questionnaire to be filled out by four separate groups: (1) conferees (2) controllees (supervisors not taking the course) (3) superiors of the conferees (4) superiors of the controllees.

The first part of the questionnaire was the "Consideration Scale" taken from the leader behavior description questionnaire originated in the Ohio State leadership studies. The second part of the questionnaire was called the Critical Incident section in which the conferee and control groups were asked to describe four types of incidents that had occurred on the job. The third and final section of the questionnaire applied to the conferees only. They were asked to rate the extent to which they felt the training course had helped them achieve each of its five stated objectives.

It was decided to conduct an extensive evaluation of the training program after the program had begun. Therefore it was not possible to make a before-and after comparison. In this study, an attempt was made to get the questionnaire respondents to compare on-the-job behavior before the program with that following the program. According to Miss Stroud, it would have been better to measure behavior prior to the program and then compare it to behavior measured after the program.

This study, called "Evaluating A Human Relations Training Program," is one of the best attempts this writer has discovered. The various evaluation results are compared and fairly concrete interpretations made.

The Sorensen Study[12]

The most comprehensive research that has been done to evaluate the effectiveness of a training program in terms of on-the-job behavior was made at the Crotonville Advanced Management Course of the General Electric Company. It was called the "Observed Changes Enquiry."

The purpose of the "enquiry" was to answer these questions:

1. Have manager graduates of General Electric's Advanced Management Courses of 1956 been observed to have changed in their manner of managing?

2. What inferences may be made from similarities and differences of changes observed in graduates and non-graduates?

First of all, the managers (graduates and non-graduates alike) were asked to indicate changes they had observed in their own manner of managing during the previous 12 months. Secondly, subordinates were asked to describe changes they had observed in the managers during the past 12 months. Thirdly, their peers (looking sideways) were asked to describe changes in behavior. And finally, the superiors of the control and experimental groups were asked to describe the same changes in behavior. This gave Sorensen an excellent opportunity to compare the observed changes of all four groups.

In this extensive research, Sorensen used experimental as well as control groups. He also used four different approaches to measure observed changes. These include the person, their subordinates, their peers, and their superiors. In this research, he did not use a before-and-after measure but rather asked each of the participants to indicate what changes, if any, had taken place during the past year.

Summary and Conclusions

The purpose of this article has been to describe briefly some of the best experiments that have been used to measure effectiveness of training programs in terms of on-the-job behavior. Only the methods and instruments used in these studies have been mentioned. The results, although interesting, cannot be borrowed by other training directors but the techniques can.

For those interested in evaluating in terms of behavioral changes, it is strongly suggested that these studies be carefully analyzed. The references following this series of articles indicate where the detailed articles can be found.

Once more I would like to emphasize that the future of training directors and their programs depends to a large extent on their effectiveness. To determine effectiveness, attempts must be made to measure in scientific and statistical terms. This article, dealing with changes in behavior resulting from training programs, indicates a very complicated procedure. But it is worthwhile and necessary if training programs are going to increase in effectiveness and their benefits made clear to top management.

It is obvious that very few training directors have the background, skill and time to engage in extensive evaluations. It is therefore frequently necessary to call on statisticians, research people, and consultants for advice and help.

Part 4—Results

The objectives of most training programs can be stated in terms of results desired. These results could be classified as: reduction of costs; reduction of turnover and absenteeism; reduction of grievances; increase in quality and quantity of production; or improved morale which, it is hoped, will lead to some of the previously stated results. From an evaluation standpoint, it would be best to evaluate training programs directly in terms of results desired. There are, however, so many complicating factors that it is extremely difficult if not impossible to evaluate certain kinds of programs in terms of results. Therefore, it is recommended that training directors begin to evaluate in terms of the three criteria described in the preceding articles.

First of all, determine the *reactions of* the trainees. Secondly, attempt to measure what *learning* takes place. And thirdly, try to measure the changes in on-the-job behavior. As has been stressed in the previous articles, these criteria are listed in increasing order of difficulty.

As I survey literature on evaluation, I find more and more articles being written on this subject. Nearly every issue of the ASTD *Journal* contains one or more articles. It is interesting to note that few of them deal with evaluation in terms of results. And this is because it is usually a difficult evaluation to make.

Certain kinds of training programs, though, are relatively easy to evaluate in terms of results. For example, in teaching clerical personnel to do a more effective typing job, you can measure the number of words per minute on a before-and-after basis.

If you are trying to reduce grievances in your plant, you can measure the number of grievances before and after the training program. If you are attempting to reduce accidents, a before-and-after measure can be made. One word of caution, however, E. C. Keachie stated it as follows in an issue of the ASTD *Journal*: "Difficulties in the evaluation of training are evident at the outset in the problem technically called 'the separation of variables;' that is, how much of the improvement is due to training as compared to other factors?" This is the problem that makes it very difficult to measure results that can be attributed directly to a specific training program.

Below are described several evaluations that have been made in terms of results. They do not offer specific formulas for other training directors to follow, but they do suggest procedures and approaches which can be effectively used.

Safety Programs

Many attempts have been made to evaluate the effectiveness of safety training programs in terms of lost-time accidents. One study was conducted by Philip E. Beekman, Plant Administrator of Salaried Personnel for the Colgate-Palmolive Company, Jersey City plant. This study was briefly described in the Number 3, 1958 *Supervisory Management Newsletter* of the American Management Associations.

A comparison was made of plant safety records for the nine-month period before the training program with a comparable period after the program. The frequency rate for lost-time accidents was measured along with the number of reported accidents. The frequency rate dropped from 4.5 percent to 2.9 percent and the number of reported accidents dropped from 41 to 32. This improvement was credited directly to the training effort because no physical changes were made which affected the accident rate.

At a 1958 Conference of The Management Institute, University of Wisconsin, Dr. G. Roy Fugal of the General Electric Company described a before-and-after evaluation of one of their safety programs. The purpose of the training was to reduce the number of accidents and to increase the regularity with which all accidents, major and minor, were reported. The training program consisted of the usual presentations, discussions, and movies which were very dramatic in describing accidents and their implications. The comprehensive evaluation indicated that the training program did not have desirable results. Therefore, a new approach to training was adopted which was more oriented to the job relationship between the foreman and each worker. An evaluation of this kind of safety training program did indicate the desired results.

Table 1   Results of training

	Total Number of Incidents	
Category	Experimental Group "A"	Control Group "B"
Negligent Accidents	5	8
Misdeliveries	21	33
Mishandling Valuable Mail	3	7
Late Reporting	35	32
Absence Without Reporting	3	6
Abuse of Sick Leave	8	12
Errors in Relay Operations	13	22
Adverse Probationary Reports	4	9
Discourtesy	4	5

Postal Carrier Training

In the September-October 1957 issue of the ASTD *Journal*, John C. Massey described a program in which he evaluated in terms of results. Experimental group "A" received 35 hours of orientation training under the post office training and development program. A comparable group called control group "B" did not receive any training. Results of this study are shown in table 1.

The design of this evaluation study includes an experimental as well as a control group. The importance of using these was emphasized in Part 3 of this series. It should also be used in evaluating results wherever possible to overcome the difficulty described by Dr. Keachie.

An Insurance Company Study

In a recent letter, S. W. Schallert of the Farmers Mutual Insurance Company of Madison, Wisconsin reported to me on an evaluation he had made. A number of their claims adjustors were enrolled in the Vale Technical Institute of Blairsville, Pennsylvania. The purpose of the three-week course was to improve the ability of adjustors to estimate and appraise automobile physical damage.

The specific technique used by Schallert was to have the adjustors keep track of their savings for approximately six months after returning from Vale. These savings were the difference between the estimate of damage by garages and the estimate of damage by the claims adjustors who had been trained at Vale. Where the final cost of the adjustment was the same as the estimate made by the Farmers Mutual adjustor, this was considered the savings.

In other words, the purpose of the training was to prepare the adjustors to make estimates which they could justify and sell. Actual dollars and cents figures could then be used to determine whether or not the cost of sending these adjustors to Vale was justified.

A Cost Reduction Institute

Several years ago, two graduate students at the University of Wisconsin attempted to measure the results of a "Cost Reduction Institute" conducted by The Management Institute of the University. Two techniques were used. The first was to conduct depth interviews with some of the supervisors who had attended the course and with their immediate supervisors. The other technique was to mail questionnaires to the remaining enrollees and to their supervisors. Following is a brief summary of that study:

A. DEPTH INTERVIEWS

Interviews with Trainees

1. Have you been able to reduce costs in the few weeks that you have been back on the job?

   Replies:
   - 13 men—yes
   - 3 men—no
   - 2 men—noncommittal or evasive
   - 1 man—failed to answer

2. How? What were the estimated savings?

   Different types of replies indicated that the 13 people who said they had made cost reductions had done so in different areas. But their ideas stemmed directly from the program, according to these trainees.

Interview of Superiors

Eight of the cost reduction actions described by the trainees were confirmed by the immediate superior and these superiors estimated total savings to be from $15,000 to $21,000 per year. The specific ideas that were used were described by superiors as well as by the trainees.

B. MAILED QUESTIONNAIRES

Questionnaires were mailed to those trainees who were not contacted personally. The results on the questionnaire were not nearly as specific and useful as the ones obtained by personal interview. The study concluded that it is probably better to use the personal interview rather than a questionnaire to measure this kind of program.

In the December 1955 issue of *The Harvard Business Review*, Willard V. Merrihue of General Electric Company and Raymond A. Katzell of Richardson, Bellows, Henry and Company described a very complex approach. According to them, "measuring performance is essential if we are to know whether the planning, the organizing, and all the other functions which preceded logically and time wise are, in fact, being discharged as well as they could or should be."

The ERI is designed to measure the extent to which groups of employees accept and perform in accordance with the objectives and policies of the company. The following indicators constituted the ERI: (1) periods of absence;

(2) separations; (3) initial visits to the dispensary for occupational reasons; (4) suggestions submitted through the suggestion system; (5) actions incurring disciplinary suspension; (6) grievances submitted through the formal grievances procedures; (7) work stoppages; and (8) participation in the insurance plan.

At the time this article was written by Merrihue and Katzell, the ERI was in its preliminary stages. Also, it did not deal directly with evaluating training programs although it indicated it might be used as a measurement yardstick. The article in its entirety should be read by those persons who are interested in the complex area of measuring training programs in terms of results. Several practical ideas might be obtained which will be helpful in establishing specific evaluation criteria and procedures.

Measuring Organizational Performance

Another sophisticated and penetrating article related to evaluation was written by Rensis Likert. It appears in the March-April 1958 issue of *The Harvard Business Review*. It shows how changes in productivity can be measured on a before-and-after basis. Two different types of groups were used; the first was a group of supervisors trained in using a democratic kind of leadership in which decision making involved the participative technique. The supervisors in the other group were trained to make their own decisions and not ask subordinates for suggestions.

In addition to measuring the results in terms of productivity, such factors as loyalty, attitudes, interest, and work involvement were also measured. Where both training programs resulted in positive changes in productivity, the "participative" approach resulted in better feelings, attitudes, and other human relations factors.

The article described another excellent study from the University of Michigan. Dr. Likert concluded by saying that "industry needs more adequate measures of organizational performance than it is now getting."

Summary

And so we see that the evaluation of training programs in terms of "results" is progressing at a very slow rate. Where the objectives of training programs are as specific as the reduction of accidents, the reduction of grievances, and the reduction of costs, we find a number of attempts have been made. In a few of them, the researchers have attempted to segregate factors other than training which might have had an effect. In most cases, the measure on a before-and-after basis has been directly attributed to the training even though other factors might have been influential.

Studies like those of Merrihue-Katzell and Likert attempt to penetrate the difficulties encountered in measuring such programs as human relations, decision making, and the like. In the years to come, we will see more efforts along this direction and eventually we may be able to measure human relations training, for example, in terms of dollars and cents. At the present time, however, our research techniques are not adequate.

Conclusion

One purpose of these four articles has been to stimulate training directors to take a penetrating look at evaluation. It has been emphasized that their future and the future of their training programs depends to a large extent on their ability to evaluate and to use evaluation results.

The second objective has been to suggest procedures, methods, and techniques for evaluating training programs. A training director should begin by measuring in terms of results as described in Part 1 of this series. A second step should be to evaluate in terms of learning as described in Part 2. Part 3 suggested ways and means of evaluating in terms of on-the-job behavior which should also be attempted. And finally Part 4 has analyzed some of the problems and approaches to measuring training programs in terms of its final objective results.

It is hoped that the training directors who have read and studied these four articles are now clearly oriented on the problems and approaches to evaluating training. As future articles on evaluation appear, we training people should carefully analyze them to see if we can borrow the techniques and procedures the writers describe.

It is also hoped that as training directors evaluate their training programs, they will describe the procedures they have used and use this magazine and others to inform others of what they have done. Progress in the evaluation of training will result if all of us will freely exchange information on objectives, methods, and criteria.

References

1. Complimentary copy available from Dr. Donald Kirkpatrick, 4380 Continental Dr., Brookfield, WI 53005.
2. Published by Martin M. Bruce, 71 Hansen Lane, Rochelle, N.Y.
3. *Personnel*, September-October, 1957, American Management Associations.
4. Fleishman, E. A., Harris, E. F., Buntt, H. E., "Leadership and Supervision in Industry," Personnel Research Board, Ohio State University, Columbus, Ohio, 1955, page 110.
5. Mann, Dr. Floyd, "Human Relations in the Industrial Setting." Survey Research Center, University of Michigan, Ann Arbor, Mich.
6. Lindholm, T. R., "Supervisory Training and Employee Attitudes," *Journal of the ASTD*, Nov.-Dec., 1953.
7. Blocker, C. E., "Evaluation of a Human Relations Training Course," *Journal of the ASTD*, May-June, 1955.
8. Tarnopol, Lester, "Evaluate Your Training Program," *Journal of the ASTD*, Mar.-Apr., 1957.
9. Moon, C. G., Hariton, Theodore, "Evaluating an Appraisal and Feedback Training Program," *Personnel*, Nov.-Dec., 1958.
10. Buchanan, P. C., Brunstetter, P.H., "A Research Approach to Management Improvement," *Journal of the ASTD*, Jan. and Feb., 1959.
11. Stroud, P. V., "Evaluating a Human Relations Training Program," *Personnel*, Nov.-Dec., 1959.
12. Sorensen, Olav, "The Observed Changes Enquiry," Manager Development Consulting Service, General Electric Company, Crotonville, New York, May 15, 1958.

The Countenance of Educational Evaluation

Robert E. Stake

President Johnson, President Conant, Mrs. Hull (Sara's teacher) and Mr. Tykociner (the man next door) are quite alike in the faith they have in education. But they have quite different ideas of what education is. The value they put on education does not reveal their way of evaluating education.

Educators differ among themselves as to both the essence and worth of an educational program. The wide range of evaluation purposes and methods allows each to keep his own perspective. Few see their own programs "in the round," partly because of a parochial approach to evaluation. To understand better his own teaching and to contribute more to the science of teaching, each educator should examine the full countenance of evaluation.

Educational evaluation has its formal and informal sides. Informal evaluation is recognized by its dependence on casual observation, implicit goals, intuitive norms, and subjective judgment. Perhaps because these are also characteristic of day-to-day, personal styles of living, informal evaluation results in perspectives which are seldom questioned. Careful study reveals informal evaluation of education to be of variable quality—sometimes penetrating and insightful, sometimes superficial and distorted.

Formal evaluation of education is recognized by its dependence on check-lists, structured visitation by peers, controlled comparisons, and standardized testing of students. Some of these techniques have long histories of successful use. Unfortunately, when planning an evaluation, few educators consider even these four. The more common notion is to evaluate informally: to ask the opinion of the instructor, to ponder the logic of the program, or to consider the reputation of the advocates. Seldom do we find a search for relevant research reports or for behavioral data pertinent to the ultimate curricular decisions.

Dissatisfaction with the formal approach is not without cause. Few highly-relevant, readable research studies can be found. The professional journals are not disposed to publish evaluation studies. Behavioral data are costly, and often do not provide the answers. Too many accreditation-type visitation teams lack special training or even experience in evaluation. Many

At the time this article was published, Robert Stake was with the University of Illinois.

From: Stake, R. E. 1967. The countenance of educational evaluation. *Teachers college record* 68:523–540. Reprinted with permission.

checklists are ambiguous; some focus too much attention on the physical attributes of a school. Psychometric tests have been developed primarily to differentiate among students at the same point in training rather than to assess the effect of instruction on acquisition of skill and understanding. Today's educator may rely little on formal evaluation because its answers have seldom been answers to questions *he* is asking.

Potential Contributions of Formal Evaluation

The educator's disdain of formal evaluation is due also to his sensitivity to criticism—and his *is* a critical clientele. It is not uncommon for him to draw before him such curtains as "national norm comparisons," "innovation phase," and "academic freedom" to avoid exposure through evaluation. The "politics" of evaluation is an interesting issue in itself, but it is not the issue here. The issue here is the *potential* contribution to education of formal evaluation. Today, educators fail to perceive what formal evaluation could do for them. They should be imploring measurement specialists to develop a methodology that reflects the fullness, the complexity, and the importance of their programs. They are not.

What one finds when he examines formal evaluation activities in education today is too little effort to spell out antecedent conditions and classroom transactions (a few of which visitation teams do record) and too little effort to couple them with the various outcomes (a few of which are portrayed by conventional test scores). Little attempt has been made to measure the match between what an educator intends to do and what he does do. The traditional concern of educational-measurement specialists for reliability of individual-student scores and predictive validity (thoroughly and competently stated in the American Council on Education's 1950 edition of *Educational Measurement*) is a questionable resource. For evaluation of curricula, attention to individual differences among students should give way to attention to the contingencies among background conditions, classroom activities, and scholastic outcomes.

This paper is not about what should be measured or how to measure. It is background for developing an evaluation plan. What and how are decided later. My orientation here is around educational programs rather than educational products. I presume that the value of a product depends on its program of use. The evaluation of a program includes the evaluation of its materials.

The countenance of educational evaluation appears to be changing. On the pages that follow, I will indicate what the countenance can, and perhaps should, be. My attempt here is to introduce a conceptualization of evaluation oriented to the complex and dynamic nature of education, one which gives proper attention to the diverse purposes and judgments of the practitioner.

Much recent concern about curriculum evaluation is attributable to contemporary large-scale curriculum-innovation activities, but the statements in this paper pertain to traditional and new curricula alike. They pertain, for example, to Title I and Title III projects funded under the Elementary and

Secondary Act of 1966. Statements here are relevant to any curriculum, whether oriented to subject-matter content or to student process, and without regard to whether curriculum is general-purpose, remedial, accelerated, compensatory, or special in any other way.

The purposes and procedures of educational evaluation will vary from instance to instance. What is quite appropriate for one school may be less appropriate for another. Standardized achievement tests here but not there. A great concern for expense there but not over there. How do evaluation purposes and procedures vary? What are the basic characteristics of evaluation activities? They are identified in these pages as the evaluation acts, the data sources, the congruence and contingencies, the standards, and the uses of evaluation. The first distinction to be made will be between description and judgment in evaluation.

The countenance of evaluation beheld by the educator is not the same one beheld by the specialist in evaluation. The specialist sees himself as a "describer," one who describes aptitudes and environments and accomplishments. The teacher and school administrator, on the other hand, expect an evaluator to grade something or someone as to merit. Moreover, they expect that he will judge things against external standards, on criteria perhaps little related to the local school's resources and goals.

Neither sees evaluation broadly enough. *Both* description and judgment are essential—in fact, they are the two basic acts of evaluation. Any individual evaluator may attempt to refrain from judging or from collecting the judgments of others. Any individual evaluator may seek only to bring to light the worth of the program. But their evaluations are incomplete. To be fully understood, the educational program must be fully described and fully judged.

Towards Full Description

The specialist in evaluation seems to be increasing his emphasis on fullness of description. For many years he evaluated primarily by measuring student progress toward academic objectives. These objectives usually were identified with the traditional disciplines, e.g. mathematics, English, and social studies. Achievement tests—standardized or "teacher-made"—were found to be useful in describing the degree to which some curricular objectives are attained by individual students in a particular course. To the early evaluators, and to many others, the countenance of evaluation has been nothing more than the administration and normative interpretation of achievement tests.

In recent years a few evaluators have attempted, in addition, to assess progress of individuals toward certain "inter-disciplinary" and "extracurricular" objectives. In their objectives, emphasis has been given to the integration of behavior within an individual; or to the perception of interrelationships among scholastic disciplines; or to the development of habits, skills, and attitudes which permit the individual to be a craftsman or scholar, in or out of school. For the descriptive evaluation of such outcomes, the Eight-Year Study (Smith and Tyler, 1942) has served as one model. The proposed National

Assessment Program may be another—this statement appeared in one interim report:

> ...all committees worked within the following broad definition of 'national assessment:' 1. In order to reflect fairly the aims of education in the U.S., the assessment should consider both traditional and modern curricula, and take into account ALL THE ASPIRATIONS schools have for developing attitudes and motivations as well as knowledge and skills...[Caps added] (Educational Testing Service, 1965).

In his paper, "Evaluation for Course Improvement," Lee Cronbach (1963) urged another step: a most generous inclusion of behavioral-science variables in order to examine the possible causes and effects of quality teaching. He proposed that the main objective for evaluation is to uncover durable relationships—those appropriate for guiding future educational programs. To the traditional description of pupil achievement, we add the description of instruction and the description of relationships between them. Like the instructional researcher, the evaluator—as so defined—seeks generalizations about educational practices. Many curriculum project evaluators are adopting this definition of evaluation.

The Role of Judgment

Description is one thing, judgment is another. Most evaluation specialists have chosen not to judge. But in his recent *Methodology of Evaluation* Michael Scriven (1967) has charged evaluators with responsibility for passing upon the merit of an educational practice. (Note that he has urged the evaluator to do what the educator has expected the evaluator to be doing.) Scriven's position is that there is no evaluation until judgment has been passed, and by his reckoning the evaluator is best qualified to judge.

By being well experienced and by becoming well-informed in the case at hand in matters of research and educational practice the evaluator does become at least partially qualified to judge. But is it wise for him to accept this responsibility? Even now when few evaluators expect to judge, educators are reluctant to initiate a formal evaluation. If evaluators were *more* frequently identified with the passing of judgment, with the discrimination among poorer and better programs, and with the awarding of support and censure, their access to data would probably diminish. Evaluators collaborate with other social scientists and behavioral research workers. Those who do not want to judge deplore the acceptance of such responsibility by their associates. They believe that in the eyes of many practitioners, social science and behavioral research will become more suspect than it already is.

Many evaluators feel that they are not capable of perceiving, as they think a judge should, the unidimensional *value* of alternative programs. They anticipate a dilemma such as Curriculum I resulting in three skills and ten understandings and Curriculum II resulting in four skills and eight understandings. They are reluctant to judge that gaining one skill is worth losing two understandings. And, whether through timidity, disinterest, or as a rational choice, the evaluator usually supports "local option," a community's privilege to set its own standards and to be its own judge of the worth of its educational system. He expects that what is good for one community will not necessarily be good for another community, and he does not trust himself to discern what is best for a briefly known community.

Scriven reminds them that there are precious few who can judge complex programs, and fewer still who will. Different decisions must be made—P.S.S.C. or Harvard Physics?—and they should not be made on trivial criteria, e.g. mere precedent, mention in the popular press, salesman personality, administrative convenience, or pedagogical myth. Who should judge? The answer comes easily to Scriven partly because he expects little interaction between treatment and learner, i.e., what works best for one learner will work best for others, at least within broad categories. He also expects that where the local good is at odds with the common good, the local good can be shown to be detrimental to the common good, to the end that the doctrine of local option is invalidated. According to Scriven the evaluator must judge.

Whether or not evaluation specialists will accept Scriven's challenge remains to be seen. In any case, it is likely that judgments will become an increasing part of the evaluation report. Evaluators will seek out and record the opinions of persons of special qualification. These opinions, though subjective, can be very useful and can be gathered objectively, independent of the solicitor's opinions. A responsibility for processing judgments is much more acceptable to the evaluation specialist than one for rendering judgments himself.

Taylor and Maguire (1966) have pointed to five groups having important opinions on education: spokesmen for society at large, subject-matter experts, teachers, parents, and the students themselves. Members of these and other groups are judges who should be heard. Superficial polls, letters to the editor, and other incidental judgments are insufficient. An evaluation of a school program should portray the merit and fault perceived by well-identified groups, systematically gathered and processed. Thus, judgment data and description data are both essential to the evaluation of educational programs.

Data Matrices

In order to evaluate, an educator will gather together certain data. The data are likely to be from several quite different sources, gathered in several quite different ways. Whether the immediate purpose is description or judgment, three bodies of information should be tapped. In the evaluation report it can be helpful to distinguish between *antecedent*, *transaction*, and *outcome* data.

An antecedent is any condition existing prior to teaching and learning which may relate to outcomes. The status of a student prior to his lesson, e.g. his aptitude, previous experience, interest, and willingness, is a complex antecedent. The programmed-instruction specialist calls some antecedents "entry behaviors." The state accrediting agency emphasizes the investment of community resources. All of these are examples of the antecedents which an evaluator will describe.

Transactions are the countless encounters of students with teacher, student with student, author with reader, parent with counselor—the succession of engagements which comprise the process of education. Examples are the presentation of a film, a class discussion, the working of a homework problem, an explanation on the margin of a term paper, and the administration of a test. Smith and Meux (n.d.) studied such transactions in detail and have provided an 18-category classification system. One very visible emphasis on a particular class of transactions was the National Defense Education Act support of audio-visual media.

Transactions are dynamic whereas antecedents and outcomes are relatively static. The boundaries between them are not clear, e.g. during a transaction we can identify certain outcomes which are feedback antecedents for subsequent learning. These boundaries do not need to be distinct. The categories should be used to stimulate rather than to subdivide our data collection.

Traditionally, most attention in formal evaluation has been given to outcomes—outcomes such as the abilities, achievements, attitudes, and aspirations of students resulting from an educational experience. Outcomes, as a body of information, would include measurements of the impact of instruction on teachers, administrators, counselors, and others. Here too would be data on wear and tear of equipment, effects of the learning environment, cost incurred. Outcomes to be considered in evaluation include not only those that are evident, or even existent, as learning sessions end, but include applications, transfer, and relearning effects which may not be available for measurement until long after. The description of the outcomes of driver training, for example, could well include reports of accident avoidance over a lifetime. In short, outcomes are the consequences of education—immediate and long-range, cognitive and conative, personal and community-wide.

Antecedents, transactions, and outcomes, the elements of evaluation statements, are shown in figure 1 to have a place in both description and judgment. To fill in these matrices the evaluator will collect judgments (e.g. of community prejudice, of problem solving styles, and of teacher personality) as well as descriptions. In figure 1 it is also indicated that judgmental statements are classified either as general standards of quality or as judgments specific to the given program. Descriptive data are classified as intents and observations. The evaluator can organize his data-gathering to conform to the format shown in figure 1.

The evaluator can prepare a record of what educators intend, or what observers perceive, of what patrons generally expect, and of what judges value the immediate program to be. The record may treat antecedents, transactions, and outcomes separately within the four classes identified as *Intents, Observations, Standards*, and *Judgments,* as in figure 1. The following is an illustration of 12 data, one of which could be recorded in each of the 12 cells, starting with an intended antecedent, and moving down each column until an outcome judgment has been indicated.

Knowing that (1) Chapter XI has been assigned and that he intends (2) to lecture on the topic Wednesday, a professor indicates (3) what

Figure 1   A layout of statements and data to be collected by the evaluator of an educational program.

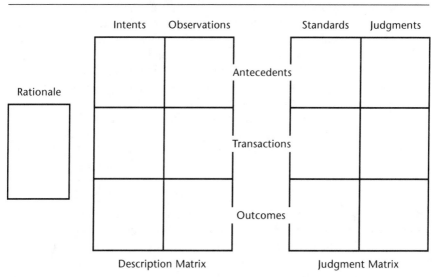

Intents   Observations   Standards   Judgments

Rationale

Antecedents

Transactions

Outcomes

Description Matrix   Judgment Matrix

the students should be able to do by Friday, partly by writing a quiz on the topic. He observes that (4) some students were absent on Wednesday, that (5) he did not quite complete the lecture because of a lengthy discussion and that (6) on the quiz only about ⅔ of the class seemed to understand a certain major concept. In general, he expects (7) some absences but that the work will be made up by quiztime; he expects (8) his lectures to be clear enough for perhaps 90 percent of a class to follow him without difficulty; and he knows that (9) his colleagues expect only about one student in ten to understand thoroughly each major concept in such lessons as these. By his own judgment (10) the reading assignment was not a sufficient background for his lecture; the students commented that (11) the lecture was provocative; and the graduate assistant who read the quiz papers said that (12) a discouragingly large number of students seemed to confuse one major concept for another.

Evaluators and educators do not expect data to be recorded in such detail, even in the distant future. My purpose here was to give twelve examples of data that could be handled by separate cells in the matrices. Next I would like to consider the description data matrix in detail.

Goals and Intents

For many years instructional technologists, test specialists, and others have pleaded for more explicit statements of educational goals. I consider "goals," "objectives," and "intents" to be synonymous. I use the category title *Intents* because many educators now equate "goals" and "objectives" with "intended student outcomes." In this paper Intents includes the planned-for environmental conditions, the planned-for demonstrations, the planned-for coverage of certain subject matter, etc., as well as the planned-for student behavior. To be included in this three-cell column are effects which are desired, those which are hoped for, those which are anticipated, and even those which are feared. This class of data includes goals and plans that others have, especially the students. (It should be noted that it is not the educator's privilege to rule out the study of a variable by saying, "that is not one of our objectives." The evaluator should include both the variable and the negation.) The resulting collection of *Intents* is a priority listing of all that may happen.

The fact that many educators now equate "goals" with "intended student outcomes" is to the credit of the behaviorists, particularly the advocates of programmed instruction. They have brought about a small reform in teaching by emphasizing those specific classroom acts and work exercises which contribute to the refinement of student responses. The A.A.A.S. Science Project, for example, has been successful in developing its curriculum around behavioristic goals (Gagné, 1966). Some curriculum-innovation projects, however, have found the emphasis on behavioral outcomes an obstacle to creative teaching (Atkin, 1963). The educational evaluator should not list goals only in terms of anticipated student behavior. To *evaluate* an educational program, we must examine what teaching, as well as what learning, is intended. (Many antecedent conditions and teaching transactions can be worded behavioristically, if desired.) How intentions are worded is not a criterion for inclusion. Intents can be the global goals of the Educational Policies Commission or the detailed goals of the programmer (Mager, 1962). Taxonomic, mechanistic, humanistic, even scriptural—any mixture of goal statements are acceptable as part of the evaluation picture.

Many a contemporary evaluator expects trouble when he sets out to record the educator's objectives. Early in the work he urged the educator to declare his objectives so that outcome-testing devices could be built. He finds the educator either reluctant or unable to verbalize objectives. With diligence, if not with pleasure, the evaluator assists with what he presumes to be the educator's job: writing behavioral goals. His presumption is wrong. As Scriven has said, the responsibility for describing curricular objectives is the responsibility of the evaluator. He is the one who is experienced with the language of behaviors, traits, and habits. Just as it is his responsibility to transform the behaviors of a teacher and the responses of a student into data, it is his responsibility to transform the intentions and expectations of an educator into "data." It is necessary for him to continue to ask the educator for statements of intent. He should augment the replies by asking, "Is this another way of saying it?" or "Is this an instance?" It is not wrong for an evaluator to teach a willing educator about behavioral objectives—they may facilitate the work. It is wrong for him to insist that every educator should use them.

Obtaining authentic statements of intent is a new challenge for the evaluator. The methodology remains to be developed. Let us now shift attention to the second column of the data cells.

Observational Choice

Most of the descriptive data cited early in the previous section are classified as *Observations*. In figure 1 when he described surroundings and events and the subsequent consequences, the evaluator[1] is telling of his Observations. Sometimes the evaluator observes these characteristics in a direct and personal way. Sometimes he uses instruments. His instruments include inventory schedules, biographical data sheets, interview routines, check lists, opinionnaires, and all kinds of psychometric tests. The experienced evaluator gives special attention to the measurement of student outcomes, but he does not fail to observe the other outcomes, nor the antecedent conditions and instructional transactions.

Many educators fear that the outside evaluator will not be attentive to the characteristics that the school staff has deemed most important. This sometimes does happen, but evaluators often pay *too much* attention to what they have been urged to look at, and too little attention to other facets. In the matter of selection of variables for evaluation, the evaluator must make a subjective decision. Obviously, he must limit the elements to be studied. He cannot look at all of them. The ones he rules out will be those that he assumes would not contribute to an understanding of the educational activity. He should give primary attention to the variables specifically indicated by the educator's objectives, but he must designate additional variables to be observed. He must search for unwanted side effects and incidental gains. The selection of measuring techniques is an obvious responsibility, but the choice of characteristics to be observed is an equally important and unique contribution of the evaluator.

An evaluation is not complete without a statement of the rationale of the program. It needs to be considered separately, as indicated in figure 1. Every program has its rationale, though often it is only implicit. The rationale indicates the philosophic background and basic purposes of the program. Its importance to evaluation has been indicated by Berlak (1966). The rationale should provide one basis for evaluating Intents. The evaluator asks himself or other judges whether the plan developed by the educator constitutes a logical step in the implementation of the basic purposes. The rationale also is of value in choosing the reference groups, e.g. merchants, mathematicians, and mathematics educators, which later are to pass judgment on various aspects of the program.

A statement of rationale may be difficult to obtain. Many an effective instructor is less than effective at presenting an educational rationale. If pressed, he may only succeed in saying something the listener wanted said. It is important that the rationale be in his language, a language he is the master of. Suggestions by the evaluator may be an obstacle, becoming accepted because they are attractive rather than because they designate the grounds for what the educator is trying to do.

The judgment matrix needs further explanation, but I am postponing that until after a consideration of the bases for processing descriptive data.

Figure 2   A representation of the processing of descriptive data.

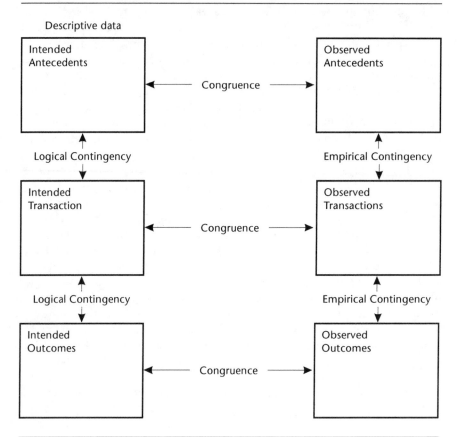

Descriptive data

Contingency and Congruence

For any one educational program there are two principal ways of processing descriptive evaluation data: finding the contingencies among antecedents, transactions, and outcomes and finding the congruence between Intents and Observations. The processing of judgments follows a different model. The first two main columns of the data matrix in figure 1 contain the descriptive data. The format for processing these data is represented in figure 2.

The data for a curriculum are *congruent* if what was intended actually happens. To be fully congruent the intended antecedents, transactions, and outcomes would have to come to pass. (This seldom happens—and often should not.) Within one row of the data matrix the evaluator should be able to compare the cells containing Intents and Observations, to note the discrepancies, and to describe the amount of congruence for that row. (Congruence of outcomes has been emphasized in the evaluation model proposed by Taylor and Maguire.) Congruence does not indicate that outcomes are reliable or valid, but that what was intended did occur.

Just as the Gestaltist found more to the whole than the sum of its parts, the evaluator studying variables from any two of the three cells in a column of the data matrix finds more to describe than the variables themselves. The relationships or *contingencies* among the variables deserve additional attention. In the sense that evaluation is the search for relationships that permit the improvement of education, the evaluator's task is one of identifying outcomes that are contingent upon particular antecedent conditions and instructional transactions.

Lesson planning and curriculum revision through the years have been built upon faith in certain contingencies. Day to day, the master teacher arranges his presentation and selects his input materials to fit his instructional goals. For him the contingencies, in the main, are logical, intuitive, and supported by a history of satisfactions and endorsements. Even the master teacher and certainly less-experienced teachers need to bring their intuitive contingencies under the scrutiny of appropriate juries.

As a first step in evaluation it is important just to record them. A film on floodwaters may be scheduled (intended transaction) to expose students to a background to conservation legislation (intended outcome). Of those who know both subject matter and pedagogy, we ask, "Is there a logical connection between this event and this purpose?" If so, a logical contingency exists between these two Intents. The record should show it.

Whenever Intents are evaluated the contingency criterion is one of logic. To test the logic of an educational contingency the evaluators rely on previous experience, perhaps on research experience, with similar observables. No immediate observation of these variables, however, is necessary to test the strength of the contingencies among Intents.

Evaluation of Observation contingencies depends on empirical evidence. To say, "this arithmetic class progressed rapidly because the teacher was somewhat but not too sophisticated in mathematics" demands empirical data, either from within the evaluation or from the research literature (Bassham, 1962). The usual evaluation of a single program will not alone provide the data necessary for contingency statements. Here too, then, previous experience with similar observables is a basic qualification of the evaluator.

The contingencies and congruences identified by evaluators are subject to judgment by experts and participants just as more unitary descriptive data are. The importance of non-congruence will vary with different viewpoints. The school superintendent and the school counselor may disagree as to the importance of a cancellation of the scheduled lessons on sex hygiene in the health class. As an example of judging contingencies, the degree to which teacher morale is contingent on the length of the school day may be deemed cause enough to abandon an early morning class by one judge and not another. Perceptions of importance of congruence and contingency deserve the evaluator's careful attention.

Standards and Judgments

There is a general agreement that the goal of education is excellence—but how schools and students should excel, and at what sacrifice, will always be debated. Whether goals are local or national, the measurement of excellence requires explicit rather than implicit standards.

Today's educational programs are not subjected to "standard-oriented" evaluation. This is not to say that schools lack in aspiration or accomplishment. It is to say that standards—benchmarks of performance having widespread reference value—are not in common use. Schools across the nation may use the same evaluation checklist[2] but the interpretations of the checklisted data are couched in inexplicit, personal terms. Even in an informal way, no school can evaluate the impact of its program without knowledge of what other schools are doing in pursuit of similar objectives. Unfortunately, many educators are loathe to accumulate that knowledge systematically (Hand, 1965; Tyler, 1965).

There is little knowledge anywhere today of the quality of a student's education. School grades are based on the private criteria and standards of the individual teacher. Most "standardized" tests scores tell where an examinee performing "psychometrically useful" tasks stands with regard to a reference group, rather than the level of competence at which he performs essential scholastic tasks. Although most teachers are competent to teach their subject matter and to spot learning difficulties, few have the ability to *describe* a student's command over his intellectual environment. Neither school grades nor standardized test scores nor the candid opinions of teachers are very informative as to the excellence of students.

Even when measurements are effectively interpreted, evaluation is complicated by a multiplicity of standards. Standards vary from student to student, from instructor to instructor, and from reference group to reference group. This is not wrong. In a healthy society, different parties have different standards. Part of the responsibility of evaluation is to make known which standards are held by whom.

It was implied much earlier that it is reasonable to expect change in an educator's *Intents* over a period of time. This is to say that he will change both his criteria and his standards during instruction. While a curriculum is being developed and disseminated, even the major classes of criteria vary. In their analysis of nationwide assimilation of new educational programs, Clark and Guba (1965) identified eight stages of change through which new programs go. For each stage they identified special criteria (each with its own standards) on which the program should be evaluated before it advances to another stage. Each of their criteria deserves elaboration, but here it is merely noted that there are quite different criteria at each successive curriculum-development stage.

Informal evaluation tends to leave criteria unspecified. Formal evaluation is more specific. But it seems the more careful the evaluation, the fewer the criteria; and the more carefully the criteria are specified, the less the concern given to standards of acceptability. It is a great misfortune that the best trained evaluators have been looking at education with a microscope rather than with a panoramic view finder.

There is no clear picture of what any school or any curriculum project is accomplishing today partly because the methodology of processing judgments is inadequate. What little formal evaluation there is is attentive to too few criteria, overly tolerant of implicit standards, and ignores the advantage of relative comparisons. More needs to be said about relative and absolute standards.

Comparing and Judging

There are two bases of judging the characteristics of a program, (1) with respect to absolute standards as reflected by personal judgments and (2) with respect to relative standards as reflected by characteristics of alternate programs. One can evaluate SMSG mathematics with respect to opinions of what a mathematics curriculum should be or with regard to what other mathematics curricula are. The evaluator's comparisons and judgments are symbolized in figure 3. The upper left matrix represents the data matrix from figure 2. At the upper right are sets of standards by which a program can be judged in an absolute sense. There are multiple sets because there may be numerous reference groups or points of view. The several matrices at the lower left represent several alternate programs to which the one being evaluated can be compared.

Each set of absolute standards, if formalized, would indicate acceptable and meritorious levels for antecedents, transactions, and outcomes. So far I have been talking about setting standards, not about judging. Before making a judgment the evaluator determines whether or not each standard is met. Unavailable standards must be estimated. The judging act itself is deciding which set of standards to heed. More precisely, judging is assigning a weight, an importance, to each set of standards. Rational judgment in educational evaluation is a decision as to how much to pay attention to the standards of each reference group (point of view) in deciding whether or not to take some administrative action.[3]

Relative comparison is accomplished in similar fashion except that the standards are taken from descriptions of other programs. It is hardly a judgmental matter to determine whether one program betters another with regard to a single characteristic, but there are many characteristics and the characteristics are not equally important. The evaluator selects which characteristics to attend to and which reference programs to compare to.

From relative judgment of a program, as well as from absolute judgment we can obtain an overall or composite rating of merit (perhaps with certain qualifying statements), a rating to be used in making an educational decision. From this final act of judgment a recommendation can be composed.

Absolute and Relative Evaluation

As to which kind of evaluation—absolute or relative—to encourage, Scriven and Cronbach have disagreed. Cronbach (1963) suggests that generalizations to the local-school situation from curriculum-comparing studies are sufficiently hazardous (even when the studies are massive,

**Figure 3   A representation of the process of judging the merit
of an educational program.**

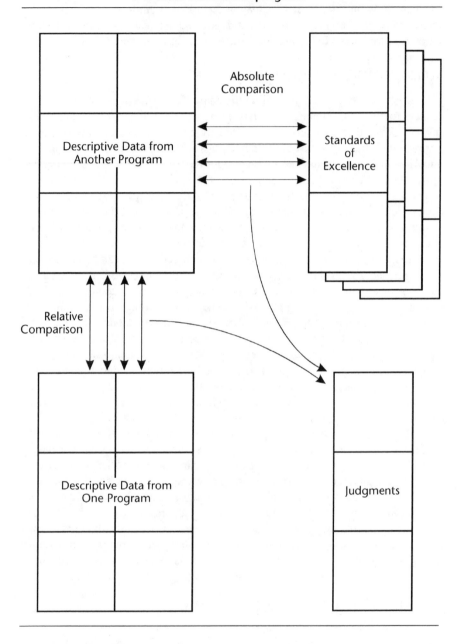

well-designed, and properly controlled) to make them poor research invest-ments. Moreover, the difference in purpose of the programs being compared is likely to be sufficiently great to render uninterpretable any outcome other than across-the-board superiority of one of them. Expecting that rarely, Cronbach urges fewer comparisons, more intensive process studies, and more curriculum "case studies" with extensive measurement and thorough description.

Scriven, on the other hand, indicates that what the educator wants to know is whether or not one program is better than another, and that the best way to answer his question is by direct comparison. He points to the difficulty of describing the outcomes of complex learning in explicit terms and with respect to absolute standards, and to the ease of observing relative outcomes from two programs. Whether or not Scriven's prescription is satisfying will probably depend on the client. An educator faced with an adoption decision is more likely to be satisfied, the curriculum innovator and instructional technologist less likely.

One of the major distinctions in evaluation is that which Scriven identi-fies as *formative* versus *summative* evaluation. His use of the terms relates primarily to the stage of development of curricular material. If material is not yet ready for distribution to classroom teachers, then its evaluation is formative; otherwise it is summative. It is probably more useful to distinguish between evaluation oriented to developer-author-publisher criteria and standards and evaluation oriented to consumer-administrator-teacher criteria and standards. The formative-summative distinction could be so defined, and I will use the terms in that way. The faculty committee facing an adoption choice asks, "Which is best? Which will do the job best?" The course developer, following Cronbach's advice, asks, "How can we teach it better?" (Note that neither are now concerned about the individual student differences.) The evaluator looks at different data and invokes different standards to answer these questions.

The evaluator who assumes responsibility for summative evaluation—rather than formative evaluation—accepts the responsibility of informing con-sumers as to the merit of the program. The judgments of figure 3 are his target. It is likely that he will attempt to describe the school situations in which the procedures or materials may be used. He may see his task as one of indicating the goodness-of-fit of an available curriculum to an existing school program. He must learn whether or not the intended antecedents, transactions, and outcomes for the curriculum are consistent with the resources, standards, and goals of the school. This may require as much attention to the school as to the new curriculum.

The formative evaluator, on the other hand, is more interested in the contingencies indicated in figure 2. He will look for covariations within the evaluation study, and across studies, as a basis for guiding the development of present or future programs.

For major evaluation activities it is obvious that an individual evaluator will not have the many competencies required. A team of social scientists is needed for many assignments. It is reasonable to suppose that such teams will include specialists in instructional technology, specialists in psychometric testing and scaling, specialists in research design and analysis, and specialists in dissemination of information. Curricular innovation is sure to have deep and widespread effects on our society, and we may include the social anthropologist on some evaluation teams. The economist and philosopher have something to offer. Experts will be needed for the study of values, population surveys, and content-oriented data-reduction techniques.

The educator who has looked disconsolate when scheduled for evaluation will look aghast at the prospect of a team of evaluators invading his school. How can these evaluators observe or describe the natural state of education when their very presence influences that state? His concern is justified. Measurement activity—just the presence of evaluators—does have a reactive effect on education, sometimes beneficial and sometimes not—but in either case contributing to the atypicality of the sessions. There are specialists, however, who anticipate that evaluation will one day be so skilled that it properly will be considered "unobtrusive measurement" (Webb, et al., 1966).

In conclusion I would remind the reader that one of the largest investments being made in U.S. education today is in the development of new programs. School officials cannot yet revise a curriculum on rational grounds, and the needed evaluation is not under way. What is to be gained from the enormous effort of the innovators of the 1960s if in the 1970s there are no evaluation records? Both the new innovator and the new teacher need to know. Folklore is not a sufficient repository. In our data banks we should document the causes and effects, the congruence of intent and accomplishment, and the panorama of judgments of those concerned. Such records should be kept to promote educational action, not obstruct it. The countenance of evaluation should be one of data gathering that leads to decision-making, not to trouble-making.

Educators should be making their own evaluations more deliberate, more formal. Those who will—whether in their classrooms or on national panels—can hope to clarify their responsibility by answering each of the following questions: (1) Is this evaluation to be primarily descriptive, primarily judgmental, or both descriptive and judgmental? (2) Is this evaluation to emphasize the antecedent conditions, the transactions, or the outcomes alone, or a combination of these, or their functional contingencies? (3) Is this evaluation to indicate the congruence between what is intended and what occurs? (4) Is this evaluation to be undertaken within a single program or as a comparison between two or more curricular programs? (5) Is this evaluation intended more to further the development of curricula or to help choose among available curricula? With these questions answered, the restrictive effects of incomplete guidelines and inappropriate countenances are more easily avoided.

Notes

1.   Here and elsewhere in this paper, for simplicity of presentation, the evaluator and the educator are referred to as two different persons. The educator will often be his own evaluator or a member of the evaluation team.

2.   One contemporary checklist is *Evaluative Criteria* (National Study of Secondary School Evaluation, 1960). It is a commendably thorough list of antecedents and possible transactions, organized mostly by subject-matter offerings.

Surely it is valuable as a checklist, identifying neglected areas. Its great value may be as a catalyst, hastening the maturity of a developing curriculum. However, it can be of only limited value in *evaluating*, for it guides neither the measurement nor the interpretation of measurement. By intent, it deals with criteria (what variables to consider) and leaves the matter of standards (what ratings to consider as meritorious) to the conjecture of the individual observer.

3. Deciding which variables to study and deciding which standards to employ are two essentially subjective commitments in evaluation. Other acts are capable of objective treatment; only these two are beyond the reach of social science methodology.

References

1. American Council on Education. *Educational Measurement.* E. F. Lindquist (ed.). Washington, D. C., 1951.

2. Smith, E. R. and Tyler, Ralph W., *Appraising and Recording Student Progress.* New York: Harper and Row, 1942.

3. Educational Testing Service, "A Long, Hot Summer of Committee Work on National Assessment of Education," *ETS Developments,* Vol. XIII, November, 1965.

4. Cronbach, Lee. "Evaluation for Course Improvement," *Teachers College Record,* 64, 1963, pp. 672-683.

5. Scriven, Michael. "The Methodology of Evaluation," *AERA Monograph Series on Curriculum Evaluation,* No. 1. Chicago: Rand McNally, 1967, pp. 39-89.

6. Taylor, Peter A., and Maguire, Thomas O., "A Theoretical Evaluation Model," *The Manitoba Journal of Educational Research,* I, 1966, pp. 12-17.

7. Smith, B. Othanel and Meux, M. O., *A Study of the Logic of Teaching.* Urbana: Bureau of Educational Research, University of Illinois. No date.

8. Gagné, Robert M., "Elementary Science: A New Scheme of Instruction," *Science,* Vol. 151, No. 3706, pp. 49-53.

9. Atkin, J. M., "Some Evaluation Problems in a Course Content Improvement Project," *Journal of Research in Science Teaching,* I, 1963, 129-132.

10. Mager, R. F., *Preparing Objectives for Programmed Instruction.* San Fransisco: Fearon Publishers, 1962.

11. Berlak, Harold. Comments recorded in *Concepts and Structure in the New Social Science Curricula.* Irving Morrissett (ed.). Lafayette, Indiana: Social Science Education Consortium, Purdue University, 1966, pp. 88-89.

12. See Bassham, H., "Teacher Understanding and Pupil Efficiency in Mathematics: A Study of Relationship," *Arithmetic Teacher,* 9: 1962, pp. 383-387.

13. Hand, Harold C., "National Assessment Viewed as the Camel's Nose," *Phi Delta Kappan,* 47, September, 1965, 8-12.

14. Tyler, Ralph W., "Assessing the Progress of Education," *Phi Delta Kappan,* 47, September, 1965, 13-16.

15. Clark, David L. and Guba, Egon G., "An Examination of Potential Change Roles in Education." Columbus: The Ohio State University, 1965. (Multilith.)

16. Webb, Eugene J.; Campbell, Donald T.; Schwartz, Richard D.; and Sechrist, Lee. *Unobtrusive Measures: Nonreactive Research in the Social Sciences.* Chicago: Rand McNally, 1966.

New Dimensions in Curriculum Development

R. Tyler

I have been asked to comment on my 1960 monograph titled *Basic Principles of Curriculum and Instruction*, indicating how this formulation came to be and to what extent I have "rethought, changed, updated, clarified my position." This is an assignment which I have found interesting, although it is provincial in focusing attention on one person's work.

The stimulus for me to construct a comprehensive outline of the questions to be answered and the steps to be taken in developing a curriculum, including the program of instruction, arose from my work with the staff of the Eight-Year Study, which officially occupied the period 1934–42. This was a monumental curriculum project for that time, since it involved 30 secondary school systems ranging across the continent from Boston to Los Angeles. This study grew out of the problems of the depression, the great increase in the proportion of youth attending high school (many of whom would have preferred to go to work but were unable to find employment), and the comparative rigidity of the high school curriculum, particularly for those students who wished to keep open the option of college attendance.

As the project began, the schools encountered great difficulty in identifying the problems to be attacked and in organizing and assigning task forces to work on these curriculum problems. There seemed to be little in common among the schools in their use of terms, in the emphasis being given to the subject fields, to student needs, and to social demands, and there was no clear-cut way in which the educational philosophies of the schools and theories of learning were considered. There were also varied views about the means of education. I was asked to devise a rationale to guide the efforts of the schools in their development of new curricula.

The rationale developed in 1936 was also employed in the Cooperative Study in General Education, a curriculum project of 22 colleges carried on in the period 1939–46. The modification which resulted from its use at the college level were incorporated in 1950 in the syllabus written for a course I taught at the University of Chicago entitled "Basic Principles of Curriculum and Instruction."

So much for the background of the monograph. The other matter I have been asked to comment on concerns changes that have taken place in "my position" since 1950. It is hard for one introspectively to chart the course of

From: Tyler, R.1966. New dimensions in curriculum development. *Phi delta kappan* 48 (September 1966):25–28. Reprinted with permission.

this thinking over 15 years in an area that has been as active as the field of curriculum, development. Hence what I have to say is likely to be incomplete and, at points, in error. I still find adequate and highly useful the original statement of the four divisions of curriculum inquiry, namely:

1. What educational purposes should the school seek to attain?
2. What educational experiences can be provided that are likely to attain these purposes?
3. How can these educational experiences be effectively organized?
4. How can we determine whether these purposes are being attained?

I also find still useful the three recommended sources for getting information helpful in deciding on objectives, these being: (1) studies of the learner, (2) studies of contemporary life, and (3) suggestions from subject specialists, along with employment of a philosophy of education and a theory of learning primarily as screens for selection and elimination among possible objectives obtained from the three sources. In working with different individuals and groups, I make clear that these sources can be used in any order, not necessarily the one presented in the syllabus, and that philosophy and psychology formulations may also be used to indicate areas for inclusion and exclusion prior to systematic studies of these sources of objectives.

In connection with investigations of curriculum objectives, the greatest change in my thinking relates to the conceptions of the learner and of knowledge and to the problem of the level of generality appropriate for an objective. The use of programmed materials in schools has involved me in observations and discussions that bring into sharp contrast the differing formulations of objectives and theories of learning, as between those who perceive the learner as being "conditioned" by the learning situation so as to respond in the way specified by the teacher or the designer of the program, and those who perceive the learner as an active agent exploring learning situations so as to learn to manipulate them for his purposes. It is somewhat like the difference implied by the cartoon showing one rat saying to another, "We've got this psychologist under control. He gives us food whenever we press the lever."

John Dewey commented more than 30 years ago on the truly educative environment as one in which there is a balance between factors under the learner's control and those that he could not influence. A learning situation in which the learner can exercise no control in terms of his purposes teaches him to conform or to rebel, but not to master. A learning situation in which all the factors are under the learner's control leads to whimsical or undisciplined behavior. Desirable learning results from the learner recognizing factors in the situation to which he must adapt and the others that he can manipulate in terms of his purposes.

I now think it is important in curriculum development to examine the concept of the learner as an active, purposeful human being. This appears to be an important psycho-philosophic factor to consider at an early stage in work on objectives.

The use of programmed material has also raised for explicit consideration in formulating objectives the question of the learner's role in developing and using knowledge. Is knowledge something outside of man that he has discovered and can now make available to learners, or is knowledge man's effort to explain phenomena with which he comes in contact, so that the learner can produce knowledge? The idea of learning by discovery, or Whitehead's comment that "knowledge is like fish, it must be caught fresh each day," takes on more meaning to curriculum workers when they treat knowledge as a growing product of man's effort to understand.

A related issue is the question of the structure of a discipline. Some programmed materials operate on the assumption that the knowledge to be learned is not primarily an organized system, such that stochastic learning processes are appropriate. However, learners can understand the structure of the discipline, that is, the question it deals with, the kind of answers it seeks, the concepts it uses to analyze the field, the methods it uses to obtain data, and the way it organizes its inquiries and findings. When they gain this understanding of the structure, they learn more effectively and efficiently the content involved in it. Hence I now seek to explore the nature of the knowledge and structure of an area before deriving and formulating objectives involved in that area.

The level of generality appropriate for an objective is perhaps the most puzzling question about objectives currently faced by curriculum workers. This problem is briefly discussed in the 1950 monograph in connection with the use of a psychology of learning, and is the third area of greatest change in my thinking relating to the formulation of objectives. In the 1950 discussion, a contrast was drawn between the highly specific objectives that are formulated when learning is viewed as building up connections between specific stimuli and specific responses as compared to objectives when learning is viewed as the development of generalizations, such as generalized ways of attacking problems, generalized modes of reaction to generalized types of situations, and generalizations which subsume many specific items. When empirical investigations are made of children's ability to generalize where no special instruction has been provided, the majority of children show a low level of accurate generalization. This, like the earlier studies of Thorndike, is often interpreted to mean that objectives should be quite specific on the ground that children are unable to learn more generalized kinds of behavior.

However, when carefully controlled studies are made with a defined level of generalization as a goal, such as generalizing the process of the addition of one-digit numbers from 20 specific illustrations, most of the 7-year-old subjects succeed. I think this is a question to be treated experimentally, aiming at as high a level of generalization as the experiments show to be successful. The purpose is to help the student perceive and use a generalized mode of behavior, as shown by his ability to deal appropriately with the specifics subsumed under the generalization. In short, he should be able to move easily from the general to the specific, and vice versa, recognizing specific illustrations of the general and recognizing the general principle that covers a number of specifics. The level of generality of the objective should then be stated in the curriculum plan, with specifics used as illustrations, rather than treating the specifics as ends in themselves.

One of the confusing aspects of this problem of level of generality has been the use of factor analysis and other methods for indicating relations among data as though they were indicators of inherent relations, inherent in the neural mechanisms, and thus subject to little, if any, change through learning. Only by recognizing that the interrelationships of responses students make to tests and other stimuli are indications that reflect not only inherent factors but also ways in which the student perceives the situation, and the connections that he has learned or not learned, have we been led to work experimentally on helping students to build new patterns of reaction representing different interrelationships among the data.

My thoughts about planning of learning experiences have been elaborated considerably since 1950. In the monograph, mention is made of five general principles that are helpful, namely:

1. The student must have experiences that give him an opportunity to practice the kind of behavior implied by the objective.

2. The learning experiences must be such that the student obtains satisfactions from carrying on the kind of behavior implied by the objective.

3. The reactions required by the learning experiences are within the range of possibility for the students involved.

4. There are many particular experiences that can be used to attain the same educational objectives.

5. The same learning experience will usually bring about several outcomes.

These five, although useful, are not adequate to give us much guidance in devising learning experiences as can be provided when use is made of experimental work both in learning and in curriculum evaluation. Hence, during recent years, I have modified the earlier five and added several others to give additional help on this task. These are now stated as 10 conditions for effective learning. The first two are the same as the first two principles given above. The other eight are:

3. The motivation of the learner, that is, the impelling force for his own active involvement, is an important condition.

4. Another condition is that the learner finds his previous ways of reacting unsatisfactory, so that he is stimulated to try new ways.

5. The learner should have some guidance in trying to carry on the new behavior he is to learn.

6. The learner should have ample and appropriate materials on which to work.

7. The learner should have time to carry on the behavior, to practice it until it has become part of his repertoire.

8. The learner should have opportunity for a good deal of sequential practice. Here repetition is inadequate and quickly becomes ineffective.

9. Another condition is for each learner to set standards for himself that require him to go beyond his performance, but standards that are attainable.

10. The tenth condition, related to the ninth, is that to continue learning beyond the time when a teacher is available, the learner must have means of judging his performance to be able to tell how well he is doing. Without these means, his standards are of no utility.

In actual use, each of these ten conditions is elaborated much more fully. They have served to focus attention on some of the places where learning experiences are likely to be inadequate.

In connection with the problem of guiding the learner in carrying on the desired behavior, I have found that students commonly observe the teacher's behavior as a model to direct their own. This is a useful guide if the teacher does frequently demonstrate the behavior the student is expected to acquire, but some teachers do not furnish an observable model of the desired learning. The teacher who lectures to a class may only be demonstrating ways of giving out information rather than showing the student how he goes about solving problems. Often when students cannot gain a clear picture of what they are to do by observing the teacher they depend upon other students to show them or tell them. This frequently results in misunderstanding of what the student is to do. In general, clear observable models are useful ways of guiding the desired behavior.

In trying to practice something new, the student needs to attend to those significant features of his behavior that serve to control it appropriately. In the case of a skill like handwriting, he needs to attend to the form of the letters he is making rather than to the gross movement of his hand and arm. In the case of a skill like swimming, he may best control his efforts by attending to critical movements of arms, legs, and body, rather than to the distance he moves through the water. In the case of problem solving, he usually needs help in noting what factors to observe and what previous knowledge to use in order to attack the problem successfully. Hence, guidance of the learning of the student includes helping him to focus his attention on those aspects of the total situation that enable him to control it and carry it on successfully.

I have also added to my own thinking about the total curriculum and the instructional program recognition of the influences upon learning of the school environment, the peer group values and practices, and the types of personality identification available in the school. We have learned a great deal from Pace and Stern about the "press" of the college environment. Using the College Characteristics Index, they have shown the variety of "presses" among the different colleges. Each type of "press" influences students somewhat differently in terms of what goals to seek, what values are acceptable, what kinds and amounts of study are approved. There is some evidence to indicate similar variations among schools. Hence the "press" of school or college is a significant matter to consider and, if necessary, to change, in order to attain desired objectives more effectively.

Within the same school or college, peer groups exert a powerful influence on the things that are learned, the efforts made, and the satisfaction obtained. Some peer groups enhance the work of teachers, some insulate the student from the influence of the faculty, and others partially counteract the efforts of teachers. In planning and developing the instructional program, peer groups should be considered and steps taken to utilize their influences constructively toward the attainment of significant educational objectives.

As children and young people grow up, they often find persons who seem particularly attractive and seek to emulate them. The young child may begin this process of identification with his mother, following her around the house and attempting to imitate her behavior. During the years of development, other persons in turn are objects of identification. This process is one of the ways in which young people learn, and with a variety of constructive personalities available, the outcomes are positive and include the acquisition of attitudes, values, and interests, as well as skills and practices. In some schools and colleges, however, the range of constructive personalities that are close enough to the students to permit attraction and emulation is too narrow, so that many children and youth find no one on the faculty enough like them to be drawn into identification. This is another consideration for instructional planning that should seek to use all important resources for learning that can be provided.

Nothing has been said thus far about changes in my thinking regarding the organization of learning experiences and evaluation. Recently, I have been giving considerable attention to the problem of organization and to the elaboration of a more helpful rationale for this area. As you know, I am also nearly over my head in a new evaluation project called "Assessing the Progress of Education." This is furnishing grist for a rather thorough reexamination of the process of evaluation. I hope later to report on these developments.

Media

The "Cone of Experience"

E. Dale

We are now equipped to consider audio-visual materials against the background of our first three chapters. Much of what we have found to be true of direct and indirect experience, and of concrete and abstract experience, can be summarized in a pictorial device. We call it the "Cone of Experience," but it is not offered as a perfect or mechanically flawless picture to be taken with absolute literalness in its simplified form. It is merely a visual aid to explain the inter-relationships of the various types of audio-visual materials, as well as their individual positions in the learning process. Even the hastiest glance at the cone shows that sensory materials can be readily classified as they move from the most direct to the most abstract kind of learning.

As you study the cone, you recognize that each division represents a stage between the two extremes—between direct experience and pure abstraction. As you travel up the cone from its base, you move in the order of decreasing directness. Thus, a "contrived experience" is one stage more direct than "dramatic participation"; "dramatic participation" is one stage more direct than "field trips," and so on. Similarly, if you travel down the cone from its pinnacle, you move in the order of decreasing abstractness: "verbal symbols" are more abstract than "visual symbols"; and "visual symbols" are more abstract than "one-sense aids," and so on.

However, you will make a dangerous error if you regard these bands on the cone as rigid, inflexible divisions. For the different kind of sensory aids often interlap and sometimes blend into one another. A few examples will register this important fact. Motion pictures can be silent or they can combine sight and sound. A dramatization is often something which you view as a spectator—and yet you might participate in it as an actor. Students may merely view a demonstration, or they may view it and then participate in it. In other words, the device of the cone must be taken for nothing more than it is: a visual metaphor of learning experiences, in which the various kinds of audio-visual materials appear in the order of increasing abstraction as one proceeds from direct experience. And remember that an abstraction is not necessarily "hard." All words used by little children or mature adults are abstractions.

Part II of this book considers each of the ten divisions in extended form. In the present chapter we shall merely define them and then take into account some related ideas to which our discussion inevitably leads. For the sake of logical simplicity, we shall consider the ten divisions starting with the base.

Direct, Purposeful Experience

The base of the cone represents direct reality itself as we experience it at first-hand. It is the rich, full-bodied experience that is the bed-rock of all education. It is the purposeful experience that is seen, handled, tasted, felt, touched, smelled. It is the unabridged version of life itself—tangible experience, which we commonly refer to as "something you can get your fingers on," "something you can sink your teeth into," etc.

It is going to the bank, preparing meals, taking a walk, taking a trip, making a piece of furniture, performing a laboratory experiment. *It is learning by direct participation with responsibility for the outcome.*

You might do well to think seriously about this purposeful direct experience and its role, not merely in the educational process, but in your own life. When you recall your childhood, your sharpest, richest memories are evoked by direct experiences—the first meadowlark's nest found on the prairie, the worn desk in the fourth-grade room in Public School 51, the earliest wild strawberries in the field, and as many other different incidents as there are lives and sensibilities. It is worth noting that this division constitutes the base of the cone, for it is in reality the *basis* of all effective learning.

But life cannot always be lived on this direct, concrete, sensory level. Even our earliest experiences involve some degree of abstraction. As very young children we learn to talk about the doll or the dog or the man or the rabbit which is not physically present. Inevitably our direct, concrete experiencing soon becomes associated with abstractions.

Contrived Experiences

The second stage in the development of increasingly abstract experience may be illustrated by the working model. It differs from the original either in size or complexity: we *simplify* it by a working model. For teaching purposes, the model may be easier to understand than the thing it stands for.

A contrived experience is *"editing" of reality*, an editing which makes the reality easier to grasp. The clutch on an automobile is hard to understand when you sit in the driver's seat and press down the pedal, but a simplified model or a cutaway model shows clearly and simply how the clutch mechanism works. For teaching purposes, therefore, the imitation is better than the reality which it imitates.

A gasoline refinery sprawling over many acres may be baffling to a visitor. It is too much for the eye to take in. But a working model of that refinery can make the processes far simpler to understand.

A "model" city presented through models often helps immensely in teaching city planning. Initially it is a better teaching method than the aimless traveling over miles of streets and viewing scores of buildings, parks, and the like. The contrived experience is a much more fruitful teaching device.

Many similar examples come to mind. Few boys and girls, for example, get the opportunity to operate the controls of an airplane. But a model which they can "fly" explains certain basic mechanisms by omitting many distracting

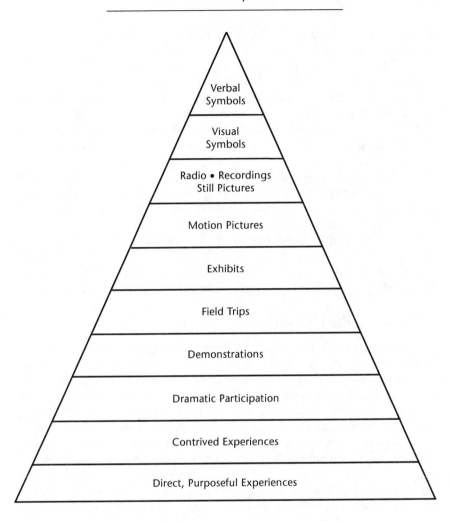

details. A miniature working model of Eli Whitney's cotton gin instantly shows the pupils the enormous savings in time secured by this device for removing seeds from cotton.

Business firms recognize the value of this teaching device. Salesmen of kitchen equipment often carry models with them to show the anxious housewife just how the new kitchen will look. Store windows frequently display small working models of washing machines. Manufacturers of machinery can usually depend on attracting crowds of fascinated onlookers when they show, for example, how paper is made by operating a miniature paper-mill at a printers' convention.

The United States Army produced a wide variety of contrived experiences as part of its aviation instruction. To learn the lighting system of a Flying Fortress first-hand is complicated and baffling. Wires are hidden, the distances between the lights are great. The Army produced a so-called "mock-up," in order to show the working of the lighting system in simplified form.

The system is set up on an exhibit board in "mock" form. However, the switches and all the rest of the equipment used are real. If you pull a particular switch, certain things happen, and they happen before your very eyes. You could not see these results if you were operating the lighting system in the airplane, but you cannot fail to see them on the mock-up. By spreading out the whole lighting plan, the Army could teach it easily. The mock-up simplifies reality.

A wrecked B-17 provided one airfield with a mock-up for teaching many facts about this plane. It was sliced in two. You could walk alongside it in the classroom and have your attention called to many details that would have been either invisible or not easily seen in the real plane.

A mock-up, then, is a device which changes and simplifies the details of the real object in order to make it more teachable. It simplifies by eliminating unnecessary detail. It emphasizes the key points. Undoubtedly this relatively new teaching device will be increasingly used both in schools and industry.

Dramatic Participation

There are a great many things we cannot possibly experience at first-hand. Life is too short. Restrictions of time and place make it impossible for any of us to experience directly much of what we need to know if we are to be educated. Besides, we cannot experience directly something that has already happened. Furthermore, some matters cannot be reduced to a contrived experience, and some ideas must of necessity be somewhat abstract and symbolic.

Dramatic participation can help us get as close as possible to certain realities that we cannot reach at first-hand. We participate in a reconstructed experience, not the original one. We re-live the hardships of Washington and his men at Valley Forge, or Jefferson at Monticello, by assuming the roles of these characters and their associates in a play, tableau, or pageant. It is, of course, commonplace for schools to dramatize the first Thanksgiving, the Mayflower Compact, the adoption of the Constitution, Lincoln's Gettysburg Address, and many other historical events. But dramatizations could be used to far greater advantage in the classroom and for teaching purposes of varied kinds.

Though it is not the thing itself, though it stands for something else, a dramatization may have certain teaching advantages over the real-life situation. It can eliminate many elements that mean little and distract attention. It can sharpen and emphasize the important ideas. By reconstructing the experience, we can focus upon the things that "matter"; thus manipulating the subject-matter for teaching purposes.

There is a distinction between participating in a dramatization and watching it. Both experiences can be fruitful, but a pupil who plays a part in dramatic reconstruction gets closer to the direct experience than a pupil who merely looks on. Thus, if we were to divide this band of our cone into two parts, "Dramatization by participation" would be the lower one (because it is a more direct experience) and "Dramatization by observation" would be the higher one. The spectator is farther away from the original reality than the participants who re-live the scenes.

The three stages that we have discussed so far all involve *doing*. The direct experience, the securing of contrived experience through the use of working models and mock-ups, and the experience of reconstructing reality by acting it out in a dramatization—in these three the individual is not a spectator but a participant.

In the next five stages on the cone, the individual is an observer. He no longer participates actively with responsibility for the outcome—he merely watches. But, as we pointed out earlier, audio-visual materials often blend into one another and interlap. Thus, the third stage of our "doing" group—dramatic participation—blends into our "observing" group, when the pupil merely watches a dramatization. He can do little to change the experiences with which he is confronted in the next five bands on the cone—demonstrations, field trips, exhibits, motion pictures, radio, recordings, and still pictures.

Demonstrations

A demonstration is another means whereby pupils can see how certain things are done. A coach demonstrates how to pass a football; a science teacher demonstrates the separation of hydrogen from oxygen by electrolysis; an arithmetic teacher demonstrates a short-cut method for multiplying.

Demonstrations may require nothing more than observation on the part of the pupil, or he may be asked to do what he has just been shown how to do. Whether the demonstration is to be followed by this "doing" on the part of the pupil, depends on the nature of the teaching problem. It may be enough for the teacher to show by electrolysis how hydrogen can be separated from oxygen. But a short-cut method in multiplying is not demonstrated by the teacher until the pupils need to use the new knowledge themselves.

You can readily see now that the cone of experience cannot be taken too literally. While the device is true as a whole, it does not imply any restrictions upon use. On the contrary, in any teaching program a variety of levels of abstraction may be effectively mixed. Indeed, in any continuous program of teaching, even in a single lesson, there will be a wide range—from direct, responsible sense-participation to a high-order level of abstraction.

Field Trips

When we make a school journey, excursion, or field trip we often see other people doing things. We watch them and note the meaning of their actions. As spectators, we are not responsible for what happens—we are on the sidelines, without authority or ability to alter the event. We merely watch it unfold.

This kind of sensory experience is so well known that extended comment at this point is unnecessary. Many schools in the eastern part of the country visit Washington, D.C. They watch the Congress at work; they go to the Mint and look on as money is printed.

If, however, they go one stage beyond observation—for example, if they interview government officials—the field trip gains in directness. When observation is combined with participation the field trip becomes more meaningful. Such a variation of the field trip indicates again how the bands of the cone interlap and blend into one another. We are beginning to see that our cone is by no means a perfect representation of the different levels of abstraction but merely a teaching device to accent certain points.

Exhibits

Where shall we place "Exhibits" on the cone? Sometimes they consist only of working models arranged in a meaningful display. Sometimes they are a series of photographs, or of photographs mixed with models and charts. Sometimes they include a demonstration or a motion picture. We shall keep our bearings if we remember that an exhibit is essentially something one sees as a spectator. A mock-up is seen by a spectator, but the spectator also operates some of the spread-out materials, or is otherwise engaged in doing. Usually one is not involved in handling anything or working the materials, though some complicated exhibits include such added sensory experiences. When they do, of course, the learning can become that much more meaningful.

Motion Pictures

Our next band, motion pictures, includes a number of variations of a single type. We may see a motion picture that is silent, or one that combines sight and sound, or one that combines sound with three-dimensional sight, and with full color.

The motion picture experience, unlike the field trip, unfolds with a compression of time and space. All the experience is not there. But this loss in directness and this compressed experience has compensating advantages. The motion picture can omit unnecessary and unimportant material and concentrate upon a few selected points. For example, in a field trip to a pottery we usually see the entire process from beginning to end. But a film on pottery-making can quickly pass over certain less important processes and emphasize the more significant ones. Besides, the mechanical devices for slow-motion enable us to sharpen up the key ideas. With slow motion, of course, we expand space and time.

Let us not forget, however, that we are *spectators* before a motion picture. We are some distance from touching, tasting, handling, feeling, from directly experiencing. We are no longer participants in the event. Neither do we get a direct or contrived experience. We are merely watching an event—perhaps seeing other people do things—and through an edited version of their experiences, in which time and space have been altered.

This is another way of saying that motion pictures present an abstracted version of the real event, with consequent losses as well as gains. It may be easier to understand than a more direct experience. A deliberate and contrived order has been imposed on the material, different from the reality itself. We can, if desirable, see the finished vase at the start of the picture and then go back to the steps involved in arriving at this result.

The motion picture can also dramatize events so effectively that we feel as though we are present at the reality itself. This is a great educational boon. For example, how clear are you as to the thinking and action in the Revolutionary period from, let us say, 1765 to 1800—a thirty-five year era unusually rich in historical meaning? Can you recall many of these events in full detail? Is Tom Paine a real flesh-and-blood character? Can you see him trudging down the streets of Philadelphia, taunted by small boys and scorned by the Tories of his time? Or is he just a vague, misty, verbal symbol?

Motion pictures can reconstruct this period with such dramatic intensity, with such realism and poignancy, that even the slowest child will react to its meaning. Unfortunately, we have not yet sufficiently used the motion picture to build a rich, memorable understanding of a great past.

Is it hard for you to think of a time when there was no such thing as capitalism? Can you visualize life in a feudal village? You have seen what a feudal castle looks like and you know something about the early methods of making clothes, tools, and the like—but can you reconstruct the ideals, attitudes, outlook, and values of feudal lord and feudal serf?

For example, can you see these things as clearly as you saw colonial life in Williamsburg in the four-reel film produced by the Eastman Kodak Company under the direction of Kenneth Edwards? Probably you cannot, because only few such materials have been made available as yet. But more undoubtedly will come, before very long, and they will be effectively used for the enrichment of both pupil and teacher.

Still Pictures, Radio, Recordings

Our next stage on the cone includes a number of devices that might be classified roughly as "one-dimensional" aids. Take motion out of the three-dimensional motion picture and you have the equivalent of a three-dimensional stereograph. If you remove the depth dimension, you have the filmstrip, the glass slide, and the photograph. The filmstrip, however, differs from both the glass slide and the photograph by using photographs in a fixed order. Radio and recordings are one-dimensional aids with similar differences as to imposed or free sequence.

These materials are roughly classified as "one-dimensional," though in terms of the central nervous system no experience can be so named. A stimulus may start through the eyes or ears, but when the impulse reaches the association centers of the brain, other neural areas are involved. The chief difference between these still pictures and the sound film is, for example, this: the still pictures are not presented in an imposed sequence. The experience of seeing them is less ordered and less formalized. Your file of pictures on Africa, consisting, let us say, of 100 separate photographs, can be used in any order you desire, and you can repeat any of them and omit as many as you wish. You can do the same, of course, with phonograph records.

It may be worth pointing out an intrinsic advantage of the projected glass slide or filmstrip: magnification. Though the pupil handles no material and is merely a spectator, he nevertheless experiences the view with more intensity. The image is large and impressive and the darkened room removes distractions and enables him to focus his attention on the subject itself.

Visual Symbols: Charts, Graphs, Maps, etc.

When we enter the next stage on the cone, we no longer have the realistic picture of the thing itself but an abstract representation. With charts, graphs, and maps, we no longer deal with literal reality but with substitutes. We communicate by means of a new language—visual symbols. A chart may use a dollar sign or a drawing of a coin to represent money, or a silhouette of a dejected working-man to symbolize one-million unemployed. It may use a pie to represent $1 of federal tax money, and a slice of the pie (part of the $1) for federal expenditure on military equipment. A graph may use a line to show growth and progress—a line which shows a rise or fall in income, production of coal, changing birthrate, and the like.

Only the simplest kinds of visual symbols are easily understood by elementary school children. High school pupils often have trouble with simple charts and graphs and may read them incorrectly. Map-reading, too, can be complicated, when many symbols are involved, and particularly when those standing for north and south, mountains and rivers, and the like are not instantly grasped. Teachers must be on guard to see that the symbolic aid is geared to the level of the pupils—that they are ready to use the new language of visual symbols.

Many purposes can be served by graphs, maps, and charts, and particularly the last. Time charts can show the progress of events over any desired period of time. Charts or diagrams can portray the stages in the operation of a gasoline engine. A chart can indicate how material progresses through a factory from the raw stuff to the finished product. A diagram may clarify the sequence of ideas in a paragraph or speech, or the organizational structure of the Congress of the United States, or the stages through which a bill becomes a law, or the plan of an association for world peace. A chart or diagram can be used whenever such a visualization can assist a pupil to understand an idea, an event, a process.

Verbal Symbols—Pinnacle of the Cone

The next and final stage brings us to verbal symbols—designations that have no resemblance to the objects or ideas for which they stand. All appearances have been removed from the original. The word *cat* does not look like a cat or sound like a cat or feel like a cat. The term *credit* does not reproduce the hundreds of specific experiences directly related to its meaning. At the pinnacle of the cone, we have abstracted everything from the original except the meaning of the term, and on this meaning we have reached more or less common agreement.

The verbal symbol may be a word (like *cat*), an idea (like *beauty*), a concept (like *credit*), a scientific principle (like the law of gravity), a formula (like H_2O), a philosophic aphorism (like *Honesty is the best policy*), and any other representation of experience that has been classified in some verbal symbolism. The range is limitless, from the elementary word *cat* to such terms as *democracy* or *truth* and *justice*. The important fact is the absolute abstractness of the symbol. Though certain words are held to be imitations of the things they stand for (onomatopoetic words like *whir*, *swish*, *crackle*), once they are conveyed through verbal symbols transcribed on paper, they have lost their last trace of direct reality. Thus, the pinnacle of the cone is not a rarefied height frequented only by the great intellects, for a child who can read and write *cat* is a user of verbal symbols. Indeed, the reading-writing processes begin at the pinnacle of the cone.

What the Cone Is and Is Not

If we realize now that the bands on the cone frequently interlap and blend into one another, and that a child who can read and write can use verbal symbols, there will be no mistaking our cone-device for a hierarchy or rank order of learning processes. It is understood for its intention—to show how sensory aids are classified in terms of more or less concreteness and abstractness. Clearly, our experiences vary all the way from direct, purposeful sense experience to the purely symbolic representations of such experiences. Certain mistaken impressions, however, may have already arisen, and it is worth our effort to remove them at once.

1. Intellectual life is impossible without abstractions and symbolizations. Through words we socialize and communicate experiences that are direct, personal, and otherwise incommunicable. But a word can stand for no more nor less than its kernel of meaning. Hence, no abstraction can be worth much if the kernel is missing—it will literally be an *empty* word.

How does this apply to the classroom? A common method of transmitting ideas from the expert to the inexpert is through reading. But the reader can get no meaning from the verbal symbol unless he puts meaning into it. Absolutely and inescapably, the reading content depends on the reactions aroused in the reader.

A youngster in Iowa who has never left his state and who has not had rich pictorial experience may find it hard to put much real meaning into the phrase about the "stern and rockbound coast." And a child living in such a New England area might have similar trouble with a phrase about a "swirling dust storm." Similarly, most adults have difficulty putting rich, concrete meaning into a term like "dialectical materialism." Empty words—empty meanings. To change our figure, verbal symbols, in order to be meaningful, must have underpinnings of concrete experience.

2. Does the cone device mean that all experience must somehow or other "travel up" this routine from base to pinnacle? Clearly and emphatically, no. There were many intelligent and learned people in the world before photography was invented and used for communicating experiences. We have seen that small children grasp simple abstractions. Before entering school they have mastered about 2,000 words, each of which is an abstraction. But abstractions range from the simplest to the most complex. Abstractions must be combined, if we are to have rich, full, deep, and broad experience and understanding. In brief, we ought to use *all the ways of experiencing* that we can.

This principle is extremely important for teachers preparing to apply audio-visual aids. Ralph Tyler's observation is well worth studying:

> The experiments in the teaching of zoology show that some students effectively learn the principles of zoology through certain types of laboratory projects, others through demonstrations and problems, others through other kinds of experiences. No one series of learning activities has proved equally effective with all students. This fact seems to me to demand a much wider range of materials in college work; that is, the learning activities in which students may engage need to be extended greatly. Furthermore, this expansion of possible learning activities should be supplemented by a means of discovering for the students where their difficulties are and of suggesting what kinds of activities will be most helpful to them in overcoming these difficulties in learning.[1]

3. Sometimes in discussing audio-visual materials, claims are made about the value of one sense over another. Actually, of course, our sensory experiences are mixed. When we listen to a speaker and think we are getting only aural experience, we are also reading lips and bodily expressions. When we look at an object with a view to picking it up, we may think we are involved exclusively in a visual experience, but we are also making judgments about its weight, feel, position, etc.

Have you ever been handed a beaker filled with mercury? You did more than "see." Your muscles were adjusted to ordinary weight and you found the beaker much heavier than your eyes had led you to expect. Similarly you may pick up a piece of something that looks heavy but is actually very light: your hand flies up quickly because you had made an incorrect muscular response. We look at a glistening object and call it "shiny," believing that it would be smooth to the touch—thus tying up touch with sight.

Experiences cannot be exclusively visual. Some extremely brilliant people have been blind from birth. This fact alone proves that one can learn effectively without sight. The following comment by Arthur I. Gates should be illuminating.

> Other things being equal, we learn quite as readily through one sense as another, with the exception, of course, of individuals whose receiving, connecting, or central mechanisms are defective. Other conditions, consequently, determine which avenue of presentation is to be preferred. Very young children learn new words better, for example, when they are presented to the ear than when presented to the eye, for the reason that their early word experience is auditory and not visual. If they have attended school, by the average age of

eight or thereabouts children memorize better material presented visually. This is mainly due to the fact that during reading the child can regulate the speed of reacting to the words to suit his capacity; he can attempt recall when and where he pleases; he can stop and repeat the especially difficult items, and disregard those already mastered.

The relative values of moving pictures, graphs, diagrams, mechanical instruments, verbal explanations, and clay models are similarly determined by past experience and mechanical advantages. The main questions are: Which method makes most clear the thing to be learned and which does it most interestingly and most economically of time, space, and money?[2]

4. You may now ask yourself: If methods other than reading are effective, why are book-reading and book-recitation so commonly used in schools? Why has this procedure retained its hold, if it has the weaknesses discussed in this chapter?

To answer this question, you must remember that through almost all of human history people have learned by direct experience and by stories passed down from father to son, from one generation to another. Learning has been a kind of apprentice system. The son learned to make shoes by apprenticeship to his father, the daughter helped her mother spin and weave. It is only in the last century that book-reading has become a common learning method for wide sections of the population. And yet even today less than half the people in the world can read and write. Indeed in some parts of the United States illiteracy is high and children are not compelled to attend school.

Textbooks are commonly used because they offer a means for teaching the vastly increased numbers of pupils in school. With their neat division of subject-matter into chapters, with subheads and questions, textbooks give the teacher a feeling of security. But the difficulty arises when one tests the quality and quantity of the learning. We have not been testing in terms of performance, of the ability of the pupil to do. We have been asking him, not "What can you do?" but "What do you remember?" And, as we have all come to realize, education involves the ability to make experiences usable.

Specialists in audio-visual materials are by no means unique in maintaining that reading and reciting on books is not enough. Extra-curricular activities, steadily on the increase throughout the country, reflect the identical conclusion. The use of great amounts of audio-visual materials in United States Army teaching, and their results, convinced countless Americans that there are excellent teaching methods that do not depend entirely on textbooks. Furthermore, able teachers interested in improving reading ability are among the most vigorous advocates of non-verbal materials. They know that you cannot read well or intelligently unless you have a sound base of experience.

5. But can we overemphasize immediate knowledge? Can we spend too much time on direct, first-hand experience? Are we in as much danger of getting our feet stuck in the concrete as we are of getting our heads lost in the clouds of abstraction? I do not think the danger is as great, but it is a danger. John Dewey, for example, points out:

> While direct impression has the advantage of being first-hand, it also has the disadvantage of being limited in range. Direct acquaintance with the natural surroundings of the home environment, as a means of making real ideas about portions of the earth beyond the reach of the sense and as a means of arousing intellectual curiosity, is one thing. As an end-all and be-all of geographical knowledge it is fatally restricted.... Just as the race developed especial symbols as tools of calculation and mathematical reasoning, because the use of the fingers as numerical symbols got in the way, so the individual must progress from concrete to abstract symbols—that is, symbols whose meaning is realized only through conceptual thinking.[3]

Summary

Experiences vary all the way from direct testing, handling, or seeing of concrete objects to the purely indirect manipulation through words and other symbols. We can roughly grade experiences in accordance with their degree of abstractness. A well-educated person has a mind stocked with a rich variety of concepts, grounded in concrete personal experiences. And such experiences are classifiable through a pictorial device—a metaphorical "cone of experience."

The cone, of course, is merely an aid to understanding this subject. It is not a mechanically flawless diagram but rather something to help explain the relationship of the various types of sensory materials, as they move from direct experience to the most abstract kind of learning. These bands of the cone, of course, interlap and frequently blend into one another. The cone as a whole conveniently subdivides into three major groups:

(1) Direct experiences (2) Contrived experiences (3) Dramatic participation	involve **DOING** in order of decreasing directness
(4) Demonstrations (5) Field trips (6) Exhibits (7) Motion pictures (8) Radio, Recordings Still Pictures	involve **OBSERVING** in order of decreasing directness
(9) Visual symbols (10) Verbal symbols	involve **SYMBOLIZING** in order of increasing abstractness

Notes

1. "Prevailing Misconceptions," in *Journal of Higher Education*, June 1933, p. 288.
2. *Psychology for Students of Education*. Macmillan, 1930, pp. 338f.
3. *Democracy and Education*. Macmillan, 1916, p. 315.

Methods and Techniques

"Good-Bye, Teacher ..."

Fred S. Keller

When I was a boy, and school "let out" for the summer, we used to celebrate our freedom from educational control by chanting:

> Good-bye scholars, good-bye school;
> Good-bye teacher, darned old fool!

We really didn't think of our teacher as deficient in judgment, or as a clown or jester. We were simply escaping from restraint, dinner pail in one hand and shoes in the other, with all the delights of summer before us. At that moment, we might even have been well-disposed toward our teacher and might have felt a touch of compassion as we completed the rhyme.

"Teacher" was usually a woman, not always young and not always pretty. She was frequently demanding and sometimes sharp of tongue, ever ready to pounce when we got out of line. But, occasionally, if one did especially well in home-work or in recitation, he could detect a flicker of approval or affection that made the hour in class worthwhile. At such times, we loved our teacher and felt that school was fun.

It was not fun enough, however, to keep me there when I grew older. Then I turned to another kind of education, in which the reinforcements were sometimes just as scarce as in the schoolroom. I became a Western Union messenger boy and, between deliveries of telegrams, I learned Morse code by memorizing dots and dashes from a sheet of paper and listening to a relay on the wall. As I look back on those days, I conclude that I am the only living reinforcement theorist who ever learned Morse code in the absence of reinforcement.

It was a long, frustrating job. It taught me that drop-out learning could be just as difficult as in-school learning and it led me to wonder about easier possible ways of mastering a skill. Years later, after returning to school and finishing my formal education, I came back to this classical learning problem, with the aim of making International Morse code less painful for beginners than American Morse had been for me (Keller, 1943).

At the time of publication, the author was on leave of absence from the University of Arizona at the Institute for Behavioral Research, Silver Spring, Maryland. This article is the text of the President's Invited Address, Division 2, American Psychological Association, Washington D.C., September 1967.

During World War II, with the aid of a number of students and colleagues, I tried to apply the principle of immediate reinforcement to the early training of Signal Corps personnel in the reception of Morse-code signals. At the same time, I had a chance to observe, at close hand and for many months, the operation of a military training center. I learned something from both experiences, but I should have learned more. I should have seen many things that I didn't see at all, or saw very dimly.

I could have noted, for example, that instruction in such a center was highly individualized, in spite of large classes, sometimes permitting students to advance at their own speed throughout a course of study. I could have seen the clear specification of terminal skills for each course, together with the carefully graded steps leading to this end. I could have seen the demand for perfection at every level of training and for every student; the employment of classroom instructors who were little more than the successful graduates of earlier classes; the minimizing of the lecture as a teaching device and the maximizing of student participation. I could have seen, especially, an interesting division of labor in the educational process, wherein the non-commissioned, classroom teacher was restricted to duties of guiding, clarifying, demonstrating, testing, grading, and the like, while the commissioned teacher, the training officer, dealt with matters of course logistics, the interpretation of training manuals, the construction of lesson plans and guides, the evaluation of student progress, the selection of non-commissioned cadre, and the writing of reports for his superiors.

I did see these things, of course, in a sense, but they were embedded deeply within a special context, one of "training" rather than "education." I did not then appreciate that a set of reinforcement contingencies which were useful in building simple skills like those of the radio operator might also be useful in developing the verbal repertories, the conceptual behaviors, and the laboratory techniques of university education. It was not until a long time later, by a very different route, that I came to such a realization.

That story began in 1962, with the attempt on the part of two Brazilian and two North American psychologists, to establish a Department of Psychology at the University of Brasilia. The question of teaching method arose from the very practical problem of getting a first course ready by a certain date for a certain number of students in the new university. We had almost complete freedom of action; we were dissatisfied with the conventional approaches; and we knew something about programmed instruction. We were also of the same theoretical persuasion. It was quite natural, I suppose, that we should look for fresh applications of reinforcement thinking to the teaching process (Keller, 1966).

The method that resulted from this collaborative effort was first used in a short-term laboratory course[1] at Columbia University in the winter of 1963, and the basic procedure of this pilot study was employed at Brasilia during the following year, by Professors Rodolfo Azzi and Carolina Martuscelli Bori, with 50 students in a one-term introductory course. Professor Azzi's report on this, at the 1965 meetings of the American Psychological Association and in personal correspondence, indicated a highly satisfactory outcome. The new procedure was received enthusiastically by the students and by the university administration. Mastery of the course material was judged excellent for all who completed the course. Objections were minor, centering around the relative absence of opportunity for discussion between students and staff.

Unfortunately, the Brasilia venture came to an abrupt end during the second semester of its operation, due to a general upheaval within the university that involved the resignation or dismissal of more than 200 teachers. Members of the original psychology staff have since taken positions elsewhere, and have reportedly begun to use the new method again, but I am unable at this time to report in detail on their efforts.

Concurrently with the early Brazilian development, Professor J. G. Sherman and I, in the spring of 1965, began a series of more or less independent applications of the same general method at Arizona State University. With various minor changes, this work has now been tried through five semesters with an increasing number of students per term (Keller, in press [a], in press [b], 1967; Sherman, 1967). The results have been more gratifying with each successive class, and there has been as yet no thought of a return to more conventional procedures. In addition, we have had the satisfaction of seeing our system used by a few other colleagues, in other courses and at other institutions.[2]

In describing this method to you, I will start with a quotation (Keller, 1967). It is from a hand-out given to all the students enrolled in the first-semester course in General Psychology (one of two introductions offered at Arizona State University) during the past year, and it describes the teaching method to which they will be exposed unless they elect to withdraw from the course.

> This is a course through which you may move, from start to finish, at your own pace. You will not be held back by other students or forced to go ahead until you are ready. At best, you may meet all the course requirements in less than one semester; at worst, you may not complete the job within that time. How fast you go is up to you.

> The work of this course will be divided into 30 units of content, which correspond roughly to a series of home-work assignments and laboratory exercises. These units will come in a definite numerical order, and you must show your mastery of each unit (by passing a "readiness" test or carrying out an experiment) before moving on to the next.

> A good share of your reading for this course may be done in the classroom, at those times when no lectures, demonstrations, or other activities are taking place. Your classroom, that is, will sometimes be a study hall.

> The lectures and demonstrations in this course will have a different relation to the rest of your work than is usually the rule. They will be provided only when you have demonstrated your readiness to appreciate them; no examination will be based upon them; and you need not attend them if you do not wish. When a certain percentage of the class has reached a certain point in the course, a lecture or demonstration will be available at a stated time, but it will not be compulsory.

> The teaching staff of your course will include proctors, assistants, and an instructor. A proctor is an undergraduate who has been chosen for his

mastery of the course content and orientation, for his maturity of judgment, for his understanding of the special problems that confront you as a beginner, and for his willingness to assist. He will provide you with all your study materials except your textbooks. He will pass upon your readiness tests as satisfactory or unsatisfactory. His judgment will ordinarily be law, but if he is ever in serious doubt, he can appeal to the classroom assistant, or even the instructor, for a ruling. Failure to pass a test on the first try, the second, the third, or even later, will not be held against you. It is better that you get too much testing than not enough, if your final success in the course is to be assured.

Your work in the laboratory will be carried out under the direct supervision of a graduate laboratory assistant, whose detailed duties cannot be listed here. There will also be a graduate classroom assistant, upon whom your proctor will depend for various course materials (assignments, study questions, special readings, and so on), and who will keep up to date all progress records for course members. The classroom assistant will confer with the instructor daily, aid the proctors on occasion, and act in a variety of ways to further the smooth operation of the course machinery.

The instructor will have as his principal responsibilities: (a) the selection of all study material used in the course; (b) the organization and the mode of presenting this material; (c) the construction of tests and examinations; and (d) the final evaluation of each student's progress. It will be his duty, also, to provide lectures, demonstrations, and discussion opportunities for all students who have earned the privilege; to act as a clearing-house for requests and complaints; and to arbitrate in any case of disagreement between students and proctors or assistants....

All students in the course are expected to take a final examination, in which the entire term's work will be represented. With certain exceptions, this examination will come at the same time for all students, at the end of the term.... The examination will consist of questions which, in large part, you have already answered on your readiness tests. Twenty-five percent of your course grade will be based on this examination; the remaining 75% will be based on the number of units of reading and laboratory work that you have successfully completed during the term.

(In my own sections of the course, these percentages were altered, during the last term, to a 30% weighting of the final examination, a 20% weighting of the 10 laboratory exercises, and a 50% weighting of the reading units.)

A picture of the way this method operates can best be obtained, perhaps, by sampling the activities of a hypothetical average student as he moves through the course. John Pilgrim is a freshman, drawn from the upper 75% of his high-school class. He has enrolled in PY 112 for unknown reasons and has been assigned to a section of about 100 students, men and women, most of whom are also in their beginning year. The class is scheduled to meet on Tuesdays and Thursdays, from 9:15 to 10:30 a.m., with a laboratory session to be arranged.

Together with the description from which I quoted a moment ago, John receives a few mimeographed instructions and some words of advice from his professor. He is told that he should cover two units of laboratory work or reading per week in order to be sure of taking an A-grade into his final examination; that he should withdraw from the course if he doesn't pass at least one readiness test within the first two weeks; and that a grade of Incomplete will not be given except in special cases. He is also advised that, in addition to the regular classroom hours on Tuesday and Thursday, readiness tests may be taken on Saturday forenoons and Wednesday afternoons of each week—periods in which he can catch up with, or move ahead of, the rest of the class.

He then receives his first assignment: an introductory chapter from a standard textbook and two "sets" from a programmed version of similar material. With this assignment, he receives a mimeographed list of "study questions," about 30 in number. He is told to seek out the answers to these questions in his reading, so as to prepare himself for the questions he will be asked in his readiness tests. He is free to study wherever he pleases, but he is strongly encouraged to use the study hall for at least part of the time. Conditions for work are optimal there, with other students doing the same thing and with an assistant or proctor on hand to clarify a confusing passage or a difficult concept.

This is on Tuesday. On Thursday, John comes to class again, having gone through the sets of programmed material and having decided to finish his study in the classroom, where he cannot but feel that the instructor really expects him. An assistant is in charge, about half the class is there, and some late registrants are reading the course description. John tries to study his regular text, but finds it difficult to concentrate and ends by deciding to work in his room. The assistant pays no attention when he leaves.

On the following Tuesday, he appears in study hall again, ready for testing, but anxious, since a whole week of the course has passed. He reports to the assistant, who sends him across the hall, without his books and notes, to the testing room, where the proctor in charge gives him a blue-book and one of the test forms for Unit 1. He takes a seat among about 20 other students and starts work. The test is composed of 10 fill-in questions and one short-answer essay question. It doesn't seem particularly difficult and, in about 10 min John returns his question sheet and is sent, with his blue-book, to the proctor's room for grading.

In the proctor's room, in one of 10 small cubicles, John finds his special proctor, Anne Merit. Anne is a psychology major who passed the same course earlier with a grade of A. She receives two points of credit for about 4 hr of proctoring per week, 2 hr of required attendance at a weekly proctors' meeting, and occasional extra duty in the study hall or test room. She has nine other students besides John to look after, so she will not as a rule be able to spend much more than 5 or 10 min of class time with each.

Anne runs through John's answers quickly, checking two of them as incorrect and placing a question mark after his answer to the essay question. Then she asks him why he answered these three as he did. His replies show two misinterpretations of the question and one failure in written expression. A restatement of the fill-in questions and some probing with respect to the essay leads Anne to write an O.K. alongside each challenged answer. She congratulates John upon his performance and warns him that later units may be a little harder to master than the first.

John's success is then recorded on the wallchart in the proctors' room, he is given his next assignment and set of study questions, and sent happily on his way. The blue-book remains with Anne, to be given later to the assistant or the instructor for inspection, and used again when John is ready for testing on Unit 2. As he leaves the room, John notices the announcement of a 20-min lecture by his instructor, for all students who have passed Unit 3 by the following Friday, and he resolves that he will be there.

If John had failed in the defense of one or two of his answers, he would have been sent back for a minimal period of 30 min for further study, with advice as to material most needing attention. If he had made more than four errors on his test, the answers would not have been considered individually; he would simply have been told that he was not ready for examination. And, if he had made no errors at all, he would probably have been asked to explain one or two of his correct answers, as a way of getting acquainted and to make sure that he was the one who had really done the work.

John did fail his first test on Unit 2, and his first two tests on Unit 4 (which gave trouble to nearly everyone). He missed the first lecture, too, but qualified for the second. (There were seven such "shows" during the term, each attended by perhaps half of the students entitled to be there.) After getting through his first five units, he failed on one review test before earning the right to move on to Unit 6. On the average, for the remainder of the course, he required nearly two readiness tests per unit. Failing a test, of course, was not an unmixed evil, since it permitted more discussion with the proctor and often served to sharpen the concepts involved.

In spite of more than a week's absence from school, John was able, by using the Wednesday and Saturday testing sessions, to complete his course units successfully about a week before the final examination. Because of his cramming for other courses during this last week, he did not review for his psychology and received only a B on his final examination. His A for the course was not affected by this, but his pride was hurt.

Sometime before the term ended, John was asked to comment on certain aspects of the course, without revealing his identity. (Remember, John is a mythical figure.) Among other things, he said that, in comparison with courses taught more conventionally, this one demanded a much greater mastery of the work assignments, it required greater memorization of detail and much greater understanding of basic concepts, it generated a greater feeling of achievement, it gave much greater recognition of the student as a person, and it was enjoyed to a much greater extent (Keller, in press).

He mentioned also that his study habits had improved during the term, that his attitude towards testing had become more positive, that his worry about final grades had diminished, and that there had been an increase in his desire to hear lectures (this in spite of the fact that he attended only half of those for which he was qualified). When asked specifically about the use of proctors, he said that the discussions with his proctors had been very helpful, that the proctor's non-academic, personal relation was also important to him, and that the use of proctors generally in grading and discussing tests was highly desirable.

Anne Merit, when asked to comment on her own reactions to the system, had many things to say, mostly positive. She referred especially to the satisfaction of having the respect of her proctees, of seeing them do well, and of cementing the material of the course for herself. She noted that the method was one of "mutual reinforcement" for student, proctor, assistant, and instructor. She suggested that it ought to be used in other courses and at other levels of instruction. She wondered why it would not be possible for a student to enroll in a second course immediately upon completion of the first, if it were taught by the same method. She also listed several changes that might improve the efficiency of the course machinery, especially in the area of testing and grading, where delay may sometimes occur.

In an earlier account of this teaching method (Keller, 1967), I summarized those features which seem to distinguish it most clearly from conventional teaching procedures. They include the following:

1. The go-at-your-own-pace feature, *which permits a student to move through the course at a speed commensurate with his ability and other demands upon his time.*

2. The unit-perfection requirement for advance, *which lets the student go ahead to new material only after demonstrating mastery of that which preceded.*

3. The use of lectures and demonstrations as vehicles of motivation, *rather than sources of critical information.*

4. *The related* stress upon the written word in *teacher-student communications; and finally:*

5. *The* use of proctors, *which permits repeated testing, immediate scoring, almost unavoidable tutoring, and a marked enhancement of the personal-social aspect of the educational process.*

The similarity of our learning paradigm to that provided in the field of programmed instruction is obvious. There is the same stress upon analysis of the task, the same concern with terminal performance, the same opportunity for individualized progression, and so on. But the sphere of action here is different. The principal steps of advance are not "frames" in a "set," but are more like the conventional home-work assignment or laboratory exercise. "The 'response' is not simply the completion of a prepared statement through the insertion of a word or phrase. Rather, it may be thought of as the resultant of many such responses, better described as the understanding of a principle, a formula, or a concept, or the ability to use an experimental technique. Advance within the program depends on something more than the appearance of a confirming word or the presentation of a new frame; it involves a personal interaction between a student and his peer, or his better, in what may be a lively verbal interchange, of interest and importance to each participant. The use of a programmed text, a teaching machine, or some sort of computer aid within such a course is entirely possible and may be quite desirable, but it is not to be equated with the course itself." (Keller, 1967.)

Failure to recognize that our teaching units are not as simple as the response words in a programmed text, or the letter reactions to Morse-code signals, or other comparable atoms of behavior, can lead to confusion concerning our procedure. A well-known critic of education in America, after reading an account of our method, sent me a note confessing to "a grave apprehension about the effect of breaking up the subject matter into little packages." "I should suppose," he said, "it would prevent all but the strongest minds from ever possessing a synoptic view of a field, and I imagine that the coaching, and testing, and passing in bits would amount to efficient training rather than effectual teaching."

Our "little packages" or "bits" are no smaller than the basic conceptions of a science of behavior and cannot be delivered all at once in one large synoptic parcel. As for the teaching-training distinction, one needs only to note that it is always the instructor who decides what is to be taught, and to what degree, thus determining whether he will be called a trainer or a teacher. The method he uses, the basic reinforcement contingencies he employs, may be turned to either purpose.

Many things occur, some of them rather strange, when a student is taught by a method such as ours. With respect to everyday student behavior, even a casual visit to a class will provide some novel items. For example, all the students seated in the study hall may be seen studying, undistracted by the presence or movements of others. In the test room, a student will rarely be seen chewing on his pencil, looking at a neighbor's blue-book, or staring out the window. In the crowded proctors' room, 10 pairs of students can be found concurrently engaged in academic interaction, with no couple bothered by the conversation of another, no matter how close by. Upon passing his assistant or instructor, in the corridors or elsewhere, a student will typically be seen to react in a friendly and respectful manner—enough to excite a mild alarm.

More interesting than this is the fact that a student may be tested 40 or 50 times in the course of one semester, often standing in line for the privilege, without a complaint. In one extreme instance, a student required nearly two terms to complete the work of one (after which he applied for, and got, permission to serve as a proctor for the following year).

Another unusual feature of our testing and grading is the opportunity given to defend an "incorrect" answer. This defense, as I noted earlier, may sometimes produce changes in the proctor's evaluation, changes that are regularly checked by the assistant or the instructor. Occasionally, a proctor's O.K. will be rejected, compelling the student to take another test, and sensitizing the proctor to the dangers of leniency; more often, it produces a note of warning, a correction, or a query written by the instructor in the student's blue-book; but always it provides the instructor with feedback on the adequacy of the question he has constructed.

Especially important, in a course taught by such a method, is the fact that any differences in social, economic, cultural, and ethnic background are completely and repeatedly subordinated to a friendly intellectual relationship between two human beings throughout a period of 15 weeks or more. Also, in such a course, a lonesome, ill-favored underprivileged, badly schooled, or otherwise handicapped boy or girl can be assured at least a modicum of individual attention, approval, encouragement, and a change to succeed. The only prerequisite for such treatment is a well-defined amount and quality of academic achievement.

Another oddity of the system is the production of a grade distribution that is upside down. In figure 1 are the results from a class of 208 students at Arizona State University during the past semester. Note the diminishing relative frequency as one moves from A to D. The category of E, indicating failure, is swollen by the presence of 18 students who failed to take up their option of W (withdrawal from the course). Grades of C and D were due to the failure of students to complete all the units of reading or laboratory before going into the final examination.

Figure 2 shows data from the class 1 year earlier. Essentially the same distribution holds, except for the category of Incomplete, which was then too easily obtainable. Discouraging the use of the Incomplete, together with the provision of more testing hours, apparently has the effect of regularizing study habits and equalizing the number of tests taken per week throughout the term.

In figure 3 (filled bars), the grade distribution is for a section of 25 students in an introductory course at Queens College (N.Y.) during the second semester of the past school year. The same method of teaching was employed as at Arizona State, but the work requirement was somewhat greater in amount. The distinctive feature here is the relative infrequency of low grades. Only four students received less than a B rating. Professor John Farmer, who provided me with these data, reports that the two students receiving F had dropped out of the course, for unknown reasons, after seven and eight units respectively.

With this teaching method, students who are presumably inferior may show up better upon examination than presumably superior students taught by more conventional procedures. Figure 4 shows two distributions of grades on a mid-term examination. The empty bars represent the achievement of 161 students of an Ivy League College, mainly sophomores, in the first semester of a one-year lecture-and-laboratory course in elementary psychology. The filled bars represent the achievement of 66 Arizona State University students, mainly freshmen, on an unannounced mid-term quiz prepared by the Ivy League instructor and from which 13% of the questions had to be eliminated on the grounds of differential course coverage.

Relevant to this comparison is that pictured in figure 3. The grade distribution obtained by Professor Farmer (and his associate, Brett Cole) is here compared with one obtained from a section of 46 students in the same course, taught in the conventional manner by a colleague who is described as "a very good instructor." The filled bars show the Farmer-Cole results; the empty ones are those from Professor Brandex.

Such comparisons are of some interest and may relieve the tedium of a lecture, but they raise many questions of interpretation, and their importance should not be over-emphasized. The kind of change needed in education today is not one that will be evaluated in terms of the percentage of A's in a grade distribution or of differences at the 0.01 (or 0.001) level of confidence. It is one that will produce a reinforcing state of affairs for everyone involved—a state

Figure 1

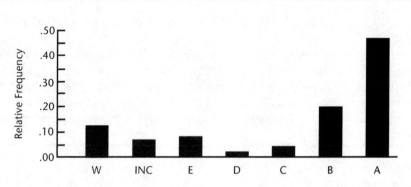

Figure 2

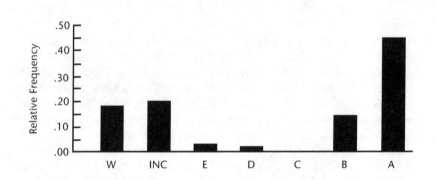

Figure 3

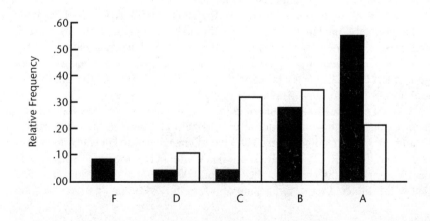

Figure 4

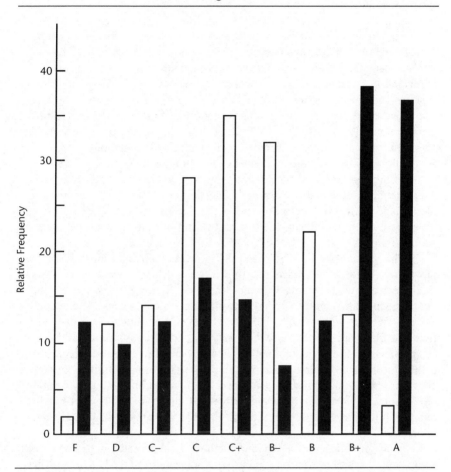

of affairs that has heretofore been reached so rarely as to be the subject of eulogy in the world's literature, and which, unfortunately, has led to the mystique of the "great teacher" rather than a sober analysis of the critical contingencies in operation.

Our method has not yet required a grant-in-aid to keep it going. On one occasion we tried to get such help, in order to pay for mimeograph paper, the services of a clark, and one or two additional assistants. Our request was rejected, quite properly, on the grounds that our project was "purely operational." Almost any member of a present-day fund-granting agency can recognize "research" when he sees it. I do think, however, that one should be freed, as I was, from other university demands while introducing a system like ours. And he should not be asked to teach more than two such courses regularly, each serving 100 students or less, unless he has highly qualified assistants upon whom he can depend.

Neither does the method require equipment and supplies that are not already available to almost every teacher in the country. Teaching machines, tape recorders, and computers could readily be fitted into the picture. Moving pictures and television could also be used in one or two ways without detriment to the basic educational process. But these are luxuries, based on only partial recognition of our problem, and they could divert us from more important considerations. (Proctors, like computers, may go wrong or break down, but they can often be repaired and they are easily replaced, at very little expense.)

The need for individualized instruction is widely recognized, and the most commonly suggested way of filling this need is automation. I think that this solution is incomplete, especially when applied to the young; and I'd like to mention a personal experience that bears upon the matter.

In the summer of 1966, I made numerous visits to a center for the care and treatment of autistic children.[3] One day, as I stood at the door of a classroom, I saw a boy get up from his chair at the end of a class period and give a soft pat to the object on the desk in front of him. At the same time, he said, with a slight smile, "Good-bye, Teaching Machine!"

This pseudo-social behavior in this fundamentally asocial child amused me at the time. It reminded me or Professor Moore's description of the three-year-old who became irritated when his "talking typewriter" made a mistake, called the device a "big bambam," requested its name, and ended by asking, "Who is your mother?" Today, however, I am not so sure that this is funny. It does suggest that affection may be generated within a child for an electromechanical instrument that has been essential to educational reinforcement. Unfortunately, such a machine, in its present form, is unlikely to generalize with human beings in the boy's world, giving to them a highly desirable reinforcing property. In fact, the growth of this type of student-machine relation, if it were the only one, would be a poor substitute for a directly social interaction.

In an earlier report upon our method, I mentioned that it had been anticipated, partially or *in toto*, in earlier studies and I described one of these in some detail. As for current developments by other workers in our field, I have not made any systematic attempt to examine the offerings, even those that deal with college or university instruction. However, I have been impressed by several of them which seem to have points in common with ours, which have met with some success, and which will probably be increasingly heard from in the future.

One of these is the Audio-Tutorial Approach to the teaching of botany, developed by S. N. Postlethwait at Purdue University (Postlethwait and Novak, 1967). Another is the Socratic-Type Programming of general psychology by Harry C. Mahan (1967) and his associates at Palomar College, in California; and a third is the Interview Technique recently applied by C. B. Ferster and M. C. Perrott (1968) in teaching principles of behavior to graduate students in education at the University of Maryland.

Professor Postlethwait's method places great emphasis upon "independent study sessions" in which students carry out each individual work assignment in the course at their own pace, by means of the extensive use of tapes and films. Teaching assistants provide for oral quizzing on major concepts and help the students with difficult assignments. Weekly "small assembly sessions" are used primarily for recitation and the discussion of problems or small research projects; and "general assembly sessions" deal mainly with motivational materials. Postlethwait reports high student interest and greatly improved performance with the use of this technique. "Grades have risen from 6% A's under the conventional system to as high as 25% A's in some semesters. Failures have decreased from 20% in the conventional system to as few as 4%."

"Socratic-Type Programming" is described by Professor Mahan as "a philosophy and technology of instruction which emphasizes student response rather than presentations by the teacher. Its basic media consist of exercises made up of questions and short answers covering the content of a standard text, the text itself, tapes for recording the questions in the exercises, a classroom tape recorder for administering tests, tape duplicating facilities, a listening center in the college library, and student owned tape recorders for home use whenever possible. Classroom time is devoted largely to the discussion of points covered by the questions. All examinations are the short-answer type and are presented aurally on tape." Students must pass three periodic tests with a score of 85% or better before they are permitted to take a comprehensive final examination. The method does not yet permit "multiple exit" from the course, but Mahan says it is "tending very much in that direction." (1967.)

The Interview Technique, as described by Ferster and Perrott, does permit students to complete the course at different times, and it also approximates the student-and-proctor feature. Progress through the course is possible by verbalizing successive units of course content in a lengthy series of short interviews. The interviews are conducted mainly between students currently enrolled in the course, and any student is free to leave the course when all of his reading assignments have been adequately covered. The interviewer may sometimes be a staff member, as at the beginning of the course, but generally he is a student who has already been interviewed by someone else on the topic in question. The interviews are highly formalized, with the interviewer playing the role of the listener, checker, appraiser, and summarizer. Each interview is an open-book affair, but of such short and sharply-defined duration (10 minutes, as a rule) that the student can do no more than cue himself by reference to the printed page.

The goal of this method is nothing less than fluency with respect to each main feature of the course. Lectures, group discussions, and demonstrations are available at certain times, contingent upon a given stage of advance. Inadequate interviews are rejected, in whole or part, without prejudice, and with suggestions for further study. A product of high quality is guaranteed through staff participation at critical points. A modification of this procedure, which is to include written tests and the employment of advanced-student proctors, is planned by Professor Ferster for the introductory course in psychology at Georgetown University during the coming semester.

In systems like these, and in the one I have centered on, the work of a teacher is at variance with that which has predominated in our time. His public appearances as classroom entertainer, expositor, critic, and debater no longer seem important. His principal job, as Frank Finger (1962) once defined it, is truly "the facilitation of learning in others." He becomes an educational engineer, a contingency manager, with the responsibility of serving the great majority, rather than the small minority, of young men and women who come to him for schooling in the area of his competence. The teacher of tomorrow will not, I think, continue to be satisfied with a 10% efficiency (at best) which makes him an object of contempt by some, commiseration by others, indifference by many, and love by a few. No longer will he need to hold his position by the exercise of functions that neither transmit culture, dignify his status, nor encourage respect for learning in others. No longer will ne need to live, like Ichabod Crane, in a world that increasingly begrudges providing him room and lodging for a doubtful service to its young. A new kind of teacher is in the making. To the old kind, I, for one, will be glad to say, "Good-bye!"

I started this paper on a personal note and I would like to end it on one. Twenty-odd years ago, when white rats were first used as laboratory subjects in the introductory course, a student would sometimes complain about his animal's behavior. The beast couldn't learn, he was asleep, he wasn't hungry, he was sick, and so forth. With a little time and a handful of pellets, we could usually show that this was wrong. All that one needed to do was follow the rules. "The rat," we used to say, "is always right."

My days of teaching are over. After what I have said about efficiency, I cannot lay claim to any great success, but my schedule of rewards was enough to maintain my behavior, and I learned one very important thing: *the student is always right*. He is not asleep, not unmotivated, not sick, and he can learn a great deal if we provide the right contingencies of reinforcement. But if we don't provide them, and provide them soon, he too may be inspired to say, "Good-bye!" to formal education.

Notes

1. With the aid of (Dr.) Lanny Fields and the members of a senior seminar at Columbia College, during the fall term of 1963–64.
2. For example, by J. L. Michael with high-school juniors on a National Science Foundation project at Grinnell College (Iowa), in 1965; and by J. Farmer and B. Cole at Queens College (New York) in a course similar to the one described here.
3. At the Linwood Children's Center, Ellicott City, Maryland.

References

Ferster, C. B., and Perrott, M. C. *Behavior principles*. New York: Appleton-Century-Crofts, 1968. Pp. 542.

Finger, F. W. Psychologists in colleges and universities. In W. B. Webb (ed.), *The profession of psychology*. New York: Holt, Reinhart and Winston, 1962. Pp. 50–73.

Keller, F. S. Studies in international morse code: 1. a new method of teaching code reception. *Journal of Applied Psychology*, 1943, 27, 407–415.

Keller, F. S. A personal course in psychology. In R. Ulrich, T. Stachnik, and J. Mabry (Eds.), *The control of behavior*. Glenview, Ill.: Scott, Foresman, 1966. Pp. 91–93.

Keller, F. S. Neglected rewards in the educational process. *Proc. 23rd Amer. Conf. Acad. Deans*, Los Angeles, Jan., 1967. Pp. 9 –22.

Keller, F. S. New reinforcement contingencies in the classroom. In *Programmiertes lernen*, Wissenschaftliche Buchgesellschaft, Darmstadt, in press.

Keller, F. S. Engineering personalized instruction in the classroom. *Rev. Interamer de Psicol.*, 1967, 1, 189–197.

Keller, F. S. and Schoenfeld, W. N. The psychology curriculum at Columbia College. *American Psychologist*, 1949, 4, 165–172.

Mahan, H. C. The use of Socratic type programmed instruction in college courses in psychology. Paper read at West. Psychol. Ass., San Francisco, May, 1967.

Postlethwait, S. N., and Novak, J. D. The use of 8-mm loop films in individualized instruction. *Annals N.Y. Acad. Sci.*, Vol. 142, Art. 2, 464–470.

Sherman, J. G. Application of reinforcement principles to a college course. Paper read at Amer. Educ. Res. Ass., New York, Feb., 1967.

The Science of Learning and the Art of Teaching

B. F. Skinner

In this article, the author discusses some recent advances made in the psychology of learning, and their implications for classroom teaching. Dr. Skinner's experimental work has been concerned with an analysis of the effects of reinforcement in learning, and the designing of techniques by which reinforcement can be manipulated with considerable precision. He points out that perhaps the most serious criticism of the current classroom is the relative infrequency of reinforcement, and suggests how the results of certain scientific research in the field of learning can be brought to bear upon practical problems in education.

In order to take advantage of recent advances in the study of learning, the teacher must have the help of mechanical devices. In presenting the advantages to be gained from instrumental help in teaching, Dr. Skinner also deals with objections which may be raised to the use of such mechanical aids in instruction.

Some promising advances have recently been made in the field of learning. Special techniques have been designed to arrange what are called "contingencies of reinforcement"—the relations which prevail between behavior on the one hand and the consequences of that behavior on the other—with the result that a much more effective control of behavior has been achieved. It has long been argued that an organism learns mainly by producing changes in its environment, but it is only recently that these changes have been carefully manipulated. In traditional devices for the study of learning—in the serial maze, for example, or in the T-maze, the problem box, or the familiar discrimination apparatus—the effects produced by the organism's behavior are left to many fluctuating circumstances. There is many a slip between the turn-to-the-right and the food-cup at the end of the alley. It is not surprising that techniques of this sort have yielded only very rough data from which the uniformities demanded by an experimental science can be extracted only by averaging many cases. In none of this work

At the time this article was published, Dr. Skinner, author of Walden Two *and* Science and Human Behavior, *was professor of psychology at Harvard University. This paper was presented at a conference on Current Trends in Psychology and the Behavioral Sciences at the University of Pittsburgh, March 12, 1954.*

From: Skinner, B. F. 1954. The science of learning and the art of teaching. *Harvard educational review.* 24(1):86–97.

has the behavior of the individual organism been predicted in more than a statistical sense. The learning processes which are the presumed object of such research are reached only through a series of inferences. current preoccupation with deductive systems reflects this state of the science.

Recent improvements in the conditions which control behavior in the field of learning are of two principal sorts. The Law of Effect has been taken seriously; we have made sure that effects *do* occur and that they occur under conditions which are optimal for producing the changes called learning. Once we have arranged the particular type of consequence called a reinforcement, our techniques permit us to shape up the behavior of an organism almost at will. It has become a routine exercise to demonstrate this in classes in elementary psychology by conditioning such an organism as a pigeon. Simply by presenting food to a hungry pigeon at the right time, it is possible to shape up three or four well-defined responses in a single demonstration period—such responses as turning around, pacing the floor in the pattern of a figure-8, standing still in a corner of the demonstration apparatus, stretching the neck, or stamping the foot. Extremely complex performances may be reached through successive stages in the shaping process, the contingencies of reinforcement being changed progressively in the direction of the required behavior. The results are often quite dramatic. In such a demonstration one can *see* learning take place. A significant change in behavior is often obvious as the result of a single reinforcement.

A second important advance in technique permits us to maintain behavior in given states of strength for long periods of time. Reinforcements continue to be important, of course, long after an organism has learned *how* to do something, long after it has acquired behavior. They are necessary to maintain the behavior in strength. Of special interest is the effect of various schedules of intermittent reinforcement. Charles B. Ferster and the author are currently preparing an extensive report of a five-year research program, sponsored by the Office of Naval Research, in which most of the important types of schedules have been investigated and in which the effects of schedules in general have been reduced to a few principles. On the theoretical side we now have a fairly good idea of why a given schedule produces its appropriate performance. On the practical side we have learned how to maintain any given level of activity for daily periods limited only by the physical exhaustion of the organism and from day to day without substantial change throughout its life. Many of these effects would be traditionally assigned to the field of motivation, although the principal operation is simply the arrangement of contingencies of reinforcement.[1]

These new methods of shaping behavior and of maintaining it in strength are a great improvement over the traditional practices of professional animal trainers, and it is not surprising that our laboratory results are already being applied to the production of performing animals for commercial purposes. In a more academic environment they have been used for demonstration purposes which extend far beyond an interest in learning as such. For example, it is not too difficult to arrange the complex contingencies which produce many types of social behavior. Competition is exemplified by two pigeons playing a modified game of ping-pong. The pigeons drive the ball back and forth across a small table by pecking at it. When the ball gets by one pigeon, the other is reinforced. The task of constructing such a "social relation" is probably completely out of reach of the traditional animal trainer. It requires a carefully designed program of gradually changing contingencies and the skillful use of schedules to maintain the behavior in strength. Each pigeon is separately prepared for its part in the total performance, and the "social relation" is then arbitrarily constructed. The sequence of events leading up to this stable state are excellent material for the study of the factors important in nonsynthetic social behavior. It is instructive to consider how a similar series of contingencies could arise in the case of the human organism through the evolution of cultural patterns.

Cooperation can also be set up, perhaps more easily than competition. We have trained two pigeons to coordinate their behavior in cooperative endeavor with a precision which equals that of the most skillful human dancers. In a more serious vein these techniques have permitted us to explore the complexities of the individual organism and to analyze some of the serial or coordinate behaviors involved in attention, problem solving, various types of self-control, and the subsidiary systems of responses within a single organism called "personalities." Some of these are exemplified in what we call multiple schedules of reinforcement. In general a given schedule has an effect upon the rate at which a response is emitted. Changes in the rate from moment to moment show a pattern typical of the schedule. The pattern may be as simple as a constant rate of responding at a given value, it may be a gradually accelerating rate between certain extremes, it may be an abrupt change from not responding at all to a given stable high rate, and so on. It has been shown that the performance characteristic of a given schedule can be brought under the control of a particular stimulus and that different performances can be brought under the control of different stimuli in the same organism. At a recent meeting of the American Psychological Association, Dr. Ferster and the author demonstrated a pigeon whose behavior showed the pattern typical of "fixed-interval" reinforcement in the presence of one stimulus and, alternately, the pattern typical of the very different schedule called "fixed ratio" in the presence of a second stimulus. In the laboratory we have been able to obtain performances appropriate to *nine* different schedules in the presence of appropriate stimuli in random alternation. When Stimulus 1 is present, the pigeon executes the performance appropriate to Schedule 1. When Stimulus 2 is present, the pigeon executes the performance appropriate to Schedule 2. And so on. This result is important because it makes the extrapolation of our laboratory results to daily life much more plausible. We are all constantly shifting from schedule to schedule as our immediate environment changes, but the dynamics of the control exercised by reinforcement remain essentially unchanged.

It is also possible to construct very complex *sequences* of schedules. It is not easy to describe these in a few words, but two or three examples may be mentioned. In one experiment the pigeon generates a performance appropriate to Schedule A where the reinforcement is simply the production of the stimulus characteristic of Schedule B, to which the pigeon then responds appropriately. Under a third stimulus, the bird yields a performance appropriate to Schedule C where the reinforcement in this case is simply the production of the stimulus characteristic of Schedule D, to which the bird then responds appropriately. In a special case, first investigated by L. B. Wyckoff, Jr., the organism responds to one stimulus where the reinforcement consists of the *clarification* of the stimulus controlling another response. The first response becomes, so to speak, an objective form of "paying attention" to the second stimulus. In one important version of this experiment, as yet unpublished, we could say that the pigeon is telling us whether it is "paying attention" to the *shape* of a spot of light or to its *color*.

One of the most dramatic applications of these techniques has recently been made in the Harvard Psychological Laboratories by Floyd Ratliff and Donald S. Blough, who have skillfully used multiple and serial schedules of reinforcement to study complex perceptual processes in the infrahuman organism. They have achieved a sort of psycho-physics without verbal instruction. In a recent experiment by Blough, for example, a pigeon draws a detailed dark-adaptation curve showing the characteristic breaks of rod and cone vision. The curve is recorded continuously in a single experimental period and is quite comparable with the curves of human subjects. The pigeon behaves in a way which, in the human case, we would not hesitate to describe by saying that it adjusts a very faint patch of light until it can just be seen.

In all this work, the species of the organism has made surprisingly little difference. It is true that the organisms studied have all been vertebrates, but they still cover a wide range. Comparable results have been obtained with pigeons, rats, dogs, monkeys, human children, and most recently, by the author in collaboration with Ogden R. Lindsley, human psychotic subjects. In spite of great phylogenetic differences, all these organisms show amazingly similar properties of the learning process. It should be emphasized that this has been achieved by analyzing the effects of reinforcement and by designing techniques which manipulate reinforcement with considerable precision. Only in this way can the behavior of the individual organism be brought under such precise control. It is also important to note that through a gradual advance to complex interrelations among responses, the same degree of rigor is being extended to behavior which would usually be assigned to such fields as perception, thinking, and personality dynamics.

From this exciting prospect of an advancing science of learning, it is a great shock to turn to that branch of technology which is most directly concerned with the learning process—education. Let us consider, for example, the teaching of arithmetic in the lower grades. The school is concerned with imparting to the child a large number of responses of a special sort. The responses are all verbal. They consist of speaking and writing certain words, figures, and signs which, to put it roughly, refer to numbers and to arithmetic operations. The first task is to shape up these responses—to get the child to pronounce and to write responses correctly, but the principal task is to bring this behavior under many sorts of stimulus control. This is what happens when the child learns to count, to recite tables, to count while ticking off the items in an assemblage of objects, to respond to spoken or written numbers by saying "odd," "even," "prime," and so on. Over and above this elaborate repertoire of numerical behavior, most of which is often dismissed as the product of rote learning, the teaching of arithmetic looks forward to those complex serial arrangements of responses involved in original mathematical thinking. The child must acquire responses of transposing, clearing fractions, and so on, which modify the order or pattern of the original material so that the response called a solution is eventually made possible.

Now, how is this extremely complicated verbal repertoire set up? In the first place, what reinforcements are used? Fifty years ago the answer would have been clear. At that time educational control was still frankly aversive. The child read numbers, copied numbers, memorized tables, and performed operations upon numbers to escape the threat of the birch rod or cane. Some positive reinforcements were perhaps eventually derived from the increased efficiency of the child in the field of arithmetic and in rare cases some automatic reinforcement may have resulted from the sheer manipulation of the medium—from the solution of problems or the discovery of the intricacies of the number system. But for the immediate purposes of education the child acted to avoid or escape punishment. It was part of the reform movement known as progressive education to make the positive consequences more immediately effective, but any one who visits the lower grades of the average school today will observe that a change has been made, not from aversive to positive control, but from one form of aversive stimulation to another. The child at his desk, filing in his workbook, is behaving primarily to escape from the threat of a series of minor aversive events—the teacher's displeasure, the criticism or ridicule of his classmates, an ignominious showing in a competition, low marks, a trip to the office "to be talked to" by the principal, or a word to the parent who may still resort to the birch rod. In this welter of aversive consequences, getting the right answer is in itself an insignificant event, any effect of which is lost amid the anxieties, the boredom, and the aggressions which are the inevitable by-products of aversive control.[2]

Secondly, we have to ask how the contingencies of reinforcement are arranged. When is a numerical operation reinforced as "right"? Eventually, of course, the pupil may be able to check his own answers and achieve some sort of automatic reinforcement, but in the early stages the reinforcement of being right is usually accorded by the teacher. The contingencies she provides are far from optimal. It can easily be demonstrated that, unless explicit mediating behavior has been set up, the lapse of only a few seconds between response and reinforcement destroys most of the effect. In a typical classroom, nevertheless, long periods of time customarily elapse. The teacher may walk up and down the aisle, for example, while the class is working on a sheet of problems, pausing here and there to say right or wrong. Many seconds or minutes intervene between the child's response and the teacher's reinforcement. In many cases—for example, when papers are taken home to be corrected—as much as 24 hours may intervene. It is surprising that this system has any effect whatsoever.

A third notable shortcoming is the lack of a skillful program which moves forward through a series of progressive approximations to the final complex behavior desired. A long series of contingencies is necessary to bring the organism into the possession of mathematical behavior most efficiently. But the teacher is seldom able to reinforce at each step in such a series because she cannot deal the pupil's responses one at a time. It is usually necessary to reinforce the behavior in blocks of responses—as in correcting a work sheet or page from a workbook. The responses within such a block must not be interrelated. The answer to one problem must not depend upon the answer to another. The number of stages through which one may progressively approach a complex pattern of behavior is therefore small, and the task so much the more difficult. Even the most modern workbook in beginning arithmetic is far from exemplifying an efficient program for shaping up mathematical behavior.

Perhaps the most serious criticism of the current classroom is the relative infrequency of reinforcement. Since the pupil is usually dependent upon the teacher for being right, and since many pupils are usually dependent upon the same teacher, the total number of contingencies which may be arranged during, say, the first four years, is of the order of only a few thousand. But a very rough estimate suggests that efficient mathematical behavior at this level requires something of the order of 25,000 contingencies. We may suppose that even in the brighter student a given contingency must be arranged several times to place the behavior well in hand. The responses to be set up are not simply the various items in tables of addition, subtraction, multiplication, and division; we have also to consider the alternative forms in which each item may be stated. To the learning of such material we should add hundreds of responses concerned with factoring, identifying primes, memorizing series, using short-cut techniques of calculation, constructing and using geometric representations or number forms, and so on. Over and above all this, the whole mathematical repertoire must be brought under the control of concrete problems of considerable variety. Perhaps 50,000 contingencies is a more conservative estimate. In this frame of reference the daily assignment in arithmetic seems pitifully meagre.

The result of all this is, of course, well known. Even our best schools are under criticism for their inefficiency in the teaching of drill subjects such as arithmetic. The condition in the average school is a matter of wide-spread national concern. Modern children simply do not learn arithmetic quickly or well. Nor is the result simply incompetence. The very subjects in which modern techniques are weakest are those in which failure is most conspicuous, and in the wake of an ever-growing incompetence come the anxieties, uncertainties, and aggressions which in their turn present other problems to the school. Most pupils soon claim the asylum of not being "ready" for arithmetic at a given level or, eventually, of not having a mathematic mind. Such explanations are readily seized upon by defensive teachers and parents. Few pupils ever reach the stage at which automatic reinforcements follow as the natural consequences of mathematical behavior. On the contrary, the figures and symbols of mathematics have become standard emotional stimuli. The glimpse of a column of figures, not to say an algebraic symbol or an integral sign, is likely to set off—not mathematical behavior—but a reaction of anxiety, guilt, or fear.

The teacher is usually no happier about this than the pupil. Denied the opportunity to control via the birch rod, quite at sea as to the mode of operation of the few techniques at her disposal, she spends as little time as possible on drill subjects and eagerly subscribes to philosophies of education which emphasize material of greater inherent interest. A confession of weakness is her extraordinary concern lest the child be taught something unnecessary. The repertoire to be imparted is carefully reduced to an essential minimum. In the field of spelling, for example, a great deal of time and energy has gone into discovering just those words which the young child is going to use, as if it were a crime to waste one's educational power in teaching an unnecessary word. Eventually, weakness of technique emerges in the disguise of a reformulation of the aims of education. Skills are minimized in favor of vague achievements—educating for democracy, educating the whole child, educating for life, and so on. And there the matter ends; for, unfortunately, these philosophies do not in turn suggest improvements for techniques. They offer little or no help in the design of better classroom practices.

There would be no point in urging these objections if improvement were impossible. But the advances which have recently been made in our control of the learning process suggest a thorough revision of classroom practices and, fortunately, they tell us how the revision can be brought about. This is not, of course, the first time that the results of an experimental science have been brought to bear upon the practical problems of education. The modern classroom does not, however, offer much evidence that research in the field of learning has been respected or used. This condition is no doubt partly due to the limitations of earlier research. But it has been encouraged by a too hasty conclusion that the laboratory study of learning is inherently limited because it cannot take into account the realities of the classroom. In the light of our increasing knowledge of the learning process we should, instead, insist upon dealing with those realities and forcing a substantial change in them. Education is perhaps the most important branch of scientific technology. It deeply affects the lives of all of us. We can no longer allow the exigencies of a practical situation to suppress the tremendous improvements which are within reach. The practical situation must be changed.

There are certain questions which have to be answered in turning to the study of any new organism. What behavior is to be set up? What reinforcers are at hand? What responses are available in embarking upon a program of progressive approximation which will lead to the final form of the behavior? How can reinforcements be most efficiently scheduled to maintain the behavior in strength? These questions are all relevant in considering the problem of the child in the lower grades.

In the first place, what reinforcements are available? What does the school have in its possession which will reinforce a child? We may look first to the material to be learned, for it is possible that this will provide considerable automatic reinforcement. Children play for hours with mechanical toys, paints, scissors and paper, noise-makers, puzzles—in short, with almost anything which feeds back significant changes in the environment and is reasonably free of aversive properties. The sheer control of nature is itself reinforcing. This effect is not evident in the modern school because it is masked by the emotional responses generated by aversive control. It is true that automatic reinforcement from the manipulation of the environment is probably only a mild reinforcer and may need to be carefully husbanded, but one of the most striking principles to emerge from recent research is that the *net* amount of reinforcement is of little significance. A very slight reinforcement may be tremendously effective in controlling behavior if it is wisely used.

If the natural reinforcement inherent in the subject matter is not enough, other reinforcers must be employed. Even in school the child is occasionally permitted to do "what he wants to do," and access to reinforcements of many sorts may be made contingent upon the more immediate consequences of the behavior to be established. Those who advocate competition as a useful social motive may wish to use the reinforcements which follow from excelling others, although there is the difficulty that in this case the reinforcement of one child is necessarily aversive to another. Next in order we might place the good will and affection of the teacher, and only when that has failed need we turn to the use of aversive stimulation.

In the second place, how are these reinforcements to be made contingent upon the desired behavior? There are two considerations here—the gradual elaboration of extremely complex patterns of behavior and the maintenance of the behavior in strength at each stage. The whole process of becoming competent in any field must be divided into a very large number of very small steps, and reinforcement must be contingent upon the accomplishment of each step. This solution to the problem of creating a complex repertoire of behavior also solves the problem of maintaining the behavior in strength. We could, of course, resort to the techniques of scheduling already developed in the study of other organisms but in the present state of our knowledge of educational practices, scheduling appears to be most effectively arranged through the design of the material to be learned. By making each successive step as small as possible, the frequency of reinforcement can be raised to a maximum, while the possibly aversive consequences of being wrong are reduced to a minimum. Other ways of designing material would yield other programs of reinforcement. Any supplementary reinforcement would probably have to be scheduled in the more traditional way.

These requirements are not excessive, but they are probably incompatible with the current realities of the classroom. In the experimental study of learning it has been found that the contingencies of reinforcement which are most efficient in controlling the organism cannot be arranged through the personal mediation of the experimenter. An organism is affected by subtle details of contingencies which are beyond the capacity of the human organism to arrange. Mechanical and electrical devices must be used. Mechanical help is also demanded by the sheer number of contingencies which may be used efficiently in a single experimental session. We have recorded many millions of responses from a single organism during thousands of experimental hours. Personal arrangement of the contingencies and personal observation of the results are quite unthinkable. Now, the human organism is, if anything, more sensitive to precise contingencies than the other organisms we have studied. We have every reason to expect, therefore, that the most effective control of human learning will require instrumental aid. The simple fact is that, as a mere reinforcing mechanism, the teacher is out of date. This would be true even if a single teacher devoted all her time to a single child, but her inadequacy is multiplied manyfold when she must serve as a reinforcing device to many children at once. If the teacher is to take advantage of recent advances in the study of learning, she must have the help of mechanical devices.

The technical problem of providing the necessary instrumental aid is not particularly difficult. There are many ways in which the necessary contingencies may be arranged, either mechanically or electrically. An inexpensive device which solves most of the principal problems has already been constructed. It is still in the experimental stage, but a description will suggest the kind of instrument which seems to be required. The device consists of a small box about the size of a small record player. On the top surface is a window through which a question or problem printed on a paper tape may be seen. The child answers the question by moving one or more sliders upon which the digits 0 through 9 are printed. The answer appears in square holes punched in the paper upon which the question is printed. When the answer has been set, the child turns a knob. The operation is as simple as adjusting a television set. If the answer is right, the knob turns freely and can be made to ring a bell or provide some other conditioned reinforcement. If the answer is wrong, the knob will not turn. A counter may be added to tally wrong answers. The knob must then be reversed slightly and a second attempt at a right answer made. (Unlike the flash-card, the device reports a wrong answer without giving the right answer.) When the answer is right, a further turn of the knob engages a clutch which moves the next problem into place in the window. This movement cannot be completed, however, until the sliders have been returned to zero.

The important features of the device are these: Reinforcement for the right answer is immediate. The mere manipulation of the device will probably be reinforcing enough to keep the average pupil at work for a suitable period each day, provided traces of earlier aversive control can be wiped out. A teacher may supervise an entire class at work on such devices at the same time, yet each child may progress at his own rate, completing as many problems as possible within the class period. If forced to be away from school, he may return to pick up where he left off. The gifted child will advance rapidly, but can be kept from getting too far ahead either by being excused from arithmetic for a time or by being given special sets of problems which take him into some of the interesting bypaths of mathematics.

The device makes it possible to present carefully designed material in which one problem can depend upon the answer to the preceding and where, therefore, the most efficient progress to an eventually complex repertoire can be made. Provision has been made for recording the commonest mistakes so that the tapes can be modified as experience dictates. Additional steps can be inserted where pupils tend to have trouble, and ultimately the material will reach a point at which the answers of the average child will almost always be right.

If the material itself proves not to be sufficiently reinforcing, other reinforcers in the possession of the teacher or school may be made contingent upon the operation of the device or upon progress through a series of problems. Supplemental reinforcement would not sacrifice the advantages gained from immediate reinforcement and from the possibility of constructing an optimal series of steps which approach the complex repertoire of mathematical behavior most efficiently.

A similar device in which the sliders carry the letters of the alphabet has been designed to teach spelling. In addition to the advantages which can be gained from precise reinforcement and careful programming, the device will teach reading at the same time. It can also be used to establish the large and important repertoire of verbal relationships encountered in logic and science. In short, it can teach verbal thinking. As to content instruction, the device can be operated as a multiple-choice self-rater.

Some objections to the use of such devices in the classroom can easily be foreseen. The cry will be raised that the child is being treated as a mere animal and that an essentially human intellectual achievement is being analyzed in unduly mechanistic terms. Mathematical behavior is usually regarded, not as a repertoire of responses involving numbers and numerical operations, but as evidences of mathematical ability or the exercise of the power of reason. It is true that the techniques which are emerging from the experimental study of learning are not designed to "develop the mind" or to further some vague "understanding" of mathematical relationships. They are designed, on the contrary, to establish the very behaviors which are taken to be the evidences of such mental states or processes. This is only a special case of the general change which is under way in the interpretation of human affairs. An advancing science continues to offer more and more convincing alternatives to traditional formulations. The behavior in terms of which human thinking must eventually be defined is worth treating in its own right as the substantial goal of education.

Of course the teacher has a more important function than to say right or wrong. The changes proposed would free her for the effective exercise of that function. Marking a set of papers in arithmetic—"Yes, nine and six *are* fifteen; no, nine and seven *are not* eighteen"—is beneath the dignity of any intelligent individual. There is more important work to be done—in which the teacher's relations to the pupil cannot be duplicated by a mechanical device. Instrumental help would merely improve these relations. One might say that the main trouble with education in the lower grades today is that the child is obviously not competent and *knows it* and the teacher is unable to do anything about it and *knows that too.* If the advances which have recently been made in our control of behavior can give the child a genuine competence in reading, writing, spelling, and arithmetic, then the teacher may begin to function, not in lieu of a cheap machine, but through intellectual, cultural, and emotional contacts of that distinctive sort which testify to her status as a human being.

Another possible objection is that mechanized instruction will mean technological unemployment. We need not worry about this until there are enough teachers to go around and until the hours and energy demanded of the teacher are comparable to those in other fields of employment. Mechanical devices will eliminate the more tiresome labors of the teacher but they will not necessarily shorten the time during which she remains in contact with the pupil.

A more practical objection: Can we afford to mechanize our schools? The answer is clearly yes. The device I have just described could be produced as cheaply as a small radio or phonograph. There would need to be far fewer devices than pupils, for they could be used in rotation. But even if we suppose that the instrument eventually found to be most effective would cost several hundred dollars and that large numbers of them would be required, our economy should be able to stand the strain. Once we have accepted the possibility and the necessity of mechanical help in the classroom, the economic problem can easily be surmounted. There is no reason why the school room should be any less mechanized than, for example, the kitchen. A country which annually produces millions of refrigerators, dish-washers, automatic washing-machines, automatic clothes-driers, and automatic garbage disposers can certainly afford the equipment necessary to educate its citizens to high standards of competence in the most effective way.

There is a simple job to be done. The task can be stated in concrete terms. The necessary techniques are known. The equipment needed can easily be provided. Nothing stands in the way but cultural inertia. But what is more characteristic of America than an unwillingness to accept the traditional as inevitable? We are on the threshold of an exciting and revolutionary period, in which the scientific study of man will be put to work in man's best interests. Education must play its part. It must accept the fact that a sweeping revision of educational practices is possible and inevitable. When it has done this, we may look forward with confidence to a school system which is aware of the nature of its tasks, secure in its methods, and generously supported by the informed and effective citizens whom education itself will create.

Notes

1. The reader may wish to review Dr. Skinner's article, "Some Contributions of an Experimental Analysis of Behavior to Psychology as a Whole," *The American Psychologist*, 1953, 8, 69–78. Ed.
2. Skinner, B. F. *Science and Human Behavior*. New York: Macmillan, 1953.

Teaching Machines

B. F. Skinner

There are more people in the world than ever before, and a far greater part of them want an education. The demand cannot be met simply by building more schools and training more teachers. Education must become more efficient. To this end curricula must be revised and simplified, and textbooks and classroom techniques improved. In any other field a demand for increased production would have led at once to the invention of labor-saving capital equipment. Education has reached this stage very late, possibly through a misconception of its task. Thanks to the advent of television, however, the so-called audio-visual aids are being reexamined. Film projectors, television sets, phonographs, and tape recorders are finding their way into American schools and colleges.

Audio-visual aids supplement and may even supplant lectures, demonstrations, and textbooks. In doing so they serve one function of the teacher: they present material to the students and, when successful, make it so clear and interesting that the student learns. There is another function to which they contribute little or nothing. It is best seen in the productive interchange between teacher and student in the small classroom or tutorial situation. Much of that interchange has already been sacrificed in American education in order to teach large numbers of students. There is a real danger that it will be wholly obscured if use of equipment designed simply to *present* material becomes widespread. The student is becoming more and more a mere passive receiver of instruction.

Pressey's Teaching Machines

There is another kind of capital equipment which will encourage the student to take an active role in the instructional process. The possibility was recognized in the 1920's, when Sidney L. Pressey designed several machines for the automatic testing of intelligence and information. A recent model of one of these is shown in figure 1. [Figure 1 was unavailable for reprint.] In using

At the time this article was published, Dr. Skinner was Edgar Pierce professor of psychology in Harvard University, Cambridge, Mass.

the device the student refers to a numbered item in a multiple-choice test. He presses the button corresponding to his first choice of answer. If he is right, the device moves on to the next item; if he is wrong, the error is tallied, and he must continue to make choices until he is right.[1] Such machines, Pressey pointed out,[2] could not only test and score, they could *teach*. When an examination is corrected and returned after a delay of many hours or days, the student's behavior is not appreciably modified. The immediate report supplied by a self-scoring device, however, can have an important instructional effect. Pressey also pointed out that such machines would increase efficiency in another way. Even in a small classroom the teacher usually knows that he is moving too slowly for some students and too fast for others. Those who could go faster are penalized, and those who should go slower are poorly taught and unnecessarily punished by criticism and failure. Machine instruction would permit each student to proceed at his own rate.

The "industrial revolution in education" which Pressey envisioned stubbornly refused to come about. In 1932 he expressed his disappointment[3] "The problems of invention are relatively simple," he wrote. "With a little money and engineering resource, a great deal could easily be done. The writer has found from bitter experience that one person alone can accomplish relatively little and he is regretfully dropping further work on these problems. But he hopes that enough may have been done to stimulate other workers, that this fascinating field may be developed."

Pressey's machines succumbed in part to cultural inertia; the world of education was not ready for them. But they also had limitations which probably contributed to their failure. Pressey was working against a background of psychological theory which had not come to grips with the learning process. The study of human learning was dominated by the "memory drum" and similar devices originally designed to study forgetting. Rate of learning was observed, but little was done to change it. Why the subject of such an experiment bothered to learn at all was of little interest. "Frequency" and "recency" theories of learning, and principles of "massed and spaced practice," concerned the conditions under which responses were remembered.

Pressey's machines were designed against this theoretical background. As versions of the memory drum, they were primarily testing devices. They were to be used after some amount of learning had already taken place elsewhere. By confirming correct responses and by weakening responses which should not have been acquired, a self-testing machine does, indeed, teach; but it is not designed primarily for that purpose. Nevertheless, Pressey seems to have been the first to emphasize the importance of immediate feedback in education and to propose a system in which each student could move at his own pace. He saw the need for capital equipment in realizing these objectives. Above all he conceived of a machine which (in contrast with the audio-visual aids which were beginning to be developed) permitted the student to play an active role.

Another Kind of Machine

The learning process is now much better understood. Much of what we know has come from studying the behavior of lower organisms, but the results hold surprisingly well for human subjects. The emphasis in this research has not been on proving or disproving theories but on discovering and controlling the variables of which learning is a function. This practical orientation has paid off, for a surprising degree of control has been achieved. By arranging appropriate "contingencies of reinforcement," specific forms of behavior can be set up and brought under the control of specific classes of stimuli. The resulting behavior can be maintained in strength for long periods of time. A technology based on this work has already been put to use in neurology, pharmacology, nutrition, psychophysics, psychiatry, and elsewhere.[4]

The analysis is also relevant to education. A student is "taught" in the sense that he is induced to engage in new forms of behavior and in specific forms upon specific occasions. It is not merely a matter of teaching him *what* to do; we are as much concerned with the probability that appropriate behavior will, indeed, appear at the proper time—an issue which would be classed traditionally under motivation. In education the behavior to be shaped and maintained is usually verbal, and it is to be brought under the control of both verbal and nonverbal stimuli. Fortunately, the special problems raised by verbal behavior can be submitted to a similar analysis.[5]

If our current knowledge of the acquisition and maintenance of verbal behavior is to be applied to education, some sort of teaching machine is needed. Contingencies of reinforcement which change the behavior of lower organisms often cannot be arranged by hand; rather elaborate apparatus is needed. The human organism requires even more subtle instrumentation. An appropriate teaching machine will have several important features. The student must *compose* his response rather than select it from a set of alternatives, as in a multiple-choice self-rater. One reason for this is that we want him to recall rather than recognize—to make a response as well as see that it is right. Another reason is that effective multiple-choice material must contain plausible wrong responses, which are out of place in the delicate process of "shaping" behavior because they strengthen unwanted forms. Although it is much easier to build a machine to score multiple-choice answers than to evaluate a composed response, the technical advantage is outweighed by these and other considerations.

A second requirement of a minimal teaching machine also distinguishes it from earlier versions. In acquiring complex behavior the student must pass through a carefully designed sequence of steps, often of considerable length. Each step must be so small that it can always be taken, yet in taking it the student moves somewhat closer to fully competent behavior. The machine must make sure that these steps are taken in a carefully prescribed order.

Several machines with the required characteristics have been built and tested. Sets of separate presentations or "frames" of visual material are stored on disks, cards, or tapes. One frame is presented at a time, adjacent frames being out of sight. In one type of machine the student composes a response by moving printed figures or letters.[6] His setting is compared by the machine with a coded response. If the two correspond, the machine automatically presents the next frame. If they do not, the response is cleared, and another must be composed. The student cannot proceed to a second step until the first has been taken. A machine of this kind is being tested in teaching spelling, arithmetic, and other subjects in the lower grades.

For more advanced students—from junior high school, say, through college—a machine which senses an arrangement of letters or figures is unnecessarily rigid in specifying form of response. Fortunately, such students may be asked to compare their responses with printed material revealed by the machine. In the machine shown in figure 2, material is printed in 30 radial frames on a 12-inch disk. [Figure 2 was unavailable for reprint.] The student inserts the disk and closes the machine. He cannot proceed until the machine has been locked, and, once he has begun, the machine cannot be unlocked. All but a corner of one frame is visible through a window. The student writes his response on a paper strip exposed through a second opening. By lifting a lever on the front of the machine, he moves what he has written under a transparent cover and uncovers the correct response in the remaining corner of the frame. If the two responses correspond, he moves the lever horizontally. This move- ment punches a hole in the paper opposite his response, recording the fact that he called it correct, and alters the machine so that the frame will not appear again when the student works around the disk a second time. Whether the response was correct or not, a second frame appears when the lever is returned to its starting position. The student proceeds in this way until he has responded to all frames. He then works around the disk a second time, but only those frames appear to which he has not correctly responded. When the disk revolves without stopping, the assignment is finished. (The student is asked to repeat each frame until a correct response is made to allow for the fact that, in telling him that a response is wrong, such a machine tells him what is right.)

The machine itself, of course, does not teach. It simply brings the student into contact with the person who composed the material it presents. It is a labor-saving device because it can bring one programmer into contact with an indefinite number of students. This may suggest mass production, but the effect upon each student is surprisingly like that of a private tutor. The comparison holds in several respects. (i) There is a constant interchange between program and student. Unlike lectures, textbooks, and the usual audio-visual aids, the machine induces sustained activity. The student is always alert and busy. (ii) Like a good tutor, the machine insists that a given point be thoroughly understood, either frame by frame or set by set, before the student moves on. Lectures, textbooks, and their mechanized equivalents, on the other hand, proceed without making sure that the student understands and easily leave him behind. (iii) Like a good tutor the machine presents just that material for which the student is ready. It asks him to take only that step which he is at the moment best equipped and most likely to take. (iv) Like a skillful tutor the machine helps the student to come up with the right answer. It does this in part through the orderly construction of the program and in part with techniques of hinting, prompting, suggesting, and so on, derived from an analysis of verbal behavior.[5] (v) Lastly, of course, the machine, like the private tutor, reinforces the student for every correct response, using this immediate feedback not only to shape his behavior most efficiently but to maintain it in strength in a manner which the layman would describe as "holding the student's interest."

Programming Material

The success of such a machine depends on the material used in it. The task of programming a given subject is at first sight rather formidable. Many helpful techniques can be derived from a general analysis of the relevant behavioral processes, verbal and nonverbal. Specific forms of behavior are to be evoked and, through differential reinforcement, brought under the control of specific stimuli.

This is not the place for a systematic review of available techniques, or of the kind of research which may be expected to discover others. However, the machines themselves cannot be adequately described without giving a few examples of programs. We may begin with a set of frames (see table 1) designed to teach a third- or fourth-grade pupil to spell the word *manufacture*. The six frames are presented in the order shown, and the pupil moves sliders to expose letters in the open squares.

The word to be learned appears in bold face in frame 1, with an example and a simple definition. The pupil's first task is simply to copy it. When he does so correctly, frame 2 appears. He must now copy selectively: he must identify "fact" as the common part of "manufacture" and "factory." This helps him to spell the word and also to acquire a separable "atomic" verbal operant.[5] In frame 3 another root must be copied selectively from "manual." In frame 4 the pupil must for the first time insert letters without copying. Since he is asked to insert the same letter in two places, a wrong response will be doubly conspicuous, and the chance of failure is thereby minimized. The same principle governs frame 5. In frame 6 the pupil spells the word to complete the sentence used as an example in frame 1. Even a poor student is likely to do this correctly because he has just composed or completed the word five times, has made two important root-responses, and has learned that two letters occur in the word twice. He has probably learned to spell the word without having made a mistake.

Teaching spelling is mainly a process of shaping complex forms of behavior. In other subjects—for example, arithmetic—responses must be brought under the control of appropriate stimuli. Unfortunately the material which has been prepared for teaching arithmetic[7] does not lend itself to excerpting. The numbers 0 through 9 are generated in relation to objects, quantities, and scales. The operations of addition, subtraction, multiplication, and division are thoroughly developed before the number 10 is reached. In the course of this the pupil composes equations and expressions in a great variety of alternative forms. He completes not only $5 + 4 = \square$, but $\square + 4 = 9$, $5 \square 4 = 9$, and so on, aided in most cases by illustrative materials. No appeal is made to rote memorizing, even in the later acquisition of the tables. The student is expected to arrive at $9 \times 7 = 63$, not by memorizing it as he would memorize a line of poetry, but by putting into practice such principles as that nine times a number is the same as ten times the number minus the number (both of these being "obvious" or already well

---

Table 1   A set of frames designed to teach a third- or fourth-grade pupil to spell the word manufacture.

---

1. **Manufacture** means to make or build. *Chair factories manufacture chairs.* Copy the word here:

   □ □ □ □ □ □ □ □ □ □ □

2. Part of the word is like part of the word **factory**. Both parts come from an old word meaning *make* or *build*.

   m a n u □ □ □ □ u r e

3. Part of the word is like part of the word **manual**. Both parts come from an old word for *hand*. Many things used to be made by hand.

   □ □ □ □ f a c t u r e

4. The same letter goes in both spaces:

   m □ n u f □ c t u r e

5. The same letter goes in both spaces:

   m a n □ f a c t □ r e

6. Chair factories □□□□□□□□□□ chairs.

---

learned), that the digits in a multiple of nine add to nine, that in composing successive multiples of nine one counts backwards (nine, eighteen, twenty-seven, thirty-six, and so on), that nine times a single digit is a number beginning with one less than the digit (nine times six is fifty something), and possibly even that the product of two numbers separated by only one number is equal to the square of the separating number minus one (the square of eight already being familiar from a special series of frames concerned with squares).

Programs of this sort run to great length. At five or six frames per word, four grades of spelling may require 20,000 or 25,000 frames, and three or four grades of arithmetic, as many again. If these figures seem large, it is only because we are thinking of the normal contact between teacher and pupil. Admittedly, a teacher cannot supervise 10,000 or 15,000 responses made by each pupil per year. But the pupil's time is not so limited. In any case, surprisingly little time is needed. Fifteen minutes per day on a machine should suffice for each of these programs, the machines being free for other students for the rest of each day. (It is probably because traditional methods are so inefficient that we have been led to suppose that education requires such a prodigious part of a young person's day.)

A simple technique used in programming material at the high-school or college level, by means of the machine shown in figure 2, is exemplified in teaching a student to recite a poem. [Figure 2 was unavailable for reprint.] The first line is presented with several unimportant letters omitted. The student must read the line "meaningfully" and supply the missing letters. The second, third, and fourth frames present succeeding lines in the same way. In the fifth frame the first line reappears with other letters also missing. Since the student has recently read the line, he can complete it correctly. He does the same for the second, third, and fourth lines. Subsequent frames are increasingly incomplete, and eventually—say, after 20 or 24 frames—the student reproduces all four lines without external help, and quite possibly without having made a wrong response. The technique is similar to that used in teaching spelling: responses are first controlled by a text, but this is slowly reduced (colloquially, "vanished") until the responses can be emitted without a text, each member in a series of responses being now under the "intraverbal" control of other members.

"Vanishing" can be used in teaching other types of verbal behavior. When a student describes the geography of part of the world or the anatomy of part of the body, or names plants and animals from specimens or pictures, verbal responses are controlled by nonverbal stimuli. In setting up such behavior the student is first asked to report features of a fully labeled map, picture, or object, and the labels are then vanished. In teaching a map, for example, the machine asks the student to describe spatial relations among cities, countries, rivers, and so on, as shown on a fully labeled map. He is then asked to do the same with a map in which the names are incomplete or, possibly, lacking. Eventually he is asked to report the same relations with no map at all. If the material has been well programmed, he can do so correctly. Instruction is sometimes concerned not so much with imparting a new repertoire of verbal responses as with getting the student to describe something accurately in any available terms. The machine can "make sure the student understands" a graph, diagram, chart, or picture by asking him to identify and explain its features—correcting him, of course, whenever he is wrong.

In addition to charts, maps, graphs, models, and so on, the student may have access to auditory material. In learning to take dictation in a foreign language, for example, he selects a short passage on an indexing phonograph according to instructions given by the machine. He listens to the passage as often as necessary and then transcribes it. The machine then reveals the correct text. The student may listen to the passage again to discover the sources of any error. The indexing phonograph may also be used with the machine to teach other language skills, as well as telegraphic code, music, speech, parts of literary and dramatic appreciation, and other subjects.

A typical program combines many of these functions. The set of frames shown in table 2 is designed to induce the student of high-school physics to talk intelligently, and to some extent technically, about the emission of light from an incandescent source. In using the machine the student will write a word or phrase to complete a given item and then uncover the corresponding word or phrase shown here in the column at the right. The reader who wishes to get the "feel" of the material should cover the right-hand column with a card, uncovering each line only after he has completed the corresponding item.

Several programming techniques are exemplified by the set of frames in table 2. Technical terms are introduced slowly. For example, the familiar term

Table 2 **Part of a program in high-school physics. The machine presents one item at a time. The student completes the item and then uncovers the corresponding word or phrase shown at the right.**

Sentence to be completed	Word to be supplied
1. The important parts of a flashlight are the battery and the bulb. When we "turn on" a flashlight, we close a switch which connects the battery with the _____ .	bulb
2. When we turn on a flashlight, an electric current flows through the fine wire in the _____ and causes it to grow hot.	bulb
3. When the hot wire glows brightly, we say that it gives off or sends out heat and _____ .	light
4. The fine wire in the bulb is called a filament. The bulb "lights up" when the filament is heated by the passage of a(n) _____ current.	electric
5. When a weak battery produces little current, the fine wire, or _____ , does not get very hot.	filament
6. A filament which is *less* hot sends out or gives off _____ light.	less
7. "Emit" means "send out." The amount of light sent out, or "emitted," by a filament depends on how _____ the filament is.	hot
8. The higher the temperature of the filament the _____ the light emitted by it.	brighter, stronger
9. If a flashlight battery is weak, the _____ in the bulb may still glow, but with only a dull red color.	filament
10. The light from a very hot filament is colored yellow or white. The light from a filament which is not very hot is colored _____ .	red
11. A blacksmith or other metal worker sometimes makes sure that a bar of iron is heated to a "cherry red" before hammering it into shape. He uses the _____ of light emitted by the bar to tell how hot it is.	color
12. Both the color and the amount of light depend on the _____ of the emitting filament or bar.	temperature
13. An object which emits light because it is hot is called "incandescent." A flashlight bulb is an incandescent source of _____ .	light
14. A neon tube emits light but remains cool. It is, therefore, not an incandescent _____ of light.	source

Table 2 Part of a program in high-school physics *(continued)*.

Sentence to be completed	Word to be supplied
15. A candle flame is hot. It is a(n) _____ source of light.	incandescent
16. The hot wick of a candle gives off small pieces or particles of carbon which burn in the flame. Before or while burning, the hot particles send out, or _____ , light.	emit
17. A long candlewick produces a flame in which oxygen does not reach all the carbon particles. Without oxygen the particles cannot burn. Particles which do not burn rise above the flame as _____ .	smoke
18. We can show that there are particles of carbon in a candle flame, even when it is not smoking, by holding a piece of metal in the flame. The metal cools some of the particles before they burn, and the unburned carbon _____ collect on the metal as soot.	particles
19. The particles of carbon in soot or smoke no longer emit light because they are _____ than when they were in the flame.	cooler, colder
20. The reddish part of a candle flame has the same color as the filament in a flashlight with a weak battery. We might guess that the yellow or white parts of a candle flame are _____ than the reddish part.	hotter
21. "Putting out" an incandescent electric light means turning off the current so that the filament grows too _____ to emit light.	cold, cool
22. Setting fire to the wick of an oil lamp is called _____ the lamp.	lighting
23. The sun is our principal _____ of light, as well as of heat.	source
24. The sun is not only very bright but very hot. It is a powerful _____ source of light.	incandescent
25. Light is a form of energy. In "emitting light" an object changes or "converts," one form of _____ into another.	energy
26. The electrical energy supplied by the battery in a flashlight is converted to _____ and _____ .	heat, light; light, heat
27. If we leave a flashlight on, all the energy stored in the battery will finally be changed or _____ into heat and light.	converted
28. The light from a candle flame comes from the _____ released by chemical changes as the candle burns.	energy

Table continued on next page

Table 2 Part of a program in high-school physics *(continued).*

Sentence to be completed	Word to be supplied
29. A nearly "dead" battery may make a flashlight bulb warm to the touch, but the filament may still not be hot enough to emit light—in other words, the filament will not be _____ at that temperature.	incandescent
30. Objects, such as a filament, carbon particles, or iron bars, become incandescent when heated to about 800 degrees Celsius. At that temperature they begin to _____ _____.	emit light
31. When raised to any temperature above 800 degrees Celsius, an object such as an iron bar will emit light. Although the bar may melt or vaporize, its particles will be _____ no matter how hot they get.	incandescent
32. About 800 degrees Celsius is the lower limit of the temperature at which particles emit light. There is no upper limit of the _____ at which emission of light occurs.	temperature
33. Sunlight is _____ by very hot gases near the surface of the sun.	emitted
34. Complex changes similar to an atomic explosion generate the great heat which explains the _____ of light by the sun.	emission
35. Below about _____ degrees Celsius an object is not an incandescent source of light.	800

"fine wire" in frame 2 is followed by a definition of the technical term "filament" in frame 4; "filament" is then asked for in the presence of the nonscientific synonym in frame 5 and without the synonym in frame 9. In the same way "glow," "give off light," and "send out light" in early frames are followed by a definition of "emit" with a synonym in frame 7. Various inflected forms of "emit" then follow, and "emit" itself is asked for with a synonym in frame 16. It is asked for without a synonym but in a helpful phrase in frame 30, and "emitted" and "emission" are asked for without help in frames 33 and 34. The relation between temperature and amount and color of light is developed in several frames before a formal statement using the word "temperature" is asked for in frame 12. "Incandescent" is defined and used in frame 13, is used again in frame 14, and is asked for in frame 15, the student receiving a thematic prompt from the recurring phrase "incandescent source of light." A formal prompt is supplied by "candle." In frame 25 the new response "energy" is easily evoked by the words "form of…." because the expression "form of energy" is used earlier in the frame. "Energy" appears again in the next two frames and is finally asked for, without aid, in frame 28. Frames 30 through 35 discuss the limiting temperatures of incandescent objects, while reviewing several kinds of sources. The figure 800 is used in three frames. Two intervening frames then permit some time to pass before the response "800" is asked for.

Unwanted responses are eliminated with special techniques. If, for example, the second sentence in frame 24 were simply "It is a(n) _____ source of light," the two "very's" would frequently lead the student to fill the blank with "strong" or a synonym thereof. This is prevented by inserting the word "powerful" to make a synonym redundant. Similarly, in frame 3 the words "heat and" preempt the response "heat," which would otherwise correctly fill the blank.

The net effect of such material is more than the acquisition of facts and terms. Beginning with a largely unverbalized acquaintance with flashlights, candles, and so on, the student is induced to talk about familiar events, together with a few new facts, with a fairly technical vocabulary. He applies the same terms to facts which he may never before have seen to be similar. The emission of light from an incandescent source takes shape as a topic or field of inquiry. An understanding of the subject emerges which is often quite surprising in view of the fragmentation required in item building.

It is not easy to construct such a program. Where a confusing or elliptical passage in a textbook is forgivable because it can be clarified by the teacher, machine material must be self-contained and wholly adequate. There are other reasons why textbooks, lecture outlines, and film scripts are of little help in preparing a program. They are usually not logical or developmental arrangements of material but stratagems which the authors have found successful under existing classroom conditions. The examples they give are more often chosen to hold the student's interest than to clarify terms and principles. In composing material for the machine, the programmer may go directly to the point.

A first step is to define the field. A second is to collect technical terms, facts, laws, principles, and cases. These must then be arranged in a plausible developmental order—linear if possible, branching if necessary. A mechanical arrangement, such as a card filing system, helps. The material is distributed among the frames of a program to achieve an arbitrary density. In the final composition of an item, techniques for strengthening asked-for responses and for transferring control from one variable to another are chosen from a list according to a given schedule in order to prevent the establishment of irrelevant verbal tendencies appropriate to a single technique. When one set of frames has been composed, its terms and facts are seeded mechanically among succeeding sets, where they will again be referred to in composing later items to make sure that the earlier repertoire remains active. Thus, the technical terms, facts, and examples in table 2 have been distributed for reuse in succeeding sets on reflection, absorption, and transmission, where they are incorporated into items dealing mainly with other matters. Sets of frames for explicit review can, of course, be constructed. Further research will presumably discover other, possibly more effective, techniques. Meanwhile, it must be admitted that a considerable measure of art is needed in composing a successful program.

Whether good programming is to remain an art or to become a scientific technology, it is reassuring to know that there is a final authority—the student. An unexpected advantage of machine instruction has proved to be the feedback to the *programmer*. In the elementary school machine, provision is made for discovering which frames commonly yield wrong responses, and in the high-school and college machine the paper strips bearing written answers are available for analysis. A trial run of the first version of a program quickly reveals frames which need to be altered, or sequences which need to be lengthened. One or two revisions in the light of a few dozen responses work a great improvement. No comparable feedback is available to the lecturer, text-book writer, or maker of films. Although one text or film may seem to be better than another, it is usually impossible to say, for example, that a given sentence on a given page or a particular sequence in a film is causing trouble.

Difficult as programming is, it has its compensations. It is a salutary thing to try to guarantee a right response at every step in the presentation of a subject matter. The programmer will usually find that he has been accustomed to leave much to the student—that he has frequently omitted essential steps and neglected to invoke relevant points. The responses made to his material may reveal surprising ambiguities. unless he is lucky, he may find that he still has something to learn about his subject. He will almost certainly find that he needs to learn a great deal more about the behavioral changes he is trying to induce in the student. This effect of the machine in confronting the programmer with the full scope of his task may in itself produce a considerable improvement in education.

Composing a set of frames can be an exciting exercise in the analysis of knowledge. The enterprise has obvious bearings on scientific methodology. There are hopeful signs that the epistemological implications will induce experts to help in composing programs. The expert may be interested for another reason. We can scarcely ask a topflight mathematician to write a primer in second-grade arithmetic if it is to be used by the average teacher in the average classroom. But a carefully controlled machine presentation and the resulting immediacy of contact between programmer and student offer a very different prospect, which may be enough to induce those who know most about the subject to give some thought to the nature of arithmetical behavior and to the various forms in which such behavior should be set up and tested.

Can Material Be Too Easy?

The traditional teacher may view these programs with concern. He may be particularly alarmed by the effort to maximize success and minimize failure. He has found that students do not pay attention unless they are worried about the consequences of their work. The customary procedure has been to maintain the necessary anxiety by inducing errors. In recitation, the student who obvi-ously knows the answer is not too often asked; a test item which is correctly answered by everyone is discarded as nondiscriminating; problems at the end of a section in a textbook in mathematics generally include one or two very difficult items; and so on. (The teacher-turned-programmer may be surprised to find this attitude affecting the construction of items. For example, he may find it difficult to allow an item to stand which "gives the point away." Yet if we can solve the motivational problem with other means, what is more effective than giving a point away?) Making sure that the student knows he doesn't know is a technique concerned with motivation, not with the learning process. Machines solve the problem of motivation in other ways. There is no evidence that what is easily learned is more readily forgotten. If this should prove to be the case, retention may be guaranteed by subsequent material constructed for an equally painless review.

The standard defense of "hard" material is that we want to teach more than subject matter. The student is to be challenged and taught to "think." The argument is sometimes little more than a rationalization for a confusing presentation, but it is doubtless true that lectures and texts are often inadequate and misleading by design. But to what end? What sort of "thinking" does the student learn in struggling through difficult material? Is it true that those who learn under difficult conditions are better students, but are they better because they have surmounted difficulties or do they surmount them because they are better? In the guise of teaching thinking we set difficult and confusing situations and claim credit for the students who deal with them successfully.

The trouble with deliberately making education difficult in order to teach thinking is (i) that we must remain content with the students thus selected, even though we know that they are only a small part of the potential supply of thinkers, and (ii) that we must continue to sacrifice the teaching of subject matter by renouncing effective but "easier" methods. A more sensible program is to analyze the behavior called "thinking" and produce it according to specifications. A program specifically concerned with such behavior could be composed of material already available in logic, mathematics, scientific method, and psychology. Much would doubtless be added in completing an effective program. The machine has already yielded important relevant by-products. Immediate feedback encourages a more careful reading of programmed material than is the case in studying a text, where the consequences of attention or inattention are so long deferred that they have little effect on reading skills. The behavior involved in observing or attending to detail—as in inspecting charts and models or listening closely to recorded speech—is efficiently shaped by the contingencies arranged by the machine. And when an immediate result is in the balance, a student will be more likely to learn how to marshal relevant material, to concentrate on specific features of a presentation, to reject irrelevant materials, to refuse the easy but wrong solution, and to tolerate indecision, all of which are involved in effective thinking.

Part of the objection to easy material is that the student will come to depend on the machine and will be less able than ever to cope with the inefficient presentations of lectures, textbooks, films, and "real life." This is indeed a problem. All good teachers must "wean" their students, and the machine is no exception. The better the teacher, the more explicit must be weaning process be. The final stages of a program must be so designed that the student no longer requires the helpful conditions arranged by the machine. This can be done in many ways—among others by using the machine to discuss material which has been studied in other forms. These are questions which can be adequately answered only by further research.

No large-scale "evaluation" of machine teaching has yet been attempted. We have so far been concerned mainly with practical problems in the design and use of machines, and with testing and revising sample programs. The machine shown in figure 2 was built and tested with a grant from the Fund for the Advancement of Education. [Figure was was unavailable for reprint.] Material has been prepared and tested with the collaboration of Lloyd E. Homme, Susan R. Meyer, and James G. Holland.[8] The self-instruction room shown in figure 3 was set up under this grant [Figure 3 was unavailable for reprint.]. It contains ten machines and was recently used to teach part of a course in human behavior to Harvard and Radcliffe undergraduates. Nearly 200 students completed 48 disks (about 1400 frames) prepared with the collaboration of Holland. The factual core of the course was covered, corresponding to about 200 pages of the text.[9] The median time required to finish 48 disks was 14½ hours. The students were not examined on the material but were responsible for the text which overlapped it. Their reactions to the material and to self-instruction in general have been studied through interviews and questionnaires. Both the machines and the material are now being modified in the light of this experience, and a more explicit evaluation will then be made.

Meanwhile, it can be said that the expected advantages of machine instruction were generously confirmed. Unsuspected possibilities were revealed which are now undergoing further exploration. Although it is less convenient to report to a self-instruction room than to pick up a textbook in one's room or elsewhere, most students felt that they had much to gain in studying by machine. Most of them worked for an hour or more with little effort, although they often felt tired afterwards, and they reported that they learned much more in less time and with less effort than in conventional ways. No attempt was made to point out the relevance of the material to crucial issues, personal or otherwise, but the students remained interested. (Indeed, one change in the reinforcing contingencies suggested by the experiment is intended to *reduce* the motivational level.) An important advantage proved to be that the student always knew where he stood, without waiting for an hour test or final examination.

Some Questions

Several questions are commonly asked when teaching machines are discussed. Cannot the results of laboratory research on learning be used in education without machines? Of course they can. They should lead to improvements in textbooks, films, and other teaching materials. Moreover, the teacher who really understands the conditions under which learning takes place will be more effective, not only in teaching subject matter but in managing the class. Nevertheless, some sort of device is necessary to arrange the subtle contingencies of reinforcement required for optimal learning if each student is to have individual attention. In nonverbal skills this is usually obvious; texts and instructor can guide the learner but they cannot arrange the final contingencies which set up skilled behavior. It is true that the verbal skills at issue here are especially dependent upon social reinforcement, but it must not be forgotten that the machine simply mediates an *essentially verbal* relation. In shaping and maintaining verbal knowledge we are not committed to the contingencies arranged through immediate personal contact.

Machines may still seem unnecessarily complex compared with other mediators such as workbooks or self-scoring test forms. Unfortunately, these alternatives are not acceptable. When material is adequately programmed, adjacent steps are often so similar that one frame reveals the response to another. Only some sort of mechanical presentation will make successive frames independent of each other. Moreover, in self-instruction an automatic record of the student's behavior is especially desirable, and for many purposes it should be foolproof. Simplified versions of the present machines have been found useful—for example, in the work of Ferster and Sapon, of Porter, and of Gilbert[8]—but the mechanical and economic problems are so easily solved that a machine with greater capabilities is fully warranted.

Will machines replace teachers? On the contrary, they are capital equipment to be used by teachers to save time and labor. In assigning certain mechanizable functions to machines, the teacher emerges in his proper role as in indispensable human being. He may teach more students than heretofore— this is probably inevitable if the world-wide demand for education is to be satisfied—but he will do so in fewer hours and with fewer burdensome chores. In return for his greater productivity he can ask society to improve his economic condition.

The role of the teacher may well be changed, for machine instruction will affect several traditional practices. Students may continue to be grouped in "grades" or "classes," but it will be possible for each to proceed at his own level, advancing as rapidly as he can. The other kind of "grade" will also change its meaning. In traditional practice a *C* means that a student has a smattering of a whole course. But if machine instruction assures mastery at every stage, a grade will be useful only in showing *how far* a student has gone. *C* might mean that he is halfway through a course. Given enough time he will be able to get an *A*; and since *A* is no longer a motivating device, this is fair enough. The quick student will meanwhile have picked up *A*'s in other subjects.

Differences in ability raise other questions. A program designed for the slowest student in the school system will probably not seriously delay the fast student, who will be free to progress at his own speed. (He may profit from the full coverage by filling in unsuspected gaps in his repertoire.) If this does not prove to be the case, programs can be constructed at two or more levels, and students can be shifted from one to the other as performances dictate. If there are also differences in "types of thinking," the extra time available for machine instruction may be used to present a subject in ways appropriate to many types. Each student will presumably retain and use those ways which he finds most useful. The kind of individual difference which arises simply because a student has missed part of an essential sequence (compare the child who has no "mathematical ability" because he was out with the measles when fractions were first taken up) will simply be eliminated.

Other Uses

Self-instruction by machine has many special advantages apart from educational institutions. Home study is an obvious case. In industrial and military training it is often inconvenient to schedule students in groups, and individual instruction by machine should be a feasible alternative. Programs can also be constructed in subjects for which teachers are not available—for example, when new kinds of equipment must be explained to operators and repairmen, or where a sweeping change in method finds teachers unprepared.[10] Education sometimes fails because students have handicaps which make a normal relationship with a teacher difficult or impossible. (Many blind children are treated today as feeble-minded because no one has had the time or patience to make contact with them. Deaf-mutes, spastics, and others suffer similar handicaps.) A teaching machine can be adapted to special kinds of communication—as, for example, Braille—and, above all, it has infinite patience.

Conclusion

An analysis of education within the framework of a science of behavior has broad implications. Our schools, in particular our "progressive" schools, are often held responsible for many current problems—including juvenile delinquency and the threat of a more powerful foreign technology. One remedy frequently suggested is a return to older techniques, especially to a greater "discipline" in schools. Presumably this is to be obtained with some form of punishment, to be administered either with certain classical instruments of physical injury—the dried bullock's tail of the Greek teacher or the cane of the English schoolmaster—or as disapproval or failure, the frequency of which is to be increased by "raising standards." This is probably not a feasible solution. Not only education but Western culture as a whole is moving away from aversive practices. We cannot prepare young people for one kind of life in institutions organized on quite different principles. The discipline of the birch rod may facilitate learning, but we must remember that it also breeds followers of dictators and revolutionists.

In the light of our present knowledge a school system must be called a failure if it cannot induce students to learn except by threatening them for not learning. That this has always been the standard pattern simply emphasizes the importance of modern techniques. John Dewey was speaking for his culture and his time when he attacked aversive educational practices and appealed to teachers to turn to positive and humane methods. What he threw out should have been thrown out. Unfortunately he had too little to put in its place. Progressive education has been a temporizing measure which can now be effectively supplemented. Aversive practices can not only be replaced, they can be replaced with far more powerful techniques. The possibilities should be thoroughly explored if we are to build an educational system which will meet the present demand without sacrificing democratic principles.

References and Notes

1. The Navy's "Self-Rater" is a larger version of Pressey's machine. The items are printed on code-punched plastic cards fed by the machine. The time required to answer is taken into account in scoring.
2. S. L. Pressey. *School and Society* 23, 586 (1926).
3. ———. *ibid.* 36, 934 (1932).

4. B. F. Skinner. "The experimental analysis of behavior." *Am. Scientist* 45, 4 (1957).

5. ————. *Verbal Behavior* (Appleton-Century-Crofts, New York, 1957).

6. ————. "The science of learning and the art of teaching." *Harvard Educational Rev.* 24, 2 (1954).

7. This material was prepared with the assistance of Susan R. Meyer.

8. Dr. Homme prepared sets of frames for teaching part of college physics (kinematics), and Mrs. Meyer has prepared and informally tested material in remedial reading and vocabulary building at the junior high school level. Others who have contributed to the development of teaching machines should be mentioned. Nathan H. Azrin cooperated with me in testing a version of a machine to teach arithmetic. C. B. Ferster and Stanley M. Sapon used a simple "machine" to teach German [see "An application of recent developments in psychology to the teaching of German." *Harvard Educational Rev.* 28, 1 (1958)]. Douglas Porter, of the Graduate School of Education at Harvard, has made an independent schoolroom test of machine instruction in spelling [see "Teaching machines," *Harvard Graduate School of Educ. Assoc. Bull.* 3, 1 (1958)]. Devra Cooper has experimented with the teaching of English composition for freshmen at the University of Kentucky. Thomas F. Gilbert, of the University of Georgia, has compared standard and machine instruction in an introductory course in psychology, and with the collaboration of J. E. Jewett has prepared material in algebra. The U.S. Naval Training Devices Center has recently contracted with the University of Pennsylvania for a study of programs relating to the machine instruction of servicemen, under the direction of Eugene H. Galanter.

9. B. F. Skinner, *Science and Human Behavior* (Macmillan, New York, 1953).

10. K. Menger, "New approach to teaching intermediate mathematics," *Science* 127, 1320 (1958).

Professions in the Audio-Visual Field

Professionalizing the Audio-Visual Field

James D. Finn

Specialization of occupation is a growing social factor in modern life. This factor is as applicable to education as to any other field. Where once there were only teachers, there are now administrators, psychologists, curriculum consultants, counselors, and many other educational specialists. Each of these specialties is developing into a profession within the general profession of education. Educators whose main responsibility lies in the preparation, distribution, and use of audio-visual materials represent another group of specialized personnel newly developed and integrated into the field of education.

In addition to the fact that people working with audio-visual materials are devoting the major share of their time to a specialized phase of education and are developing special interests, techniques, etc., there is also the fact that the audio-visual field itself is somewhat unique in that it embraces all branches of the communication arts and technology and brings new disciplines to bear upon the problems of education. This second fact makes the audio-visual field even more of a specialized educational activity than, say, the teaching of reading.

In recent years audio-visual workers have become sensitive to the professional problems of their specialty. Questions have been raised as to the possible degree of professionalization of the movement; as to what, if any, certification requirements should be set up for audio-visual directors, and as to the long-range professional objectives of associations such as the Department of Audio-Visual Instruction of the NEA (DAVI). DAVI has set up a Committee on Professional Education to study the general problem of professionalization.

At the time this article was published, Dr. Finn was associate professor of education and chairman of audio-visual education at the University of Southern California. He was also Chairman of the DAVI Committee on Professional Education.

From: Finn, J. D. 1953. Professionalizing the audio-visual field. *Audio-visual communication review* 1(1):6–18. Reprinted with permission of Association for Educational Communications and Technology.

Editor's Note: In this paper, citations to numbered references appear in parentheses, like this: (16).

It is the purpose of a series of papers, of which this is the first, to present a study of the problem of professionalization to the membership of DAVI from the Committee on Professional Education. These papers will analyze the present status of the field to determine, if possible, the degree of professionalization that has been developed, to review the historical development of this status, and to suggest some problems that must be met and some possible solutions that might be developed in order to move the field further in the direction of a true profession.

It is hoped that these studies will stimulate the membership of DAVI and other people working in the field to undertake appropriate action. It is very significant to the Committee on Professional Education that this series of papers is inaugurated in the first issue of the new professional magazine of the Department of Audio-Visual Instruction.

Tools of a Profession

In considering the audio-visual field as a possible area of professionalization, a good place to begin is with the question: What are the characteristics of a profession?[1] A profession has, at least, these characteristics: (a) an intellectual technique, (b) an application of that technique to the practical affairs of man, (c) a period of long training necessary before entering into the profession, (d) an association of the members of the profession into a closely-knit group with a high quality of communication between members, (e) a series of standards and a statement of ethics which is enforced, and (f) an organized body of intellectual theory constantly expanding by research.

The statements identifying these characteristics need little comment. That a profession is primarily intellectual in character can be readily seen by viewing the activities of any profession; a doctor who did not reflectively think before prescribing is inconceivable. That a profession applies its knowledge directly to the benefit of man is also obvious.

The long periods of training necessary to develop specialists such as design engineers or oral surgeons are common examples of the third characteristic. Professional associations which began their evolution in the Middle Ages are a part of every civilized society. They identify the members who have successfully passed through the long training stage and, in fact, even control to a great degree the nature of that training. Communication between members of the profession is carried on by meetings, journals of high quality, consultations, and other means.

Architects, actuaries, engineers all have their codes of conduct or statements of ethics and various forms of standards. Coupled with this ethical formulation is a means of enforcing it in the more highly organized professions. Sometimes this enforcement responsibility rests with the professional association, sometimes with the state as a licensing body, and sometimes with both. Although there is much criticism of many professions at this point and some evidence[11] that many codes are window dressing to protect the profession from public interference and are not enforced except to the advantage of the profession as against the public, the fact remains that the idea of an ethic with the power of enforcement places a personal responsibility on each member of a profession not associated with other types of occupations.

Finally, the most fundamental and most important characteristic of a profession is that the skills involved are founded upon a body of intellectual theory and research. Furthermore, this systematic theory is constantly being expanded by research and thinking within the profession. As Whitehead says, "...the practice of a profession cannot be disjoined from its theoretical understanding or *vice versa*.... The antithesis to a profession is an avocation based upon customary activities and modified by the trial and error of individual practice. Such an avocation is a Craft...." (16:557) The difference between the bricklayer and the architect lies right here.

Professional Status of Audio-Visual Education

We can now examine the present status of audio-visual education when measured by these six tests of a profession. Are audio-visual personnel, in fact, professionals? By audio-visual personnel is meant, for the moment, those individuals who spend fifty per cent or more of their time working with audio-visual programs in schools and colleges as directors, supervisors, producers, consultants, etc., or those who engage in in-service and pre-service teacher training or research in this area.

An Intellectual Technique

First, the audio-visual worker does possess an intellectual technique. He has to think reflectively in such varied areas as the critical evaluation of materials, the visualization of abstract concepts, the improvement of instruction, and in many aspects of planning and administration. Audio-visual personnel, as a group, meet this criterion fairly well.

Practical Application of the Technique

Second, audio-visual techniques and materials justify their existence only as they become operative in classroom communication. Hence the test of practical application is completely met. Here the personnel of the field is at its best. The practical problems of classroom design, equipment, and materials are the meat and drink of most audio-visual people. As will be indicated below, there is, perhaps, even an overemphasis on this point.

Long Period of Training

The test of a high degree of professionalization of the audio-visual field, however, breaks down completely against the third criterion, a long period of rigorous training for the members of a profession. Most professions not only require this long period of training but are also in substantial agreement as to the nature of this training. This results in the professional associations specifying the nature of the training either through state regulation of some sort or through a system of accrediting training institutions.

The teaching profession as a whole does maintain training standards. But specific training for audio-visual directors and other personnel, with few exceptions, is still in the thinking stage. Although there have been directors of programs since before World War I, McClusky's bibliography lists only fifteen articles in the literature which discuss the requirements for audio-visual personnel.[14] An examination of these articles reveals that only four are pertinent. [6, 7, 12, 15] The others are devoted to administrative relationships and duties of principals, building coordinators, students, and miscellaneous problems. There has been practically no thoughtful consideration of this problem by audio-visual people and no attempt to develop standards.

The history of all professions reveals that the lengthy and rigorous training programs came after a long period of evolution. So it is not surprising to find that the audio-visual field has not made an organized effort as yet to develop such a program. The audio-visual field has developed rapidly and has surmounted many professional problems without showing all the required characteristics of a profession. Now, in 1953, the field is really, for the first time, in a position to take a good look at the problem of professional training. The State of Indiana has already taken action, and proposals have been published in other states as to the training necessary for an audio-visual director and pointing to some form of certification. The Committee on Professional Education of DAVI has this as one of its direct concerns.

The nature and content of professional education for audio-visual directors and other workers presents many problems that must be solved before audio-visual education can claim the status of a profession. The system of apprenticeship training that has been in operation is no longer adequate. Trained audio-visual personnel will not stay in their present jobs forever, and there is no longer the reservoir of service-experienced people to draw upon. Obviously, a graduate program that can provide the competencies generated by service and industrial experience coupled with a better theoretical background is required immediately. The audio-visual field cannot be upgraded into a profession until this occurs. Other unsolved problems include the nature of certification standards, admission standards and practices, and placement.

Association and Communication Between Members

The fourth criterion of a profession—a closely-knit association with a high quality of communication between members—is another point at which the audio-visual field does not measure up. Considering, first, professional association, the best that can be said at present is that a professional association is in the process of *becoming* and will someday emerge.

For many years DAVI was a comparatively weak organization held together by a small group of stalwarts. DAVI went through several reorganizations and managed to survive a depression and a war, but only in the last two or three years has the organization shown anything like the potential it can develop. The present arrangement which ties in the organization with the NEA through its executive secretary, with working national committees dealing with important problems, and with an increasing and interested membership promises much for the future.

The audio-visual field has also suffered from too many organizations. It is a moot question whether the organizations which represent special applications of the field such as The Association for Education by Radio-Television (AERT), the Educational Film Library Association (EFLA), and the Film Council of America (FCA) should remain outside of the main stream of the DAVI or become divisions within it in order to develop the best possible organization for the profession. The men and women who founded and carried on these organizations deserve nothing but commendation for their continual struggle and achievements, but the field as a profession would probably benefit more by merger than by continued separatism. At least this possibility should be thoroughly explored.

At the state and local levels, the structure of audio-visual organization has not yet even approached the professional. There are some fine state units, to be sure. The Audio-Visual Education Association of California, one of the oldest and strongest, is a professional organization in every sense of the word. AVID of Indiana has achieved national recognition, and AVDO of Ohio is rapidly growing in strength. And there are others. But much work remains to be done on the state and local levels.

It is at the other half of the concept of association—the idea of a high quality of communication between members—that the audio-visual movement as a whole had failed until the decision was made to publish the journal in which this paper appears. With the exception of Edgar Dale's *Newsletter*, all of the journals serving the field had difficulty presenting professional content. This was true of *Educational Screen, Audio-Visual World, See and Hear, Audio-Visual Guide, Business Screen, The Journal of the AERT, Film News,* and all the rest. Most of the time these magazines were not able to print thorough and scholarly papers on the theoretical bases of audio-visual education; research studies for the most part were ignored and left to journals outside the field. When compared to the *Psychological Review, The American Journal of Sociology*, or a hundred other professional periodicals, the audio-visual magazines have simply not measured up professionally. There were good and sufficient reasons for this, but the fact remains.

This is not to say that these other audio-visual journals have failed to contribute as the audio-visual field struggled through its infancy. They have done their share in developing the field. In particular, Nelson Greene made a great contribution through the years with the *Educational Screen*. Greene was a scholar and had an intensive interest in professionalizing audio-visual education. Some examples of this interest were the publication of Krows' somewhat dull but important account of the development of the non-theatrical film, carried serially over two years; David Goodman's abortive column on research abstracts; and an attempt to carry a column which critically reviewed the literature of the field.

In general, the journals until now have made a contribution by carrying information on materials and equipment, occasionally publishing an article of professional merit, and everlastingly promoting and crusading for things audio-visual. This is a sign of the childhood and adolescence of the audio-visual movement. Audio-visual education is here to stay. Promotion and professionalization, while both are necessary, are not the same things. The time has come to add the dimension of professional content to the field's journals and it is hoped that the *Audio-Visual Communication Review* will fill the gap.

Professional communication is also carried on in meetings and conferences. The same criticisms leveled at the quality of the journals can apply to the quality of most audio-visual meetings. The meeting agenda seem to be of two types. One is a type designed to appeal to the practicing teacher and consists of a rehash of one or more chapters of Dale, Hoban, or Kinder carried on for two or three days! To the audio-visual professional, this type of meeting is about as intellectually stimulating as a plateful of unsalted grits would be to Oscar of the Waldorf. The other type appeals to the ever-present gadgeteer in audio-visual circles and, while it may not be concerned any more with the "F-value" of lenses, the topics have merely changed to more efficient booking forms, the JAN projector, or the heat and pressure necessary to laminate a 20 × 24 print.

The writer is not arguing for the elimination of meetings designed primarily for teachers nor for the abolishing of the technical problems of the audio-visual field from consideration. Certainly thousands of teachers need help with the elementary concepts of audio-visual instruction;[2] certainly the audio-visual field will always be plagued with technical problems which must be solved. But professional meetings are not professional meetings if they are limited to these two areas. The first can be best dealt with in regular gatherings of teachers rather than at audio-visual meetings, and the second area should be reduced to a section or two of professional audio-visual conferences to restore perspective.

Again, improvement in recent years has been noted. The agenda for the Boston and St. Louis meetings of DAVI showed many signs of professionalization not present at earlier meetings. Many state meetings have been improving programs. Nevertheless, the improvement of audio-visual conferences has a long way to go.

In summary, then, to achieve a real professional status, the audio-visual movement needs to develop a strong and creative association at the national and state and local levels; it needs to develop true professional journals, and it needs to improve conferences and meetings. When these things are done, audio-visual personnel can say they have met the requirements of the fourth criterion—the criterion of association and communication.

Code of Ethics and Standards

The fifth measuring point, ethics, standards and their enforcement, is a function of the fourth, a strong association. Statements of ethics and publications of standards are developed by professional associations. Audio-visual personnel, as members of the teacher profession, are subject to the ethics of the profession. As yet, nothing has been done to develop a separate code of ethics for the audio-visual movement.

In the field of standards, there are signs that professionalization is under way. The Committee on Buildings and Equipment of DAVI is studying standards in its field, and has produced an excellent publication.[17]

However, the publication of codes of ethics and manuals of standards in itself guarantees nothing. Professionalization occurs when enforcement is possible and vigorous. Thus, the American Medical Association wages war on quacks and malpractice; engineers and architects write building standards into the law, and the courts can disbar a lawyer for illegal practice.

Enforcement is closely tied in with admission to the profession by a licensing system (a function of criterion three—training), with placement which assures that licensed personnel are hired, and, most fundamentally, with an obligation on the part of each professional to the ethics and standards of his profession.

In view of the fact that the entire education profession has not met this criterion to the degree that the other professions have, it is questionable whether the audio-visual group will ever completely measure up to this point. And it is even questionable whether such a rigorous arrangement is either necessary or desirable. However, the audio-visual movement will at least have to reach the stage where it has a well-defined code of ethics, a series of standards based upon fundamental research, and a form of certification somewhat related to them. At the moment the field is not at this stage and does not meet criterion five.

Intellectual Theory and Research

As was indicated in the introductory phase of this paper, the most important characteristic of a profession was the sixth and last, that the technique of a profession is founded upon a body of systematic theory and research constantly being expanded by research and thinking within the profession. When the audio-visual field is measured against this characteristic, again the conclusion must be reached that professional status has not been attained.

Audio-visual workers have put a premium on "practicality" and have been criticized for this by colleagues within the field of education and by the *literati* from without. There is some merit to this criticism. For years, even at audio-visual meetings, someone has always been taking cracks at the "gadgeteers." As the writer has indicated above, it is his position that the audio-visual field is a result of the fruits of technology applied to the educational process and a certain amount of gadgeteering will always be necessary. Too much, however, reveals a poverty of thought.

The audio-visual field has never been too clear on the point that theory and practice must constantly interact in any intellectual activity of man. In line with some other mistaken educators, many audio-visual people have insisted that they want to be "practical" and not "theoretical," and that "experience" is the thing. This is, in part, an honest reaction against an older viewpoint that placed theory up somewhere near the Milky Way where it had no relation to practice except to cause aesthetic chills to chase up the spine of some professor.

This attitude, however, also represents a complete misunderstanding of the nature of reflective thinking, scientific progress, and the wellsprings of human behavior. As Dewey[4] has said, "...we find that experience when it is experimental does not signify the absence of large and far-reaching ideas and purposes. It is dependent upon them at every point." Without these large and far-reaching ideas any field, and this is particularly true of the audio-visual field, can go only so far and then has to stop.

Many of the criticisms listed above, lack of content at meetings, journals with little intellectual meat, etc., are merely symptoms of this greater trouble—lack of theoretical direction. Without a theory which produces hypotheses for research, there can be no expanding of knowledge and technique. And without a constant attempt to assess practice so that the theoretical implications may be teased out, there can be no assurance that we will ever have a theory or that our practice will make sense.

The audio-visual movement is new and growing, but it is in danger of becoming stunted if it is left to its present theoretical formulations. The present theory guiding the movement can be summed up in three references.[2, 8, 10] The basic concept around which all three have oriented is the notion of the concrete-abstract relationship in learning. This is perhaps most thoroughly explored in Hoban. Dale adds material on retention and forgetting with a brief historical section, and Kinder expands to a very short history of communication and deals slightly with perception and imagery. All also emphasize the gamut of materials approach to learning, the concept of utilization, the experience theory of learning, and the strengths and weaknesses of the various aids.

The remainder of audio-visual theory is scattered throughout the literature. McClusky (13) has related audio-visual techniques to learning theory in a somewhat unique fashion; Brooker[1] began a line of thinking of promise in his discussion of communication which remains to be explored; Exton's[5] contribution of the concept of "optimum synthesis" has not received the attention it merits. All of these are but examples of the scattering of notions throughout audio-visual literature which, when brought together, might constitute a beginning of a fruitful theory.

To these examples, of course, much more would have to be added: most of the writings of Hoban, many of Dale's essays in the *Newsletter*, reports on the proceedings of conferences, generalizations derived from successful practice, generalizations derived from research, etc. The audio-visual field cannot rest its theoretical formulation on the contents of several textbooks designed for teacher training that do not include even all the useful theory to be found in audio-visual literature.

Because of the nature of the audio-visual field, however, useful theory is not confined to its own literature. As most workers realize, there is a literature of the film, of photography, of the museum, of dramatization, etc.; there is also the literature of educational method and curriculum; there is the literature of educational psychology, of social psychology, of social anthropology; there is the literature of art and design; finally and perhaps most important, there is the growing literature of communication. In fact, research and thinking in some parts of the physical sciences (neurology, physiology, acoustics, etc.), the social sciences (social communication and control, learning theory, etc.), and the humanities (art, music, etc.) are each pertinent to the field. We need to understand the filmic expression ideas of Slavko Vorkapich, the visual experiments of Samuel Renshaw, and the communication philosophy of Susanne Langer.

Viewed in this light, most people in the audio-visual field are still guided by a theory which is fragmentary; theory as now guiding the field (the generalizations held by many of the workers) is not even inclusive of the notions contained in audio-visual literature; it has never worked in most of the pertinent generalizations available from outside these narrow limits.

On the important test of theory the audio-visual field does not meet professional standards. Its workers are craftsmen, not professionals, in the majority of instances because they are operating, in Whitehead's words, on "customary activities modified by the trial and error of individual practice." Absolutely fundamental to the development of audio-visual education as a profession in the sense that DAVI is now using the term is the prior development of an all-inclusive body of theory upon which to assess and guide practice and base research. Once this is done, many of the other criticisms stated above will no longer be valid because their source will have disappeared.

The status of audio-visual research also reflects on professionalization. Not that research does not exist or that it is not being pursued. A recent bibliography[3] lists 163 titles through 1946, and this is by no means all-inclusive. Because of the journal policy discussed above, research pertinent to audio-visual education is published throughout the literature of the social sciences and needs a staff of detectives to trace it down. Very little of it has been reported in audio-visual meetings. This means that many audio-visual workers must be "flying blind"—a black mark for professionalization.

The post-war years have brought an increase in research activities in audio-visual education and related areas. Much of this research is government sponsored and financed, but it is being published in pamphlet form, in psychological journals, or in other places more or less inaccessible to the practicing worker in the audio-visual field. A true profession, such as medicine, makes this information more easily available to its practitioners. Furthermore, outside of the volume by Hoban and van Ormer,[9] there is not much evidence that research is influencing the formulation of theory. Many of the hypotheses now being tested have been derived from learning theory and the "social perception" theories which have been developed by a number of social psychologists. *The audio-visual field is in the peculiar position of having much of its research carried on by workers in other disciplines using hypotheses unknown to many audio-visual workers, and reporting results in journals that audio-visual people do not read and at meetings that audio-visual people do not attend.* While the research is expanding the intellectual background of the profession it seems to be having little effect. A tremendous amount of integration is necessary before this part of the criterion six can be met.

Summary

In summary, then, of the six criteria set forth in this paper: (a) intellectual technique, (b) application of technique to practice, (c) long training period, (d) association of members with a high quality of communication, (e) a series of standards and an enforced statement of ethics, and (f) an organized body of intellectual theory constantly expanding by research, audio-visual personnel meet only the first and second completely. The fourth and fifth are met to a degree which is not satisfactory but which is improving. And the third and sixth tests rate such low scores that failure is the only possible grade. This adds up, in the opinion of the writer, to the simply stated fact that *the audio-visual field is not yet a profession.*

Notes

1. The best quick source on the nature and development of the professions with special reference to the teaching profession may be found in Smith.[16] Part Four of this volume, "The Nature and Status of the Teaching Profession," contains pertinent articles by A. M. Carr-Saunders, Abraham Flexner, A. N. Whitehead, and William O. Stanley. Many of Flexner's other works also consider this problem. See also articles relating to the professions and professionalization in the Encyclopedia of Social Sciences. A good idea of the development of a profession to a status closely resembling medicine may be obtained by studying the last four or five years of the *American Psychologist.* In this journal reports of committees on standards, ethics, training, etc., are particularly revealing.

2. See, for example, the recording: Edgar Dale and James D. Finn, "The Improvement of Teaching Through Audio-Visual Materials," Educational Recording Services, Los Angeles, 1951, an aid for teachers' meetings, illustrating the position of the writer on this point.

References

1. Brooker, F. Communication in the modern world. In *Audio-visual materials of instruction.* 48th Yearbook, Part I. Chicago: National Society for the Study of Education, 1948. Pp. 4–27.

2. Dale, E. *Audio-visual methods in teaching.* New York: Dryden Press, 1946.

3. Dale, E., Finn, J. D., and Hoban, C. F. Research on audio-visual materials. In *Audio-visual materials of instruction.* 48th Yearbook, Part I. Chicago: National Society for the Study of Education, 1948. Pp. 253–293.

4. Dewey, J. *The quest for certainty.* New York: Minton, Balch, 1929.

5. Exton, W., Jr. *Audio-visual aids to instruction.* New York: McGraw-Hill, 1947.

6. Finn, J. D. Adequate training for a director of audio-visual education. *Education,* 1941, 61, Pp. 337–343.

7. Frazier, A. How much does the audio-visual director need to know? *School Review,* 1949, 57, Pp. 416–424.

8. Hoban, C. F., Hoban, C. F., Jr., and Zisman, S. B. *Visualizing the curriculum.* New York: Cordon, 1937.

9. Hoban, C. F., Jr., and van Ormer, E. B. *Instructional film research 1918–1950.* Port Washington, Long Island, New York: Special Devices Center, U.S. Navy, 1951.

10. Kinder, J. D. *Audio-visual materials and techniques.* New York: American Book Co., 1950.

11. Landis, B. Y. *Professional codes: a sociological analysis to determine applications to the teaching profession.* Contributions to Education, No. 267, New York: Teachers College, Columbia University, 1927.

12. Lewin, W. (Ed.) Duties of school audio-visual coordinators. *Film and radio guide,* 13, 1947, Pp. 10–11.

13. McClusky, F. D. *Audio-visual teaching techniques.* Dubuque, Iowa: Wm. C. Brown Co., 1949.

14. McClusky, F. D. *The A-V bibliography*. Dubuque, Iowa: Wm. C. Brown Co., 1950.
15. Shreve, R. The superintendent hires an A-V supervisor. *See and hear*. 1950, 5, P. 35.
16. Smith, B. O., et al. *Readings in the social aspects of education*. Danville, Illinois: Interstate Printers and Publishers, 1951.
17. *Planning schools for use of audio-visual materials, No. 1, Classrooms*. Washington: Department of Audio-Visual Instruction, National Education Association, 1952.

Bibliography

This bibliography follows the organization of the book. It does not list the articles that are included in this publication. It contains books and related articles that are considered to be classics in the field of instructional technology. Many items have been suggested by individuals who reviewed the original list of proposed titles. Other listings come from frequency counts of citations in the literature of the field. The bibliography is not comprehensive. It is selective based on the following criteria used to nominate articles for inclusion in this volume:

1. The article or chapter is one of the first to introduce important concepts.
2. It is original and does not borrow extensively from other sources.
3. It is often quoted as a primary reference by current authors.
4. It is recognized by academics who are experienced in the field.
5. It has lasting value; it is not just a historic document that was popular at the time it was published.

Some readers may be concerned about the dates of the writings cited here. An attempt was made to find the origin of the idea, principle, or concept. In some cases, for example, Dick and Carey (1978), Gagné (1965), and Rogers (1962), there have been several later editions of the original title. The first date of publication is used since one purpose of this volume is to explore the primary reference rather than to review its current interpretations and applications.

Definition and Conceptual Background

The Field and Its Definition

Anglin, G. J., ed. 1995. *Instructional technology: past, present and future*. 2d ed. Englewood, Colo.: Libraries Unlimited.

Association for Educational Communications and Technology. 1977. The definition of educational technology: A summary. In *The definition of educational technology*, 1–16. Washington, D.C.: AECT.

Charters, W. W. 1945. Is there a field of educational engineering? *Educational research bulletin* 24:(2)29–37, 53.

Davies, I. K. 1978. Educational technology: Archetypes, paradigms and models. In *Contribution to education technology*, vol. 2, edited by J.A. Hartley and I. K. Davies, 9–29. London: Kogan Page.

Ely, D. P., ed. 1963. The changing role of the audiovisual process in education: A definition and a glossary of related terms. *AV Communication Review* 11:(1) Monograph No. 1, Supplement No. 6.

Ely, D. P., and T. Plomp. 1986. The promises of educational technology: A reassessment. *International review of education* 32:(2)231–249.

Eraut, M. R. 1989. "Educational technology: Conceptual frameworks and historical development." In *The international encyclopedia of educational technology*, edited by M.R. Eraut, 11–21. Oxford: Pergamon Press.

Heinich, R. M. 1973. Is there a field of educational communications and technology? *Audiovisual instruction.*

Reiser, R. A. 1987. "Instructional technology: A history." In *Instructional technology: Foundations*, edited by R.M. Gagné, 38–48. Hillsdale, N.J.: Lawrence Erlbaum.

Rosenberg, M. 1982. Our instructional media roots. *Performance and Instruction*, 21:(3)12–15, 33.

Saettler, P. 1968. *A history of instructional technology.* New York: McGraw-Hill.

―――. 1990. *The evolution of American educational technology.* Englewood, Colo.: Libraries Unlimited.

Seels, B. B., and R. C. Richey. 1994. *Instructional technology: The definition and domains of the field.* Washington, D.C.: Association for Educational Communications and Technology.

Tickton, S. 1970. *To improve learning: An evaluation of instructional technology.* New York: Bowker.

Theory and Rationale

Banathy, B. H. 1968. *Instructional systems.* Belmont, Calif.: Fearon Press.

Berlo, D. K. 1960. *The process of communication.* New York: Holt, Rinehart, and Winston.

―――. 1963. You are in the people business. *Audiovisual instruction* 8, 372–381.

Bruner, J. R. 1966. *Toward a theory of instruction.* Cambridge, Mass.: Belknap Press.

Churchman, C. W. 1965. On the design of educational systems. *Audiovisual instruction* 10(5):361–365.

Finn, J. D. 1960. Technology and the instructional process. *AV communication review* 8:(1)5–26.

―――. 1962. A walk on the altered side. *Phi delta kappan* 44(1):29–34.

Flechsig, K. H. 1975. *Towards a critical appraisal of educational technology theory and practice.* Strasbourg: Steering Group on Educational Technology, Council for Cultural Cooperation, Council of Europe.

Gagné, R. M. 1965. *The conditions of learning.* 1st ed. New York: Holt, Rinehart, and Winston.

Glaser, R. 1962. Psychology and instructional technology. In *Training research and education,* edited by R. Glaser, 1–21. Pittsburgh: University of Pittsburgh Press.

Heinich, R. 1984. The proper study of instructional technology. *Educational communications and technology journal* 32:(2)67–87.

Hoban, C. F. Jr. 1977. A systems approach to audio-visual communications (1956 Okoboji speech). In *Okoboji: A 20 year review of leadership 1955–1974,* edited by L. W. Cochran, 67–72. Dubuque, Iowa: Kendall/Hunt.

Hoban, C. F., F. H. Hoban, and S. B. Zisman. 1937. *Visualizing the curriculum.* New York: Dryden Press.

Jonassen, D. H. 1991. Objectivism vs constructivism: Do we need a new paradigm? *Educational technology research and development* 39(3):5–14.

Lunsdaine, A. A. 1964. Educational technolgoy, programed learning, and instructional science. In *Theories of learning, and instruction: The sixty-third yearbook of the National Society for the Study of Education, Part 1,* edited by E. R. Hilgard, 371–401. Chicago: Univ. of Chicago Press.

Meierhenry, W. C., ed. 1961. Learning theory and AV utilization. *AV communication review* 9:(5) Supplement No. 4.

Norberg, K., ed. 1962. Perception theory and AV education. *AV communication review* 10:(5) Supplement No. 5.

Reigeluth, C. M., ed. 1983. *Instructional design theories and models: an overview of their current status.* Hillsdale, N.J.: Lawrence Erlbaum.

Schramm, W. 1954. *Process and effects of mass communication.* Urbana, Ill.: University of Illinois Press.

Shannon, C., and Weaver, W. 1949. *The mathematical theory of communications.* Champaign-Urbana: Univ. of Illinois Press.

Design and Development Functions

Design and Development

Andrews, D. H. and L. A. Goodson. 1980. A comparative analysis of models of instructional design. *Journal of instructional development* 3:(4)2–16.

Briggs, L. J. 1977. *Instructional design: Principles and applications.* Englewood Cliffs, N.J.: Educational Technology Publications.

Dick, W., and L. Carey. 1978. *The systematic design of instruction*, 1st ed. Glenview, Ill.: Scott, Foresman.

Fleming, M., and H. Levie. 1978. *Instructional message design: Principles from the behavioral sciences*, 1st ed. Englewood Cliffs, N.J.: Educational Technology Publications.

Gagné, R. M. 1968. Learning hierarchies. *Educationl psychologist* 6:1–9.

Gagné, R. M., and L. J. Briggs. 1979. *Principles of instructional design.* New York: Holt, Rinehart, and Winston.

Gustafson, K. L. 1981. *A survey of instructional development models*, 1st ed. Syracuse, N.Y.: ERIC Clearinghouse on Information Resources.

Keller, J. M. 1987. Development and use of the ARCS model of motivation design. *Journal of instructional development* 10(3):2–10.

Mager, R. F. 1962. *Preparing objectives for programmed instruction.* Belmont, Calif.: Fearon Press.

Merrill, M. D. 1983. Component display theory. In *Instructional design theories and models: An overview of their current status*, edited by C. M. Reigeluth, 279–333. Hillsdale, N.J.: Lawrence Erlbaum.

Merrill, M. D., A. Li, and M. K. Jones. 1990. The second generation instructional design research program. *Educational technology* 31:(5)45–53.

Reiser, R., and R. J. Gagné. 1982. *The selection of media for instruction.* Englewood Cliffs, N.J.: Educational Technology Publications.

Romiszowski, A. M. 1981. *Designing instructional systems: Decision making incourse planning and curriculum design.* London: Kogan Page.

———. 1984. *Producing instructional systems.* London: Kogan Page.

Rossett, A. 1987. *Training needs assessment.* Englewood Cliffs, N.J.: Educational Technology Publications.

Rowntree, D. 1974. *Educational technology in curriculum development*, 1st ed. London: Harper and Row.

Tosti, D., and R. Ball. 1969. A behavioral approach to instructional design and media selection. *Audiovisual communication review* 17(1):5–26.

Evaluation

Kaufman, R. 1972. *Educational system planning.* Englewood Cliffs, N.J.: Prentice Hall.

———. 1977. Needs assessments: internal and external. *Journal of instructional development* 1(1):5–8.

Kaufman, R., and F. English. 1979. *Needs assessment: concept and application.* Englewood Cliffs, N.J.: Educational Technology Publications.

Kirkpatrick, D. L. 1979. Techniques for evaluating training programs. *Training and development journal* (June 1979):178–192.

Scriven, M. 1967. *The methodology of evaluation.* AERA Monograph Series on Curriculum Evaluation, No. 1. Chicago: Rand McNally.

Stake, R. E. 1967. The countenance of educational evaluation. *Teachers college record* 68:523–540.

Stufflebeam, D. L. 1983. The CIPP model for program evaluation. In. *Evaluation models: Viewpoints on educational and human services evaluation,* edited by G.F. Madaus, M. Scriven, and D.L. Stufflebeam. Boston: Kluwer–Nijhoff.

Tyler, R. W. 1942. General statement on evaluation. *Journal of Educational Research* 35, 492–501.

————. 1966. New dimensions in curriculum development. *Phi delta kappan* 48 (September 1966):25–28.

Delivery Options

Media

Carpenter, C. R., and L. P. Greenhill. 1956. *Instructional film research reports,* Vol. 2 (Technical Report No. 269-7-61). Port Washington, N.Y.: U.S. Navy Special Devices Center.

Clark, R. E. 1983. Reconsidering research on learning from media. *Review of educational research* 53, 445–459.

Clark, R. E., and G. Salomon. 1986. Media and education. In *Handbook of research on teaching,* 3d ed., edited by M. Wittrock. New York: Holt, Rinehart, and Winston.

Dale, E. 1946. The "cone of experience." In *Audio-visual methods in teaching,* 1st ed., 37–51. New York: Dryden Press.

Knowlton, D., and J. Tilton. 1929. *Motion pictures in history teaching.* New Haven, Conn.: Yale University Press.

May, M. A., and A. A. Lumsdaine. 1958. *Learning from films.* New Haven, Conn.: Yale University Press.

Meierhenry, W. C. 1952. *Enriching the curriculum through motion pictures.* Lincoln: University of Nebraska Press.

Suppes, P., and E. Macken. 1978. The historical path from research and development to operation use of CAI. *Educational technology* 18:(4)9–12.

Wood, B., and F. Freeman. 1929. *Motion pictures in the classroom.* Boston: Houghton Mifflin.

Methods and Techniques

Block, J. H. 1979. Mastery learning: The current state of the craft. *Educational leadership* 37, 114–117.

Bloom, B. S. 1968. Learning for mastery. *Evaluation comment* 1:(2).

Carroll, J. B. 1963. A model of school learning. *Teachers college record* 64, 723–733.

Keller, F. S. 1968. "Good-bye, teacher ..." *Journal of applied behavior analysis* 1: 79–89.

Postlethwait, S. N., J. Novak, and H. T. Murray, Jr. 1982. *The audio-tutorial approach to learning,* 3d ed. Minneapolis: Burgess.

Skinner, B. F. 1954. The science of learning and the art of teaching. *Harvard educational review.* 24:86–97. Copyright 1954 by the President and Fellows of Harvard College. All rights reserved. Reprinted with permission.

————. 1958. Teaching machines. *Science* 128:969–977.

Applications in Institutional Settings

Implementation

Berman, P., and M. McLaughlin. 1975. *Federal programs supporting educational change, Volume 5: The findings in review.* Santa Monica, Calif.: RAND Corporation.

Fullan, M., and A. Pomfret. 1977. Research on curriculum and instruction implementation. *Review of educational research* 47:(1)335–397.

Fullan, M. 1984. Curriculum implementation. In *International encyclopedia of education,* 1st ed.

Hall, G., and S. Loucks. 1977. Developmental model for determining whether the treatment is actually implemented. *American educational research journal* 14:(3)263–276.

Rogers, E. M. 1962. *Diffusion of innovations.* New York: Free Press.

Management

Branson, R. K. 1987. Why the schools can't improve. The upper limit hypothesis. *Journal of instructional development* 10:(4)15–26.

Heinich, R. 1970. *Technology and the management of instruction.* Association for Educational Communications and Technology Monograph No. 4. Washington, D.C.: AECT.

Romiszowski, A. M. 1981. Troubleshooting in educational technology or why projects fail. *Programmed Learning and Educational Technology* 18:(3)168–189.

The Profession

Finn, J. D. 1953. Professionalizing the audio-visual field. *Audio-visual communication review* 1(1):6–18.

Hawkridge, D. G. 1976. Next year, Jerusalem! The rise of educational technology. *British journal of educational technology* 1:(7)7–30.

Morgan, R. M. 1978. Educational technology—Adolescence to adulthood. *Educational communication and technology journal* 26, 142–152.

Index